Anticapitalist Economy in

Rojava

The Contradictions
of Revolution
in the Kurdish Struggle

Azize Aslan

Daraja Press

Published by Daraja Press
https://darajapress.com
Wakefield, Quebec, Canada

ISBN 9781990263712

First published in Spanish as
Economía anticapitalista en Rojava:
Las contradicciones de la revolución en la lucha kurda
published by Bajo Tierra A.C. and
Benemérita Universidad Autónoma de Puebla, Mexico, 2022
978-607-99301-9-6

Cátedra

Recipient of the Jorge Alonso Chair Award in 2021

Translation edited by Gwendolyn Schulman

Thanks to John Michael Colón, Elsa García, Brian Feldman Clough,
Sasha Hoffman and Arturo Castillon for their help with translations.

Cover and interior design: Kate McDonnell

Library and Archives Canada Cataloguing in Publication

Title: Anticapitalist economy in Rojava : the contradictions of revolution in the Kurdish
    struggle / Azize Aslan.
Other titles: Economía anticapitalista en Rojava. English
Names: Aslan, Azize, author.
Description: Translation of: Economía anticapitalista en Rojava. | Includes bibliographical
    references.
Identifiers: Canadiana 20230534821 | ISBN 9781990263712 (softcover)
Subjects: LCSH: Autonomous Administration of North and East Syria. | LCSH: Anti-
    globalization movement—Syria. | LCSH: Kurds—Syria—Economic conditions. | LCSH:
    Kurds—Syria—Social conditions. | LCSH: Kurds—Syria—Politics and government.
Classification: LCC DS94.8.K8 A8513 2023 | DDC 956.91/00491597—dc23

Rojava is a multi-ethnic region, bringing together several peoples who have fought for their freedom, autonomy and recognition for more than a century. This is a book that tells of the racism that the Kurdish people have experienced, but also about how to organize in the face of violence linked to racism that is promoted by the State.

This book is about revolution, but not the revolution of traditional leftist thought that seeks power, but rather of a new revolution without organization, without party, without political leaders, without vertical structures, with horizontal relations that overcome the class struggle and expand it to other social dimensions, the economic one in particular. It is about the contradictions faced by people who are committed to changing the world, their world. It is a book about colonialism, about academic coloniality and about the coloniality of power.

It is a book about emotions, creative emotions, says Azize: the pain, rage, rebellion and power of the Kurdish population that move the community and the organization. It is about the state's ability to generate shame in a person's essential identity; about the construction of another, alternative, resistance, autono-mous, social, supportive, trans-formative, feminist, anti-capitalist, communal or democratic economy, which allows us to reflect on these other ways of doing economics. This is also a feminist book, which highlights the self-managed nature of the social economy from a vision of organizing a democratic, ecological and libertarian communal economy for women.

> – **Marcela Ibarra**, Director of the Economic and Social Innovation Laboratory of the Universidad Iberoamericana Puebla

This book delves into the anti-capitalist process that is being experienced in Rojava, of which many authors and analysts find similarities with the Zapatista movement in Chiapas. It is the product of months of fieldwork in situ and written by a Kurdish academic who knows the movement intimately. Azize Aslan details in depth her observations on the revolutionary process in the region. This is supported by interviews that express the perception of active participants. She emphasizes not so much the results but the processes: the paradigm shift from an anti-hierarchical perspective and the Revolution as a living and unfinished process in which it is experienced, created, destroyed and transformed.

She highlights the role of women in the economy and in capitalism as a consequence of patriarchal logic. She points out the cooperative model and the approach to the economy based on "use value" and not on "exchange value"; in production based on the needs and possibilities of society, and not of the capitalist market.

The great value of this work is that it brings us closer to a process that seems far away and establishes the basis of a serious, critical and direct dialogue that allows us to exchange experiences on the anti-capitalist movements of the world

> – **Sebastián Estremo**, born in Mexico City in 1991, has a degree in Geography from the Faculty of Philosophy and Letters of the Universidad Nacional Autónoma de México and a Master's in Asian and African Studies with a specialization in the Middle East from El Colegio de México.

Table of Contents

To Hevrin Khalaf,
with the memory of her dignified smile...

Acknowledgments

The writing of my acknowledgements is the most difficult part of this book. Because, like any concrete production, the book is the result of collective work, of thinking and dreaming together. For this reason, I find myself unable to express the totality of my gratitude to each person who has contributed in some way to this voyage, to this route, to this march... Because in this life I have met so many valuable and worthy people who have made decisions that I could write, and you can hold this book in your hands. So many collective existences and social processes that embraced me, opened their spaces to me, told me about their struggles, shared with me their homes, meals, dreams, created this book.

Therefore, there are no words to express my gratitude to the people of Rojava who have been fighting for freedom, an anti-capitalist world and a communal life during these long years of resistance. I am very grateful both to their struggle for a dignified life and for allowing me to be part of it. Every word they shared with me, the place they showed me, the discussions we had not only created this book, but also recreated my subjectivity. Despite all the cruelty of war, they shared with me hope, tea and gave me life in their communes: I appreciate all the people of the Social Economy and the women of the Aboriyajin (Women's Economy) organizations at Rojava and Northern Syria. And most especially I would like to thank the *heval* (comrades) who made me feel and live what is the *rêhevaltî*[1] from Rojava to all nooks of Kurdistan.

It was also very inspiring and fundamental to live this process with the accompaniment of the Zapatista Movement (EZLN) during my stays in Chiapas. By telling me about their struggle, they taught me that it is possible to understand each other in any language when you listen with your heart. Their resistance and rebellion and their hope for "another world is possible" deeply inspired this work. Many thanks to the promoters of the Centro de Español y Lenguas Mayas Rebelde Autónomo Zapatista (CELMRAZ) for contributing to build real solidarity between Chiapas and Kurdistan.

This book would not have been written if John Holloway had not invited me to be his student at the ICSyH of the Benemérita Universidad Autónoma de Puebla. Being his student not only fills me with pride, but it also gave me the possibility to think freely and to be critical, that is, to inhabit the world in a

---

1 For me this feeling does not have a translation, the closest and most distant word may be "camaraderie".

different way. I am always grateful for John's unconditional support; he changed a destiny. I would like to thank colleagues from the entire Sociology department of ICSyH-BUAP, not only for their academic contribution, but for their loving friendship with "la kurda" of the institute.

The book was translated into English by John Michael Colón, Elsa García, Brian Feldman Clough and Sasha Hoffman, who have woven their lives around solidarity with the Rojava Revolution. Their excellent work was perfected by the meticulous editing of Gwendolyn Schulman. Another friend who deserves thanks is Sebastian Estremo, who prepared all the maps for the book. Thanks to Kate McDonnell for the cover and interior design. I owe a very special thanks to my beloved editor Firoze Manji and to all the workers of Daraja Press, whose patience, care, and enthusiasm made the book possible.

Finally, and forever, I thank my mother, sisters, brothers and nieces and nephews who, despite the distance and longing to never lose their trust in me, and for constantly making me feel missed, loved, and valued.

A home in Mexico, 2023

Foreword

A fabulous book. Just read the introduction and you realise that this is a special book, not just because of its theme, but because of the way that the theme is approached: politically, personally, critically. A book on the Kurdish revolution, a book from the inside, by someone who has grown up in that movement, who is strongly committed to it but is conscious of its difficulties and contradictions. Azize writes about the Kurdish process not as a *they* but as a *we*. That is important because for us readers too, the movement is a *we*.

For many of the readers of this book, myself included, Kurdistan is a long way away geographically. Yet the struggles of the people there are our struggles. *Our* struggles because they are fighting to create a different world in practice, a different way of organising society, a different form of collectivity, a radical change in the relations between women, men and others.

The old slogan of "another world is possible", proclaimed by the alterglobalisation movement of twenty years ago, has always existed on the edge of ridicule: how is it possible, where is it, show it to me, stop dreaming! As this century advances, it often seems that the idea of a different world becomes more ridiculous. Revolution is a word that becomes harder and harder to even pronounce, much less imagine. And yet it is clear that that which we cannot even pronounce is becoming more urgent than ever: climate catastrophe, the threat of nuclear war, growing inequality, the rise of the extreme right, destruction of the natural preconditions of human existence. A world ruled by money, by capital, by profit, is taking us deeper and deeper into catastrophe.

Where are the revolutionary leaders, the revolutionary parties, that can save us? Nowhere. Thank goodness. The old idea of revolution, centred on parties and leaders, caused enormous suffering and certainly did not lead to the creation of attractive alternatives to the capitalism that is destroying us. We are lost. Lost in history. The highway to revolution, so visible a hundred years ago, no longer exists. The catastrophe into which the rule of money is taking us is unprecedented in scale, the urgency of radical change is clearer than ever, but revolution remains a question, not an answer.

There are many, many attempts to find a way forward, many, many resistances to the destructive assault of money. Of these, two stand out. Both as persistent, deep-rooted demonstrations in practice that another world is indeed possible, difficult but possible. And as astonishingly fertile, amazingly inspiring rethinkings of what revolution means. The first is the Zapatista movement in Mexico, which will be celebrating its thirty years of public existence just as this book is published. And the other is the movement centred on Rojava in the north-eastern part of Syria. These are movements that are not "over there", they cannot be thought of in the third person: they change the world in which we live, they open up windows in our minds and in our actions, they give new colour to the world of our children.

Azize came to Mexico (I say "came" because I live in Mexico) to study the similarities and differences between these two great movements of hope; and, in doing so, also gave me the enormous privilege of being the supervisor of her doctoral thesis. There is probably no one with such a profound knowledge of the two movements. Her knowledge of the Zapatista movement is not an explicit theme in this book, but it does give an extra dimension to her discussion. It deepens her awareness of both the strength and the difficulty of this creation of another world.

The book, largely written in or close to Zapatista territory, although based on research in Rojava carried out in conditions that were often terrifying, is outstanding in its knowledge of the process in Rojava and the depth of its questions, and also in the way that it confronts the dilemma of any rebellious study of a rebellious movement. How do we talk about a movement that we admire, especially when we know that it is in danger, attacked on all sides both physically and ideologically? We do not want to weaken the movement, so there is always a danger of idealising it, of closing our eyes to the contradictions or failings that we see in it. But if we do not criticise, then we easily find ourselves participating in the creation of a movement in which there is no room for critical discussion, strengthening tendencies towards the creation of the sort of authoritarian structures that the movement explicitly rejects. Azize tackles these problems head-on, taking us into the detail of the process of building an anti-capitalist economy in Rojava, the debates, the contradictions, the difficulties. She shows how these questions are far from being technical issues but make sense only in the context of the communal and anti-patriarchal process of social reinvention that is taking place in Rojava. Her book is important both for those with specialist knowledge who want to know more of the details of the process and also for all of us who cling to the insane and necessary idea that another world is possible.

Enough! Or too much. You must read this book. Better if you get on with it, starting with the wonderful Introduction, I fall silent, in happy and enthusiastic admiration.

– John Holloway
Professor, Posgrado de Sociología,
Instituto de Ciencias Sociales y Humanidades "Alfonso Vélez Pliego",
Benemérita Universidad Autónoma de Puebla

Introduction

This book looks at the anti-capitalist economy and the organization of social relations in the context of the revolution and autonomy of Rojava (Kurdistan-Syria). It questions both the limitations and the historical problems of the phenomenon of revolution, and the conflicts and contradictions that emerge in this process.

This work also draws from the conflicts and contradictions I have consistently felt as a "political subject" who wants to change the world, especially through my experience in the Kurdish struggle and the Kurdish Movement. For this reason, every question I raise and attempt to answer in this book—in reference to the Kurds, Rojava, and the world in general, involves my own subjectivity.

The idea and dream of revolution has existed since humans created systems of domination. Indeed, revolution, meaning the liberation from systems of domination, has undoubtedly been one of the most discussed subjects in history. There have been moments when the possibility of revolution has been clearer, and there have also been certain agreements on what it is and how to get there, but it has never been something completely definable. This continues to be true today. This book does not intend to provide a definition of this great phenomenon, rather it looks at the revolutionary practices that create emancipating realities, and embraces revolution as an undefined, contradictory and dynamic process. Although history has traditionally been written by the rulers, the history of social struggles has been and is still being created by many revolutionary and transformational processes. The future is being shaped on the basis of desired revolutions and of the struggles that, in turn, transform their own actors, the people. Therefore, the desire and quest of the Kurdish people for liberation from the colonial rule of the nation-states of the Middle East—the subject of this book—has always been directly linked to the phenomenon of revolution.

Approximately one year after the beginning of the civil war in Syria, in 2012, the Kurdish Movement of Syria—which had adopted the ideas and objectives of the Kurdistan Worker's Party (PKK) and Abdullah Öcalan[1]—declared de facto autonomy in the smallest part of western Kurdistan, Rojava, where contradictions and social conflicts have always been more intense. It then set out to build democratic autonomy through military control in the regions predominantly

---

1 In Syria, the armed struggle is represented by the YPG – Yekîneyên Parastina Gel (Peoples' Defence Unit) – and the YPJ – Yekîneyên Parastina Jin (Women's Defence Unit), and the political and social struggle by the PYD – Partiya Yekîtîya Demokratik (Democratic Union Party).

inhabited by Kurds (Afrîn, Kobanê, Cezîre). In 2015, it extended this to the entire region of northern Syria up to the Euphrates River, including Tabqa, Raqqa and Deir-ezzor, where the Arab population is concentrated.

The process that developed with the declaration of autonomy in Rojava was defined as a "Revolution" by the Kurds, who resisted the division of their territory just as they had resisted colonization and the negation of their existence for a century. The Kurdish Movement defined autonomy as the process of "construction of the Rojava Revolution." One of the most significant debates in those days was "Is Rojava a revolution?" During the years I lived in Istanbul, this question led to heated discussions between the Turkish Left and the Kurds who identified with the Rojava Revolution despite their different political leanings. In fact, a similar discussion took place in Syria too, where Syrian opposition groups accused the Kurds of betraying the *Syrian Revolution*. These discussions and conflicts—in which I was directly or indirectly involved—were amongst the first and defining factors that prompted me to conduct this research.

For us Kurds, there was no point in discussing whether or not Rojava was a revolution. The question for us, from the outset, was "What type of revolution was being organized in Rojava?" A question I seek to answer in this book. These discussions, which intensified with the revolution in Rojava and became much more concrete, were not new for us Kurds, for the Kurdish struggle has always been accused of being a nationalist, not socialist struggle. In fact, similar discussions had paved the way for the separation of the socialist Kurdish Movement from the Turkish Left and, later, the founding of the PKK in 1978, the most important Kurdish organization representing this movement. For me personally, these debates emerged based on my discussions and feelings on issues such as whether class struggle came before the struggle for national liberation. These took place within a Turkish leftwing group where I first became politically conscious in the early 2000s, when I was 15 years old.

When I was seven years old, my family was forced to emigrate from Bakur (Kurdistan-Turkey) to a Turkish city in west Turkey because of Turkish aggression against our people. After almost two years of living in a tent and working in Turkish fields and in servitude, we were able to save enough money to rent a house on the outskirts of the city, where there was no electricity and no road access. There were many Kurdish families like mine in this neighborhood, and only a few Turkish families. These Turks illegally sold state-owned land to the Kurds. We knew that they were Turks and that they were selling us land with no legal documents, but we had no other way of putting a roof over our heads. What I was not old enough to understand, however, was why they called us "dirty Kurds, Kurds with a tail."

According to the Turkish Constitution, all those who live in Turkey are Turks, that is, there are no Kurds. As children at school, we were forced to take an oath every morning that proclaimed, "how fortunate are those who say I am a Turk!" In other words, the Turkish state is shaped on the basis of negating different, non-Turkish ethnic identities. In practice, what defined everyday life in Turkey was the conversion of the non-Turks. Wherever we went, it was obvious that we were Kurds: the color of our hair, of our eyes, the fact that our skin was slightly darker than that of the Turks, revealed we were not Turks, and this was a major problem when we wanted to speak. So, we would not speak Kurdish outside our homes—our parents told us not to speak it. Indeed, it was banned. But we could not speak Turkish well, for our throats are not suited to the phonetics of the Turkish language. As a result, when we spoke it, we immediately gave ourselves away. Once exposed, we would become the target of racism that affected all aspects of our everyday lives, a violence, humiliation and fear that tried to turn us into Turks, negate and uniformize us, and dishonor our Kurdish essence. Our language, culture, family ties, history, roads and cities, our names, our work, all that we have and all that we are were the object of racist negation. This act of dishonor has always enraged me ever since I was a child.

Later—I do not know why, maybe because of the birds, as Ahmed Arif[2] says—the idea of freedom entered my consciousness. Freedom was linked to dignity in every book and every poem I read, in every song I heard. Freedom, therefore, was a struggle for dignity. I was probably not aware of these definitions at the beginning; I was only able to define them much later. Initially, for me freedom was an abstract, vague possibility. But by the time this possibility began to occupy a place in my life and in my thoughts, I had already embarked on the search and the path that would lead me to write this book. That is how I came to know the ideas and practices of the Left, and that is how I discovered my own contradictions and conflicts. For how can we attain liberation if we do not acknowledge our contradictions and conflicts?

The first lesson I learned about socialism, which is presumably the social system that follows capitalism, was that it constituted a transition towards a final objective: a communist society in which we would all be free and, above all, that we had to transcend capitalism as a social and economic system. This required understanding capitalism and organizing ourselves to destroy it. Therefore, I joined a socialist party. My comrades told me that if I wanted to understand capitalism, I should read Karl Marx, for how could we transcend capitalism without

2 "There are also birds, your honor / They are the reason for everything.../ They put freedom into the mind of the people.../ Look, they are flying like terrorists, terrorists..." (Poem by Ahmed Arif)

fully understanding it? This inspired me to study economics at a university in Istanbul. I was very lucky in that, at a time when Marxism was disappearing from academia, I was attending a university where there were still Marxist professors. While I learned the laws of liberal economics (required courses), I also attended courses that criticized this economy (most of these were elective). Furthermore, great comrades from the party in which I was a member were in Istanbul, many of whom were from a traditional faction of the Turkish Left. Apart from the economics classes I was attending, I read the works of Marx, Lenin, Engels, Stalin, Trotsky, so as to discuss "Revolution" and "What is to be done?" with these comrades.

The party defined itself as Leninist and acknowledged the existence of Kurds in Turkey; even the party program supported the Kurds' struggle for their nation, which could only be achieved through a revolution of the working class and socialism. However, the prevailing opinion in the Left was that the Kurds were not fighting a class struggle, they were fighting for their national rights and their only goal was to establish Kurdistan. They argued that the Kurds should partake in the working-class struggle in Turkey and, once they had taken power, the Turks would acknowledge the right of the Kurds to self-determination. I agreed—and still agree—with the idea that the struggle should be a class struggle; that is why this book is about anti-capitalism. But at that time, I was unable to achieve an emotional synthesis. When Kurds who were organized in different leftwing organizations tried to speak of these feelings that we could not synthesize, we were considered nationalists or, at best, nationalists of an oppressed nation. We were told that we had either not read enough on communism or, if we had, we had not fully understood it. Then the feminists began to express the same idea, that as Kurdish women, we had not read enough on feminism or, if we had, we had not fully understood that either. But the same question kept repeating itself in my head: Why should Turks give us the right to self-determination? That is how I first became aware of contradiction within politics: communists did not acknowledge the Kurdish dimension.

What I wished for in those years was to be taken care of and to be accepted as a Kurd too. I was a communist, but I was also a Kurd, and my soul was scarred as a result of being a Kurd. I had not taken a beating at school because I was a communist. We were beaten for being Kurds or, rather, for playing in Kurdish. And we were not only beaten; we were taught Turkish by force, and our Turkish was never enough to satisfy them. I do not know what could be more difficult for one than disciplining the mouth to speak with a force that had been well-learned. In other words, to be a communist during that period was, in the best of cases, romantic; but there was nothing romantic about being a Kurd. To be a Kurd was to want and to not want to be a Kurd all at the same time.

Just as I was experiencing this emotional conflict with the Left, on November 21, 2004, Uğur Kaymaz, a 12-year-old Kurdish boy, was murdered by the Turkish police in front of his house in Qoeser, Mêrdîn. He was shot 13 times. The city's main state authority announced that two terrorists had been "annihilated." On the following day, I learned that Kurds were to gather to read a communiqué for Uğur Kaymaz and his father. We suggested that we go to the meeting as a party, but that did not happen. In the end, only one comrade from the party, also a Kurd, and I went—two communist Kurds went individually to protest the murder of a Kurdish boy. Once the public communiqué had been read, people began to take the megaphone to express their feelings about the murder. An old man said: "To be a Kurd in Turkey is to die of 13 bullets at the age of 12." These words hit me hard. Thirteen bullets at the age of 12! From that day on, when speaking of Uğur Kaymaz, his name is not mentioned. Instead, "13 bullets at the age of 12!" is the common name for Uğur and for all the other Kurdish children who have been murdered by the state.

With Uğur's murder, the classic Left narrative of "the worker's revolution comes first and national liberation follows" lost its meaning for me. It was an absurd political stance in the face of the constant massacre that a people, my people, were experiencing. In fact, I left the leftwing party a while later. However, this divergence did not have to do with Left thinking or with the idea of organization; it was the partisanship of the Left that led me to distance myself. For a short time, I became involved in the Kurdish youth movement.

The Kurds I met in Istanbul were not like the Kurds I had grown up with. Most of my friends were from the university and had arrived in Istanbul directly from Kurdish cities. They did not deny they were Kurds, they did not struggle to speak Turkish correctly as I did. In fact, they taught me that to speak Turkish badly was a form of resistance. In these Kurdish students houses, I became acquainted for the first time with the experience of the commune, which will come up often in this book, as well as with the Kurdish Movement. We read Abdullah Öcalan, we described ourselves as a youth movement. No one declared it openly, but we knew we sympathized with the PKK. We were critical of the Left, but we always expressed that our struggles had common objectives, although we Kurds had certain specific political goals that required an organization of our own. This organization and the community, student life, made me feel more integrated emotionally with the struggle. However, that did not mean I felt no contradictions. In fact, I later understood that to be in struggle is to be in contradiction.

In the first chapter of this book, "Debating Revolution and Emancipation in the Kurdish Struggle," I raise questions on the basis of these contradictions. For, in time, I understood that these are not contradictions that I alone have experienced, they are not even contradictions experienced only by the Kurds; they are also experienced by the Maya, in Chiapas and the Aymara, in Bolivia, as peoples in struggle. These contradictions are fueled by a series of problematic and controversial issues in the socialist revolution, the political concepts and objectives of the traditional Left, the dominant perspectives, identity politics rooted in postmodernism, and the national struggles that are focused on the construction of the state. In the case of the Kurds, they are closely linked to how the Kurdish struggle is understood and discussed, especially in academia, where Kurds are talked about in terms of "The Kurdish Issue." Put simply, the struggle is a "problem."

The first part of this book talks about the Kurds and the Kurdish struggles, and stresses that neither are homogeneous. The Kurds, whose territory was divided between the nation-states that were established in the region after the First World War (Iran, Iraq, Turkey, Syria), have risen up many times and have been fighting in the four parts of Kurdistan for over a century. However, the movements and organizations of Kurdistan have always been controversial. What will the liberation of Kurdistan and the Kurds look like, and what forms and methods of struggle will lead to emancipation?

Until the early 2000s, a united and independent Kurdistan was seen as the only solution, by the nationalist and socialist movements alike. However, in time, the Kurdish Movement led by the PKK and Abdullah Öcalan, which was initially launched with the objective of creating the socialist state of Kurdistan, was transformed. It undertook a process of self-criticism as a party and concluded it had been wrong to consider the state as a path to emancipation. Thus, in 2003, it proposed democratic autonomy as a new horizon of struggle under the paradigm of democratic confederalism. The subject and main question of the first chapter is why and how the Kurdish Movement, which emerged as a Leninist party (PKK), gradually became a popular movement and underwent this intellectual transformation. To understand this transformation, an analysis was required of the revolutionary approach of the traditional Left, which focused on taking power, and of the 21st-century approach of the spontaneous revolution, which emerged following the negation of organization (the party). The transformation of the PKK seeks to overcome both revolutionary approaches (purely hierarchic or horizontal) and to construct a revolutionary process in which the people are the subject. This section of the book often refers to the Zapatista Movement. Despite their different social dynamics and histories, their similar perspectives led me to reflect on the relationship between the Kurdish and the Zapatista movements.

The intellectual and organizational transformation of the Kurdish Movement and, through its self-critical transformation, the adaptation of autonomy as a new politics of emancipation are not only the historical backdrop that led to the Rojava Revolution; they also define Rojava in the present. The fact that the Kurdish Movement first problematized power, in the sense of breaking with the idea of the state; then realized—through its own experience of gender-based conflict within the movement—that power relations can emerge in all areas where patriarchy is dominant; and finally turned criticism and self-criticism into a methodology of organization against the rise of powers, led to a change that allows the movement to have a dynamic and transformative capacity. In this sense, Rojava is a revolutionary experience that combines the intellectual and organizational transformation of the Kurdish Movement with social transformation. Consequently, the book also addresses the question of autonomy as expressed as a process of constructing revolution and how social transformation is produced.

Before analyzing the autonomy of Rojava, I believe it is necessary to first tell the story of the resistance of Rojava in order to understand the social foundations of its revolution and the subjectivities of the people who revolt. The second chapter, "The Common History of Resistance," is based on a fundamental critique: the history of colonialism is always told from the perspective of (colonizing) domination. While colonized people have always resisted to defend their freedom, as in Rojava, the historiography or social sciences ignore this resistance and treat these people as victims of colonialism. This viewpoint reproduces the dominant power of the colonizer. The second chapter underlines the fact that the quest for autonomy always walks hand in hand with resistance and has worked its way into the common memory of resistance of the Kurds in Rojava.

In the third chapter, "The Autonomy of Rojava as a Movement," I analyze democratic autonomy and democratic confederalism—which have been the concepts of struggle of the Kurdish Movement since 2003—in terms of theory and practice. The negation of power constitutes the foundation of these new objectives of struggle. The understanding of autonomy, which repudiates nationalization and all types of relations of domination between the state and society, points toward a new social, democratic and ecological organization and towards women's liberation. It turns autonomy into a practice of coexistence and of decision-making between different ethnic and religious identities from the standpoint and the practice of the democratic nation. I highlight that the process of constructing autonomy in Rojava has not been defined in the seven years that have passed since the declaration of autonomy, and that this autonomy has transformed as its practices emerged. As such, it is an ongoing process. I discuss what tendencies exist within these practices and what is revealed by their transformation.

The conditions of hot war and the policies against the insurgents compel an institutionalization of autonomy, as well as the acceptance of the relations and forms of domination of the nation-state. Consequently, the process of transformation of the first popular assemblies in Rojava into the Federation of North and East Syria has unfolded at the risk of institutionalization, as has occurred with other experiences of autonomy. However, I argue that popular assemblies and the experiences of the communes can overcome this risk by creating practices that mobilize the peoples from below. Therefore, the possibility of the "Kurdish state" walks hand in hand with the revolutionary process and the construction of autonomy as an emotional contradiction, especially in the context of violent attacks against the villages.

The main argument in this chapter is that Rojava, the communes and the popular assemblies have overcome the issue of representation and democracy, and the act of assembly has become a movement; the commune has become the daily way of life in Rojava, and autonomy informs the relations around which life is organized. The practices of popular organization, the creation of relations and spaces for collective decision-making, and the capacity of the community to make decisions a reality are fundamental social transformations that motivate the autonomous government to deepen the autonomy by creating more autonomous practices, and distancing itself from state or capitalist institutionalization. The fact that women participate equally (50%) in all these autonomous practices and have their own organization makes it possible to move autonomy away from patriarchy.

The last part of the book addresses the practice of an anti-capitalist economy in Rojava. Many revolutions have been relegated to the pages of history because they were unable to organize an anti-capitalist economy that liberated labor from the rule of capital. Also, many autonomy experiments have attained political autonomy but have not been able to become independent from global capitalism; they produced a local capitalism and were unable to bring about true social emancipation. What determines the future of the revolution and autonomy is the capacity for liberation from capitalist relations and the creation of a life guided by use value. The risk of capitalization is also present in the Rojava Revolution and its autonomy. I examine the capacity of the revolution and autonomy of Rojava to transcend and destroy capitalism, by focusing on the organization of an anti-capitalist economy, expressed as a "social economy" in Rojava.

The social economy is one of the organizational dimensions of democratic autonomy; its goal is to socialize production and communalize property from the general (mixed) economy and the women's economy (*Aboriya Jin*). From 2014, with the beginning of committee organizing, and later through coordination, many different methods have been employed to organize this dimension. While there are many customs and practices of the peoples in many walks of life, spontaneous experiences also arise in such conditions. However, organizing a non-capitalist economy and eliminating capitalist relations is one of the most demanding challenges for the Kurdish Movement and the autonomous government of Rojava. The experiences and problems of past revolutions are also evident in the Rojava Revolution. The main reason it is so difficult to eliminate capitalism is the totality with which it is enmeshed in the state and the patriarchate and, now, in the ongoing war. However, it is also due to the Kurdish Movement's analysis of capitalism and its communal economy perspective.

The main objective of this book is to discuss the theoretical and practical limitations of the communal economy in the face of the totality of capitalism. Consequently, in the first part of the final chapter, I focus on the contradictions between the communal economy perspective and practice. I argue that the communal economy perspective can sometimes miss, and indeed has missed, many of the potentially revolutionary experiences and practices that emerge in the process of organizing the economy. This is because politics, the political leaders and the people have not sufficiently internalized and valued the need for an anti-capitalist economy. In addition, critical reflections are needed about cooperativism, for the communal economy perspective is based on cooperatives. I conclude the chapter with an analysis of how cooperatives in Rojava are organized and their characteristics, dynamics and limitations. This analysis demonstrates that cooperatives in Rojava are experienced not merely as structures of production but as something relational.

While my experience as a Kurd and as a participant in the Kurdish struggle for many years permeates the entire book, this is particularly true in the last chapter, which is strongly influenced by the time I spent on the economics committee in Bakur, where we organized and supported cooperatives just like Rojava. Many of the questions and issues I discuss in the last chapter are rooted in this experience and the research I conducted in Rojava.

While writing this book, I visited Rojava twice, with an interval of approximately two years, and I conducted research in a broad field. My first visit took place between January and April 2018, and the second from November to December 2019. Since 2011, the whole of Syria has been experiencing a tough war; it is fair to say that the region of Rojava, although not as isolated as other regions of Syria, is under constant attack. In fact, during my first visit and second visits to the Afrîn canton, the regions of Serîkanîyê and Girêsipîyê were attacked by a joint invasion of the Turks and the jihadists. My research was conducted in that context. However, despite the war and the climate of insecurity, especially for women, I was able to observe that the people are uniting more and more each day around democratic autonomy; resistance, hope and social transformation, as well as the transformation of individuals who are being turned into subjects of autonomy, made me feel that writing on this revolutionary and transformative process is much more vital than writing on the destruction and violence that the war has caused.

I have not limited my field research to a specific geographic region; the social diversity in Rojava and in the north of Syria has created a richness in which each territory—even each village—has its own subjectivities. I did not wish to limit these differences to a geography that represents the region in scientific terms. I defined the field of investigation in terms of the relations created by the organization of the non-territorial economy. In other words, I conducted my research following the communities that are part of the organization of the social economy.

The research consisted of individual and group interviews, participation in and observation of meetings of cooperatives, popular assemblies and communes, and visits to cooperatives and economic projects. Although most of my field research focuses on the organization of the economy, I also conducted numerous interviews and observations outside this realm. I met with the co-presidents of the autonomous government of the Cezîre region, as well as with the co-president of the economic council, and I attended the meetings of the cantonal assemblies of Qamishlo and Hesekê as a listener and an observer. Apart from these interviews and meetings, most of which are recorded, many unrecorded interviews, meetings, discussions and observations also informed the arguments in this book.

During my time in Rojava, I stayed in the commune houses of the women's movement (Kongra-Star) and thus had the opportunity to experience communal life and community processes. One of the most important experiences that impressed me in Rojava was that, beyond the commune houses, through autonomy, communal life in Rojava and in north and east Syria has expanded and become incorporated into the local culture of solidarity and sharing.

During my research, I needed almost no money; I received incredible support from all these networks, relations and communal spaces. Wherever I went, I was offered food and tea, and then engaged in extensive discussions. The members of the coordination body of the social economy of Rojava provided all the liaisons for my meetings. I personally chose the people I would interview. Being familiar with the organizational structure and forms of the Kurdish Movement helped me make those choices, and create a relationship of trust with my interviewees.

On my first visit, I met with the leaders of the economic committees of TEV-DEM (Democratic Society Movement) and Kongra-Star, who organized the economic sphere, to understand the organizational structure of the social economy. I scheduled my visits to the cooperatives with the cooperative committee and met with the members of the cooperatives as well as with the Houses of Cooperatives (*Mala Kooperatîfan*), the Cooperatives Unit (*Yekîtîya Kooperatîfan*) and the Economy Council (*Destaye Aborî*). I also had the chance to visit innumerable communes, to follow the popular congregations of "a cooperative for each commune" organized by the cooperativist movement, and launched by the committee of the women's economy (*Aborîya Jin*).

On my second visit, I once again met with members of the coordination body of the economy so as to understand the changes and transformations that had taken place between my first visit and the end of 2019. I visited cooperatives, although many I had visited in 2018 no longer existed. To understand how the economy is linked and integrated with other dimensions of autonomy, I met with the women's movement, the academy of Jineolojî, the women's village (Jinwar), members of the coordination body of the municipalities and ecology, the autonomous government, and the co-presidents of the cantonal assemblies. I took part in numerous mass gatherings, such as solidarity campaigns organized by the communes for the displaced populations of Afrin and Girêsipîyê-Serîkanîye. I also visited tree plantations and attended marches against the invasion, celebrations of Newroz, and women's marches. In this sense, although the social economy is at the core of my research, the time I spent in Rojava was a process in which I experienced anti-capitalist life and was able to experiment and observe and, most importantly, talk with people.

One of the greatest difficulties I encountered while researching this book was working within a process of constant change and transformation. Consequently, in this book, you will not find final assertions on the revolution and the process of construction of autonomy in Rojava; on the contrary, I tried to underline the tendencies of autonomy, the collective efforts to overcome contradictions, conflicts and time constraints. For, in Rojava, the revolution is occurring through peoples' experimentation and is not ruled by any institution or predefined thinking.

I must point out that my experience in Rojava occurred hand in hand with getting to know the Zapatista Movement in Chiapas during my stay in Mexico. The peoples of Mesopotamia and the Land of the Maya led civilizations and

Neolithic revolutions thousands of years ago, and they continue to do so today. They continue fighting to make the world a better and more livable place. When I became aware of the fact that their struggles have been ongoing for thousands of years, and that for democracy to be fair and, above all, to be free, for these peoples it is not only a political quest but also a way of life, I understood, thousands of years later, why these lands continue to be the global center of hope. That is why, as a Kurdish woman from Mesopotamia, touching the soul of the Maya lands is the most beautiful, hopeful and motivating experience I could ever have. It is not easy for a book to describe the immensely rich totality of these experiences, for life is always more than a book, and the struggle is sometimes more than life itself. However, if it manages to create a thread for the bridge that connects these two centers of hope, it will have achieved its objective.

CHAPTER 1

Debating Revolution and Emancipation in the Kurdish Struggle

The Valley of the Butchers

The wind carried the smell of basil & thyme & tobacco—our contraband.
The tall little windows of the houses with their low roofs
disseminated their pale light into the night.
The howling of the dogs blended itself with our fears.
It propped up those fears.
Later, when doubtful gunshots sounded in the mountains,
hearts convulsed before the barrel of a gun...
Our lament reached up as echoes into those mountains.
Our doors were broken open, our loves, our hopes, our dreams,
and everything that could belong to human beings...
And blood flowed in our rivers.
Zilan, Munzur, the valley of the butchers...
suffering locked itself away
in all the rivers of our country.
No creature of God could hear us in that place.
And when the dove alighted into that black night, we dreamed of the mountains.
All that's left for the Kurds is the good fight.
Resistance is another name for life...

–Musa Anter[1]

---

1 Musa Anter (1920–September 20, 1992), also known as *Apê Musa* (Kurdish for "Uncle Musa"), was a Kurdish writer, journalist and intellectual who was assassinated by Turkish JITEM, the unofficial and illegal intelligence agency-like paramilitary organization. The name of the poem refers to the Kasaplar Deresi (*Newala Qesaba* in Kurdish, Kasaplar Stream in English), which was used as a mass grave in the 1980s by the Turkish army. Even today no research is allowed in this area. Original translation by Azê (author).

The Kurds and their struggle

To date, there have been many studies of the so-called "Kurdish Question" or "Kurdish Problem"—its substance, its history, cultural analyses and ethnographies from diverse perspectives—that have addressed the subject of the Kurdish people's struggle for liberation in its various forms (Jabar and Mansour, 2019; Gunes and Zeydanlioglu, 2014; Stansfield and Shareef, 2017). Research in this area has led to the emergence of such concepts as "kurdology" and "kurdologists"[2] (Bruinessen, 2012). The "question" tends systematically to be identified as a "problem," and the whole notion of a "Kurdish Question" (*Kürt Sorunu*, in Turkish) emerged from beneath this hegemonic gaze. Indeed, this phenomenon, which the preferred lenses of state-backed research refer to as a Kurdish problem, that is, a crisis created by those who seek the liberation of the Kurds, is, in essence, a crisis of the ideology of the nation-state itself, of its very possibility in the Middle East. The struggle of the Kurdish people to be, to exist or be visible, represents in itself the larger crisis of the nation-state. Though defined as a political or sociological problem, and all too often in the most superficial manner as merely an economic problem, the Kurdish phenomenon is, in fact, proof of the crises and contradictions of capitalist and statist systems. As such, it is one of the most important objects of political and academic research around the world.

The main reasons for this can be outlined as follows:

- In the past, the Kurds' historical and cultural lands were divided up between various empires (the Ottomans, the Persians); today, they are divided up between various nation-states (Turkey, Iraq, Iran and Syria).
- This division has meant and continues to mean the oppression of the region's people.
- Battles are ongoing between several major capitalist actors in the Middle East, owing principally to the distribution of the region's oil.
- There is an ongoing need among capitalist nation-states to consolidate power and exert control by means of the extraction and sale of oil, as well as other natural resources.
- All of this has resulted in years of war, displacement, migration, violence, disappearances, and so on.

That all these factors have turned the region into a place riddled with social conflict—with political and communal violence—has attracted the attention of many social science researchers. Thousands of these researchers, financed by

---

2 Kurdology refers to a complex of human sciences studying the languages, history, literature, folklore, culture and ethnology of people speaking Kurdish languages. Kurdologist refers to the researcher of Kurdish history, culture and language.

this or that state, are sent out to the Middle East on a regular basis to compile information that, no doubt, will prove of some use in the inter-imperial struggle itself. However, many of these investigations have been motivated by the fact that the Kurdish liberation struggle and the alternative way of life it proposes have become a source of enormous hope for many people, organizations, collectives and movements who oppose the dominant global system. And this has resulted in a considerable number of people studying, observing, consulting, comparing their experiences to, and ultimately aligning themselves with the Kurdish struggle, all for the purpose of nurturing and growing this hope.

Hope, yes, but as always, hope that is measured in concrete achievements and in expected outcomes. All too often, it seems that concepts such as "the struggle," or more concretely "the revolution," must be related to the attainment of certain specific victories, to the established objectives of the revolution. This sort of thinking focuses only on outcomes, instead of studying the process of struggle itself and how it comes to be. In written sources, there is a similar kind of thinking that concerns itself either with the human, geographic or political forces that have destroyed the hegemonic system, or with objectives that the struggle has yet to realize.

For my part, I am concerned with the contradictions, the conflicts, and the journey that arise in the course of struggle, rather than its simple outcome. Of course, the consequences of a struggle are important, however, I do not regard the struggle for liberation as something that ends at some particular moment, after realizing certain specific objectives. Because the struggle for liberation is not a conflict with limited aims, it has always been the single most stimulating element of human history.

When I say "the journey of the Kurdish people," I do not take this to refer to a homogenous phenomenon, as many studies have done. Their journey, their search for liberation, has taken varied forms through the course of their long history, and it remains quite diverse in its forms today. Indeed, these ways of thinking and this diversity can all manifest themselves in one and the same struggle. The Kurdish people are extremely heterogeneous in terms of class, religion, culture and way of life. That they have not become nationalized in the course of their history, that is, they have neither founded a Kurdish state nor all been governed by one sovereign power, has ensured the preservation of social diversity within their ranks. Kurdish society has never existed as a single hegemonic mentality or a statist way of thinking. Of course, the Kurds wanted to establish a state, but this never became a concrete reality. And the desire to found a state should not be confused with the enshrinement of the state in one's mind as the affirmation of one's identity. This continues to be true even today. The history of the Kurds, seen in this way, clearly facilitates their acceptance of a more radical idea of democratic autonomy.

Although the Kurdish people have not been repressed, regulated or forced into conformity with the creation of their own state, they nonetheless experience various forms of oppression and exploitation under the centralized hegemony of other nation-states. What is unique about Kurdish society is that they experience these daily conditions of oppression and exploitation due to their being Kurdish. And, therefore, it is precisely their being "different" by being Kurdish—or more precisely their Kurdishness, that is, their embrace of the Kurdish identity—that serves as a kind of self-defense in the face of that oppression. This creative act imbues the Kurdish community with a sense of their common destiny. In his article on Kurdish nationalism, the renowned Turkish historian Hamit Bozarslan affirms that this sense of a shared destiny exists despite the fragmentation of the community across a number of nation-states, and that this fragmentation has not eliminated the existence of a "common sociology" amongst the Kurds:

> All the Kurdish movements perceive Kurdish reality by means of a shared map, a shared founding myth (*Kawa*), a shared national holiday (*Newroz*), a shared national anthem (*ey Reqib*), and the conjoined histories of the Iraqi-Kurdish Barzani leader and the PKK in Turkey. These sources and reference points determine the symbolic universe of all the Kurdish movements of the Middle East. For this reason, any movement that upon starting gains momentum in one country can in short order become a regional movement, mobilizing the Kurdish Movement in other countries, or at the very least compelling them to take a stance. (Bozarslan, 2008, p. 843)

Every journey seeking liberation among the Kurds is ultimately directed towards the overthrow of these conditions of oppression, violence and exploitation. And every journey is nourished by the aforementioned sense of a common history, a shared sociology, a unified symbolic universe. Though it must also be said that these journeys and these struggles vary, depending on their context, and based on their different answers to the key question of how to achieve freedom. In other words, they become diversified with respect to the means and the ends by which they struggle. As such, there exist many struggles for national liberation, movements that are nationalist, statist, independent, liberal, and so on in their demands. And there are also struggles that, undergirded by Marxist notions of class struggle and the right to self-determination among nations, and so on, have their own notable history in Kurdistan (Abdurrahim Özmen and Emir Ali Türkmen, 2014).

What project, what set of demands can liberate the Kurdish people? This is a controversial subject today, as it has been throughout history. And it should be noted that this is far from exclusively a theoretical discussion. This debate will just as much be determined by emotions, by interventions in the world of meaningful symbols, by dominant ideologies—and these are more decisive than anything else. Listen to people's conversations over tea on any street in Kurdistan, and you will find that the most hotly debated matter in Kurdish society is the question of liberation. How will the Kurds emancipate themselves? How will Kurdistan be free? These conversations form a part of everyday life.

When Kurds discuss the question of their own emancipation, they often construct a language around their ethnic identity. In other words, the subject who is discussing their freedom is Kurdish; hence, many studies address the quest for Kurdish liberation in the context of the national liberation of the Kurdish people and identity. This struggle began when the Kurdish people rebelled against the conditions of oppression and exploitation they experienced by the mere fact of their Kurdishness. But, today, there can be no doubt that their demands go far beyond those stated at the outset. Often, in the context of nationalist ideology, the Kurdish struggle is reduced and restricted to aspects pertaining to the recognition of cultural identity rights, the sharing of sovereignty, or, at its logical conclusion, the establishment of a Kurdish state. But when asked today what it is they want, the Kurds talk about their struggle in terms of more universal values such as freedom, democracy, equality and world peace.

One particular Kurdish movement—led politically and ideologically by the PKK (Kurdistan Workers' Party) and Abdullah Öcalan since 1978—now signifies a far broader popular movement, one that reaches deep into the population regardless of whether they are sympathizers of the PKK and/or Öcalan. Nor is it simply a movement for national liberation; from its beginnings, it has engaged in a powerful critique of the capitalist system, not solely an analysis of the national question. The language of struggle, which in its early period was formed principally on the basis of identity and cultural rights, has been superseded by a grammar of anti-capitalist revolt that also analyzes and critiques, in turn, the traditional Left's ideas concerning revolution. In fact, none of the movement's objectives today has to do with the "national" liberation of the Kurds; rather, the struggle has been reoriented towards the destruction of the system of capitalist modernity that dominates the world.

From the day it emerged, the Kurdish Movement has affirmed its desire to create an anti-capitalist form of social life—a goal it expresses in its communiques through the concept of *avakirin*, or "construction" (DTK, *Demokratik Özerklik İlan Belgesi*, 2011). Avakirin, at its root, is the act of collectively building or assembling something, a task that can only be completed successfully through

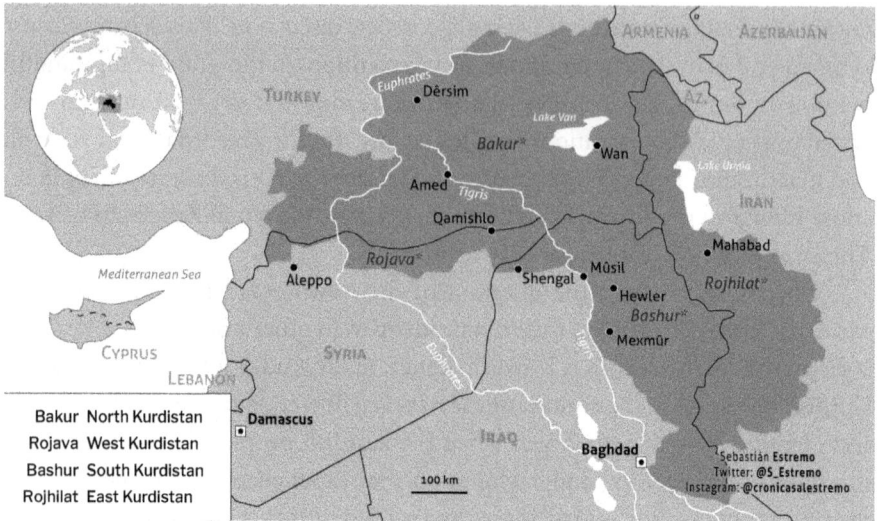

Regions of Kurdistan

the active participation of the people in that process. In precisely this manner, people in different parts of Kurdistan have begun to weave together the pieces of anti-capitalist social relations. The de facto autonomy built up in Rojava in northeastern Syria over the past ten years is only the most lasting and permanent demonstration of these concrete efforts.

The Kurdish Movement today is therefore the expression of something far greater than a simple nationalist movement. The idea of autonomy in the thought of the Kurdish Movement, which it calls "democratic confederalism," is a project based fundamentally on the critique of the nation-state (Öcalan, 2005). The demands of autonomy go further than the struggles of an oppressed ethnicity for civil rights and the social recognition of their identity. The movement also defends the peace between different ethnicities through its notion of the "democratic nation" (Öcalan, 2016). Furthermore, the struggle for autonomy is driven by the struggle against patriarchy, the fight to liberate women, that they may not once again become mere subjects (Jineoloji Academy, 2016). This battle is realized not only in theory, but also through the anti-patriarchal construction of the autonomous institutions themselves. These model institutions, such as communes and cooperatives, guarantee an economic community, instead of what Öcalan refers to as "monopoly capitalism" (Aslan, 2015).

It should be noted that Öcalan analyzes capitalism through several different conceptual lenses across his work. When he uses the term "monopoly capitalism," I understand him to be referring to how the capitalist system is controlled and dominated by large firms that have outsized control over the world's capital. The result, according to him, is that many other forms of economic activity—although not themselves capitalist—are immersed in and subordinated to the totalizing and totalitarian logic of capitalist relations. We find a similar idea in J.K. Gibson-Graham's[3] book *The End of Capitalism (As We Knew It): A Feminist Critique of Political Economy* (2010, p. 61), in which the authors talk about how islands of alternative modes of production exist within the global system but are frequently re-absorbed by capitalism's hegemonic manner of organizing production, and totalizing patterns of thought.

The Kurdish Movement has arrived at similar reflections in its attempts to break with capitalism. This impacts its methods and approaches. Later in this analysis we will see how, in order to aid the construction of a communal economy, the movement establishes a dialogue with small capitalist producers. While these petty capitalists are indeed often dominated by monopoly capitalists, the attempt to engage them in building an anti-capitalist system creates a deep contradiction in the political economy of the autonomous zone.

The theoretical and political evolution of the Kurdish Movement has been the result of moments of rupture from its own history and traditions. The revolutionary movement draws on practices of criticism and self-criticism through which its theories and practices are constantly destroyed and reconstructed in order to leave it stronger and better prepared to confront the challenges of the concrete situation. And, crucially, the Kurdish struggle has an existence that transcends Kurdish identity: when the movements speak of autonomy, it is not speaking only of the autonomy of Rojava's Kurds but also that of all the peoples of northeastern Syria. Rojava's Social Contract—the first founding text of the Autonomy of Rojava—clearly expressed that all peoples and religious groups living in the region would have autonomy and participate jointly in the construction of a new society:

> We the peoples of the areas of self-administration of Democratic Kurds, Arabs and Assyrians (Assyrian Chaldeans, Arameans), Turkmen, Armenians, and Chechens, by our free will have announced this to materialize justice, freedom and democracy in accordance with the principle of ecological balance and equality without discrimination on the basis of race, religion, creed, doctrine or gender, to achieve the political and moral fabric of a democratic society in order to function with mutual understanding and coexistence within diversity and respect for the

3 A pseudonym for two critical geographers, Julie Graham and Katherine Gibson, who collaborated on their books. – *Translator's note*

principle of self-determination of peoples, and to ensure the rights of women and children, the protection, defense and respect of the freedom of religion and belief. (Rojava Social Contract, 2014)

However, the introduction of the Contract indicates that autonomy will not accept any state or form of power: "Democratic Autonomous Region Administrations; It does not accept the nation-state, military and religious state understanding, as well as central government and power" (Rojava Social Contract, 2014). In its journey for freedom from capitalism, the Kurdish Movement has envisioned a world and prefigured a life beyond national liberation.

The tension between nationalism and socialism in the Kurdish struggles

The Kurdish struggles have articulated critiques of an anti-capitalist character since about the 1960s. Before 1960, Kurdish movement had a more traditional and nationalist character. Specifically, Bozarslan (2008, p. 841) states that Kurdish nationalism was a cultural nationalism until 1914, only to then gradually become a political nationalism.

If we read the politicization of Kurdish nationalism as a process of escalating conflict with the central governments of the various countries where Kurds resided, we can see how this politicization played an important role in rebellions organized by representatives of those regions' feudal social order—*aga* (rural landowners), *şex* (Muslim tribal leaders) and *mir* (aristocratic landlords). These leading classes of the ancien regime sought to regain the privileges they had lost with the rise of modernized nation-states, especially after the First World War, such as the right to have soldiers of their own or to collect local taxes and fees.

The Kurds lived in large tribes led by feudal actors of a sort, who to this day continue to impact Kurdish society. These feudal classes have always established alliances with the Turkish authorities. Within the framework of these alliances, they participated in the Armenian genocide (Çelik, 2020), for example, which was carried out for the purpose of nationalizing capital during the Turkish war of independence and contributed to the establishment of Turkey as a nation-state. After the liberation war, however, the nation-states established in the territory of what had been the Ottoman Empire denied the cultural and political exis-tence of the Kurds, on the grounds that Kurdishness threatened their self-image as a unitary nation. In accordance with this understanding, they confiscated the social wealth in Kurdish lands and began the process of forcefully assimilating the people. The new nation-states made no distinction between different social classes, imposing extreme pressure on propertied and penniless Kurds alike.

That such policies applied equally to all segments of Kurdish society had the effect of smoothing over and concealing class differences—and, therefore, the contradictions and exploitation of the class system—within Kurdish society. Consequently, in this period, there is no real evidence of class struggle among the Kurds due to the cross-class unity and solidarity created by a shared experience of national oppression.

Abdullah Öcalan defines the period up to the Kurdish Republic of Mahabad as the age of primitive nationalism. This republic, also known as Iranian Kurd-istan (*Rojhilat*), declared its existence with the support of the USSR in 1946, only to collapse when it lost that support. And, indeed, after the collapse of Mahabad it seems all Kurdish rebel movements died out until the 1960s. Many researchers, such as Baskın Oran, Hamit Bozarslan and İsmail Beşikçi, refer to the era that followed as the period of "silence" and "intimidation" or as "the wordless period." However, although we cannot speak of organizational mobilization or outright rebellion during this period, this picture omits much that is of great impor-tance to understanding future developments. This was a time when the youth were avidly reading the Syrian Kurdish poet Cigerxwîn; a moment when the intellectual Musa Anter was being published by *Kaniya Dîcleyê* (Tigris Source), the Kurdish-language newspaper in Diyarbakır. Therefore, it is incorrect to call this a "period of silence." Rather, it was a period in which resistance had to be conducted in a passive way, a deep way, existing beneath the surface.

Resistance cannot always manifest itself in the form of political action or formal organization. The organization of everyday life against the dominant system can in itself be a form of resistance worthy of a dignified people. As the Zapatistas say:

> [W]e Zapatistas turned silence into a weapon of struggle that [the system] did not know and against which it could do nothing, and against our silence the prickling lies, the bullets, the bombs, the blows crashed again and again. Just as after the combat of January 1994 we'd discov-ered that the word was our weapon, now we did it with silence. While the government was presenting everyone with the threat of death and destruction, we were able to learn and teach ourselves and teach another form of struggle, that with reason, truth, and history it's possible to fight and win...by keeping silent. (CCRI-EZLN, 1998)

In the 1960s, this worthy form of resistance broke down, and the nationalist movements led by the class interests of the feudal actors were replaced by Kurdish socialist movements led by students and leftist intellectuals. These included the TKPD, PSK, DDKD-KIP, PKK, Rizgari and Kawa ve Têkoşin. Although Kurdish nationalism continued to influence these socialist movements, the change in the class character of the rebel forces also transformed the grammar of resistance. From this point on, there began to be revolutionary arguments against capitalism, expressed in the struggle for the rights of Kurdish worker-peasants.

In these years, the USSR became a decisive political force in the Middle East because of the hope for socialism it generated among the peoples of the region. This was aided by many other historical factors as well, including the revolutionary impact of the 1968 youth movements in Turkey—the Eastern Public Rallies (*Doğu Mitingleri*) organized by the Workers' Party of Turkey (*Türkiye İşçi Partisi*, or TIP) in the cities of the Kurds—Amed, Batman, Sêwreg and Dersîm. And then there was the Algerian War of Independence (1954–1962), the liberation struggle of the Kurds in Iraq (1961–1970) led by Mustafa Barzani, the ETA's struggle for the liberation of the Basque Country, and so on.

All this allowed for the emergence of movements pushing for socialist revolution. Kurds began to consider themselves colonized people. In Marxism-Leninism, they found a justification for the national struggle that also entwined them organically with leftist currents around the world (Bozarslan, 2008, p. 842). Bozarslan notes that the Kurdish Movement and the Kurdish Left became almost synonymous in the 1960s (Jongerden, Akkaya and Şimşek, 2015, p. 71). Ahmet Hamdi Akkaya (2013), for his part, argues that this identification became more evident from the 1970s onwards. Certain traditionally nationalist demands—such as for recognition of identity-based rights and freedom of expression in the Kurdish language—never disappeared, but were now fought for under the banner of socialism.

By the 1970s, after much discussion of the notion that "Kurdistan is colonized," the Kurdish movements began to split off from the Turkish left and highlight their own struggle for independence by means of their own organizations. This process eventually resulted in the founding of the Revolutionary Cultural Eastern Hearths (Devrimci Doğu Kültür Ocakları, or DDKO), a Kurdish student organization that existed from 1969 to 1971.

It is difficult to find a detailed reading on the reasons why the Kurds split from the Turkish Left. Memoirs written after the fact state that this was "felt" to be a necessity. I can point to two main reasons that come to the fore in my research on this period. One is that the Turkish Left consistently subordinated the emancipation of the Kurds to the socialist revolution and accused those who highlighted the Kurdish question of splitting the revolutionary forces. The second is that—as can be seen in the judgments of the socialists in the TIP—the Turkish Left was against the forced assimilation of the Kurds into Turkish identity, but was perfectly willing to accept their "organic" assimilation. Such tendencies are to be found in the discussions of the Turkish Left even today. Yet for all that, the Turkish Left was itself divided into factions and experiencing many conflicts without the help of ethnic minorities. The Kurds, it seems, did not want to wait patiently for a revolution that clearly was not going to happen in order to secure their national rights (Fırat, 2006, p. 179). And so it was that leftist Kurds who exited the TIP and other socialist formations founded the DDKO, the Kurds' own first socialist organization, in 1969. The DDKO was not a party; it took the form of a student club where young Kurdish socialists gathered. It was initially organized in Istanbul and Ankara, where there were university students, and later spread to the regions where Kurds live: Batman, Amed and Hezzo.

According to Bozarslan (2008, p. 856), the DDKO in this period represents an important organizational development for the Kurdish Left. Akkaya, for his part, points out that the DDKO has been one of the main sources of an autonomous and independent Kurdish lineage within the Turkish socialist movement of the 1970s. One of the main reasons for the break has to do with the approach Turkish socialists took to the Kurdish/Kurdistan question, which could be summed up as the assertion that "the Kurdish question is solved by socialism" (Akkaya 2013, p. 95).

Bozarslan (2008) asserts that this organizational development was followed by two important theoretical developments that reinterpret the Kurdish problem:

> The most important theoretical developments accepted that Kurdistan was not a part of Iran, Iraq, or Turkey, but rather was colonized and fragmented by these countries. The second theoretical development, a natural consequence of this, was that each Kurdish movement saw itself as part of the whole Kurdish history of the Middle East and did not reject an independent and united Kurdistan as a legal right and a political possibility. (2008, p. 856)

This means that the Kurdish Left, which was autonomous from the experience of the DDKO, began to discuss the idea of revolution around the national question. The result was an inference that corresponded to the theoretical tendencies of the Left of that period: the socialist nation-state as an answer to the national problem. In fact, today's Kurdish Movement—the one making the revolution in Rojava and building a broader sort of democratic autonomy— was initially born with this objective: the construction of a united, independent and socialist Kurdistan.

Overcoming revolutionary history

Social problems are inseparably linked to the question of revolution. This situation is in turn a response to the fact that the phenomenon of revolution represents a very special moment in the flow of social relations. Because revolution is the reality of historical society, total and concentrated; it is a moment of metaphysical transcendence that reaches audacious heights; it corresponds to the very moment when the enthusiasm of the crowd and the individual heartbeat meet in their acceleration. And this period of time is connected to freedom. (Erdal, 2018, p. 20)

Histories of the Kurdish struggle mention some 29 major rebellions (Karayılan, 2011). All but the current revolution were suppressed, through massacres perpetrated by the colonialist states. Rebellion and massacre are two phenomena that are always invoked in the common memory of Kurds. For Kurds, rebellion is associated with death, not only their own, but in terms of mass killings. And it is believed that dying oneself is a kind of salvation, inasmuch as it is better than living with the memory of a massacre. For this reason, revolt, pain and anger are the most important elements that make the community and organize its struggle everywhere.

Raúl Zibechi (2006, p. 51), referring to Negri, emphasizes that pain "is a key that opens the door to community" and that community is not something that arises spontaneously. "Community doesn't exist, it is made; it is not an institution, not even an organization, but a form taken by the links between people. Far more important than defining a community is to see how it works" (Zibechi R., 2006, p. 38).

Undoubtedly, grief can sometimes serve as firmer terrain for a community than a shared physical territory. But at the same time, it is difficult to say that pain is a revolutionary or emancipatory emotion. For on its own, pain just as often terrifies, intimidates and disperses as it unites. Pain is a powerful emotion that can gather a community joined together in bitterness, but all too often it walks arm in arm with fear. It renders inert the natural form of community. Grief fixes memory in a particular moment, in its own time, and those who feel the pain become trapped there. After a great common pain, time seems to remain stuck in that instant forever.

For example, my generation—which had to emigrate from what was then Kurdish territory within Turkey in the 1990s—grew up in deafening silence and denial after the pain of what happened to our families. We know few things about Kurdistan in 1990, because it is still very difficult for our parents to tell the story. Our Kurdish parents, who tried to forget their suffering, demonstrated a frequent rejection or denial of their own Kurdishness by not teaching us our mother tongue, for instance. Yıldırım Türker (2011), who worked as a journalist in the region in the 1990s, says this about Amed (Diyarbakır) of the 1990s:

> People don't live here, they hide. Being able to name what they hide from is perhaps the first step to understanding this geography. The people of Diyarbakır do not hide from soldiers, nor from the PKK, nor from imaginary or imaginable enemies. They hide from their own identity, from their history erased with a rancor they cannot understand, in short, from being Kurds. It's called a state of emergency. (Türker, 2011, s. 11)

The 1990s altered the sociological makeup of Kurds in many respects. The Kurdish Movement declared itself to be in *serhildan* (rebellion) under the leadership of the PKK in 1989, and until 1993 the insurrection spread throughout the Kurdish population of Turkey. During these years, Kurds living in Turkey witnessed popular uprisings and violent conflicts in almost the entire region.

In this period, the Turkish state launched a security program establishing so-called *koruculuk*, or village guards, in rural areas, paramilitary groups recruited from the population to fight against and prevent popular support for the PKK. This is a phenomenon that has occurred in other parts of the world where paramilitary units similar to the village guard system have been formed, such as the "united self-defense forces" in Colombia, and the "Kadyrov followers" (*Kadyrovtsy*) in Chechnya (Göc-Der, 2013, p. 1). With this system, the Turkish state specifically wanted to arm the border villages to operate in its favor. Although some people accepted the village guard, most villages in general, refused the idea of using weapons against the PKK. This decision resulted in one of the most extensive episodes of displacement in Kurdish history.

As a result of the burning of villages and increasing political pressure, the Kurdish population of these areas—then numbering in the millions—was forced to migrate to the large cities in the east and then to the western Turkish provinces. Kawar village, which I visited in 2014 to learn about its cooperative process, is one of the villages that was burned, destroyed and its residents displaced in 1993. The people of Kawar started to return to their village in 2005, in an attempt to re-establish their community life. In our conversation, one of the villagers, who spent about 15 years under torture, imprisonment, threats and forced migration, expressed the following regarding why they did not accept to be village guards:

> Actually, we were just giving bread to the PKK; who can starve their own children? They are our children. We were just giving bread and cheese to the PKK, the PKK were the ones who helped us—if we lose an axe, say, we go to the PKK. Because they're fair; if there's a dispute, they settle it without offending anyone. They always settle blood feuds. Before the PKK, we didn't know what justice was. No one treated us like humans. They even solve the problems between husbands and wives; for example, I used to behave very badly with my wife, but now I don't behave badly because the guerrilla women used to talk to me a lot and tell me how beautiful my wife is, how hard she works for the family [...] Now I know that my wife is the rose of my house and she has the right to do whatever she wants to do. (Interview with a villager from Kawar, 2014)

Contrary to the propaganda and threats of the Turkish state in those years, the PKK was hardly a scourge upon the people. With the coming of the PKK, Kurdistan's society was changing in favor of the poor for the first time. One of the inhabitants of Kawar, who refused to be a village guard, tells Nurcan Baysal how Kawar was burned in *That Day (O Gün)*:

> It was the night of December 28, 1993. Soldiers arrived, first they set fire to the mountains. After 01:00, Special Operations soldiers (*Özel Harekat*) entered the village with Panzers. At that time there was no one left in Düzcealan,[4] everyone went to other villages. There was no one left. They shot our uncle, they smashed his arms. They crushed him with a Panzer [...] Then we heard that our village was set on fire. There was cannon fire and shooting. The man was going crazy. They told us, "That village was burned, that person was killed." I went crazy, they killed my relatives, my uncle. We could not go to the village. We decided to go through the mountains. It was the next day when we came to our village from the mountains. We are afraid that we came. The village is burned, we can't say anything to anybody. There were three or four big Panzers where the school is. We tried to go down to the village and they shot at us. [...] There was a smell of burning grass and burning trees. The houses were still burning. Nobody intervened. Pillows and sofas were still burning. We couldn't go in because of fear.

---

4 Düzcealan is the official name of the Kawar village. After the founding of Turkey, the Turkish state began to rename cities, municipalities and villages that originally had Kurdish and Armenian names.

No one was there. Everyone fled to other places. We sat and cried with my friend [...]. (Baysal, 2014, p. 77)

Although forced migration was a politico-military measure imposed by the Turkish state to control the Kurdish liberation movement, it was also the most rapid and complete process of dispossession and proletarianization since the Armenian genocide (Yörük, 2012). According to data provided by the State Governorate of the State of Emergency in November 1997, 820 villages and 2,345 burghs in four provinces forming the contiguous area with six cities under state of emergency were evacuated. A total of 378,335 people, except returnees, from 57,314 house-holds in 3,165 settlements migrated to various cities. When the residents of 85 villages and 178 burghs were later evacuated and forced to migrate were added to these figures, the number of victims increased to 450,000 people (CHP Merkez Yönetim Kurulu Somut Politikalar Çalışma Grubu, 1998). Informal data indicate that the number of people affected by forced migration between 1993 and 1996 exceeded 1.5 million. According to the report of the "Survey on Migration and Displaced Population in Turkey" in 2004, some 3 million people were affected by forced migration (Hacettepe University Institute of Population Studies, 2004). To this must be added thousands of cases of torture, disappearance, unidentified murder, rape and imprisonment. The displaced Kurds were not only economi-cally impoverished, they were stripped of their memories, culture, language and community life.

The great pain caused by the Turkish state's violence and the subsequent forced migrations led to great fear. My generation needed a stronger feeling in order to overcome the fear that reached deep into every crevice of daily life. Maybe pain does make us a community—and in fact we displaced Kurds have established new lives as migrants in the places where we end up. But pain does not make us a community on the move; it makes us an isolated and enclosed community.

And yet, it is emotions that also give us strength to fight, to change, and to imagine that another world is possible. I refer not to passive emotions, like pain, but to active and creative ones. The Zapatistas call this "dignified rage." I guess in Kurdish that translates into berxwedan (resistance). Although in many languages, resistance refers to an action, in the symbolic world of the Kurds, it has to do with a feeling—the feeling of living. For Kurds to resist means to exist, and this is expressed by two words that can be found in so many of our poems and songs, and graffitied on the walls of our streets and alleys: *Berxwedan Jiyane*, Resistance is Life! This slogan was politicized by Kurds who were tortured in prison in the 1980s. When it was discovered by others, too often it was translated incorrectly as "life is resistance"—because when we Kurds say "Berxwedan Jiyane," what we mean is that resistance is the only way of truly experiencing life, a way of thinking or seeing life that changes you forever. This is why so many Kurds identify themselves with the famous phrase, "better a flower in the mountains of freedom than a rose in the garden of obedience," from Yılmaz Güney's poem *Freedom*. Resistance is not an ideology or a political discourse; it is the common sense of existing. It is precisely this sentiment that drives the Kurdish struggle today.

I dwell on this point in order to underline that the revolution has not been forged by ideologies but by emotions. Today, when we look at the revolutionary movements that are changing the relations of domination across the world, the most important thing they teach us is that: "From the Zapatistas we have learned that without the pain and rage of those from below (or better: without our dignified rages, without the centrality of us) the word revolution has no meaning" (Tischler, 2008, p. 18).

In other words, any revolutionary process that has been bureaucratized, that has been torn away from the creative sentiments of society, has not provided true emancipation. Ultimately, all these movements also ended up demanding that society obey the new power, one rationalized by the idea of "administration of society." And this has also meant the reversion of the revolution to patriarchy.

How to make a revolution?

When we think of revolution based on the concepts of the traditional Left, certain fundamental debates come to mind: the seizure of state power, the representative role of the political party, the role of the vanguard, the central position of the proletariat, and so on. In the 20th century, thanks to Engels' scientific socialism (1880), the idea of the revolution was rationalized in the context of an ideology that discussed it as a practical project rooted in material conditions. Society, based on the struggle of antagonistic classes, would need the state to move from capitalism to socialism, and this need would diminish as the working class began more and more to self-manage (Engels, 1978).

Similarly, Lenin in *State and Revolution* considers that state seizure is necessary to create "the conditions for replacing the state." In Holloway's words, this implies the penetration of the idea of "power-over" into the heart of revolutionary theory, which for a century reduced the idea of revolution to the seizure of state power (Holloway, 2011, p. 164). This was certainly not a spontaneous idea. The suppression of the Paris Commune with violence and massacres led to this inference (Ross, 2015). Thus, the main task of the party and revolutionaries was to "inject consciousness," bring the "truth to the masses" and "lead" them to triumph (Gutiérrez Aguilar, 2014, p. 34). "The professional revolutionary" could use "revolutionary violence" when deemed necessary. The revolutionaries who fought to seize power thought they could overcome the power structure they overthrew by imitating its dominant methods. And so, the revolutionary movement was built as a mirror image of power, "army against army, party against party" (Holloway, 2011, p. 59), becoming its opposite. None was able to create a real process of emancipation, because, in the end, all built up systems of absolute power analogous to the ones they had overthrown. Moreover, the working class was never transformed in such a way as to end its exploitation and so to come to an end as a working class. On the contrary, its existence was affirmed and even celebrated as necessary for the economic development of the socialist state, and it continued to exist under a form of capitalist exploitation, only now under a socialist power structure. That is, the conditions of capitalist domination were not eliminated. To the contrary, they were further strengthened.

In the end, the collapse of the Soviet bloc made it clear that emancipation or communism cannot be realized through state power, even if that power is in the hands of the proletariat. This is why it is not said that the idea or hope of revolution collapsed but rather that it "implied the liberation of revolutionary thought, the liberation from the identification between revolution and the conquest of power" (Holloway, 2011, p. 37).

Today, when we speak of revolution, it comes with a critique of the vertical order. It involves the more heterogeneous and non-hierarchical practices of social movements that emerged at the turn of the 21st century. This way of thinking points towards a spontaneous revolution, with neither organization (party) nor political leaders (vanguard). In the popular revolts and insurrections of the last decades in different parts of the world, revolutionary moments and practices of direct action are considered more important than the total revolution of 20th-century thought (Graeber, 2012, p. 9). Furthermore, the current revolutionary discussion does not define social problems only in terms of the conflict between classes and capitalist exploitation, the dominant terms of analysis in Marxist theory. Rather, the social question of the traditional Left is read today within the context of a broad diversity of power relations. Instead of there being a single social question (the exploitation of labor by capital), many social problems are raised (patriarchy, racism, border control, ecological destruction, etc.). Instead of there being only one revolutionary subject (the working class), diverse revolutionary subjects (women, environmentalists, Black people, Indigenous people, Kurds) are emerging on the scene. It is in this context that one so often hears about movements for democracy, about the need for diversity within the movement, and about the politics of the multitude.

People who reject the hierarchical Leninist revolutionary organization and the conception of revolutionary militancy define themselves as activists and consider the most important constructive political activities to be happening within open collectives, where they can establish more horizontal relations instead of receiving and completing assignments from a top-down party. In open collectives, there is no discussion of entry or exit from the collective. The activist can be part of the action when they want to; when they do not, it does not mean they are out of the collective. This should not be interpreted as arbitrariness. The notion that membership in the group requires a mandatory minimum time to fulfill the requirements of the organization—to hang banners, write slogans, attend political meetings, march, and so on—on a full-time and permanent basis has disappeared, giving way to the idea of voluntary time dedicated to voluntary actions. The division of collective labor seems to be a more urgent and important question in such spaces than the revolutionary meaning of those tasks. The initial and final meetings determined by the discipline of the party organization now take place in those forums, assemblies or collectivities that are to be found in spontaneous marches, in large gatherings in public spaces, in the occupation of squares and parks, and so on.

These horizontal experiences contribute to the democratization of social relations and create alternative ways in which people learn to listen to each other. All people, regardless of their roots, color, age, or wisdom, can express their opposition, their right to say "no," their shout of dissent. And not only speaking but listening to each other is becoming an important ethic. The democratization of space and the relationships within it necessarily involves listening to one another. Those who participate in these spaces try to apply forms of democracy other than the merely representative, such as direct or radical democracy, to every aspect of their lives.

It is clear that these new revolutionary practices also have their problems. It takes a long time to make common decisions supported by all and then implement them—which is why, after a while, people in those forums and neighborhood assemblies get bored and gradually abandon them. It is precisely for this reason that after a rebellion in which millions are mobilized by such methods, there are not many permanent spaces left active that can change social relations in the long run. Although spontaneous experiences have made significant contributions to revolutionary thought and moved us past the 20th century, they have often disappeared as quickly as they appeared. Once the peak of great mobilization has passed, what remains are assemblies in which few people participate; occupied spaces, which many times are closed or become an innocuous social centers; occupied factories that could not break the logic of capitalist accumulation; and so on. In quite the same manner as the movements of the 20th century, which sought to take state power with the idea of the proletarian party-state, the movements of the 21st century—which promote horizontal relations without order, without a specific organization, and without leader—have found themselves unable to create real change, that is, the destruction of capitalism and social emancipation in the most radical sense of the term.

And so, the struggle has led us once again to the same question: how are we going to change the capitalist order as it manifests itself in our everyday life? How are we going to really make the revolution? The struggles of the Zapatistas in Mexico and the Kurds in the Middle East have, over the past few decades, accumulated important experiences that can help us answer these fundamental questions.

Thinking and re-thinking: a self-critical organization for a popular revolution

Let creativity be power!
–Suphi Nejat Ağırnaslı[5]

The Zapatista and Kurdish movements have distinguished themselves from the rest of the aforementioned 21st century tendencies towards revolutionary strategies of spontaneity, voluntarism and direct democracy, of which they are otherwise a part. Their breaks from practices common in other radical movements have been very fruitful and interesting. Often, the difference has to do with the meaning of the revolution. As I see it, here are the main ways the Zapatista and Kurdish movements differ:

- The revolution has become what I call a popular revolution.
- The question of organization and the practice of organizing are central to both movements.
- As revolutionary organizations, they have the capacity to adapt to the needs of the struggle and to translate these changes into practical politics.
- They are, in other words, capable of continually changing and transforming organizational structures and guaranteeing the functioning of the new structures over time. They accomplish this by establishing

5 Suphi Nejat Ağırnaslı (1984–2014) died in Kobanê in 2014 under the *nom de guerre* Paramaz Kizilbas (*Hayal Gücü iktidara!*). This is the last line of his farewell letter.

processes for internal transformation (the Kurds refer to these processes as criticism-self-criticism, *tekmil*, and the *platform*; for the Zapatistas they are *interpellar*, *vigilar*, etc.). These self-critical processes also prevent the creation of micropowers within the movement. In addition to these mechanisms, the main objective of permanent meetings, political formations and publications is to help the collective construction of the individuals who built the revolution as a revolutionary people. This construction means the transformation of the subject in the sense of creator-defender of a moral-political project.

- Use-value (rather than exchange-value) has become the dominant element of community relations, and autonomy is based on these relations.
- The antagonistic role of women has proved decisive in determining the processes of struggle, revolution, and autonomy.
- They have been able to establish and maintain international solidarity networks and put time and energy into internationalizing the revolution.
- Struggle and life are one and the same in these movements.

I call "popular revolution" the revolutions in which the peoples of a region are the revolutionary subjects, not the party-organization, that is, a revolution where the popular base is fundamentally integrated into the process of revolution—like those of the Zapatistas in Chiapas and the Kurds in Rojava. Instead of thinking of the people as being determined by the consciousness-raising, the decrees and the policies of the revolutionary organization, a popular revolution is guided by the understanding that it is the self-determination of the people, struggling to secure their material sustenance, that directs the revolutionary struggle and serves as its protagonist. This has been the crucial dynamic for the continuation of these revolutions: that the organization has accepted the people (the Kurdish society and the Zapatista society) as the subjects of the revolution.

The Zapatistas tend not to refer to their process of social transformation with the specific (Western) concept of revolution. Nonetheless, a text by Subcomandante Marcos contains three points that clearly account for a whole theoretical conception of revolution along the lines of what I have been calling the popular revolution (albeit this is a revolution in lower case, he explains, so as to avoid misunderstanding and polemics with the various vanguards and safeguards who dogmatically defend "*The* Revolution" as classically conceived):

> The first point refers to the character of revolutionary change, of this particular revolutionary change. It is a character that incorporates different methods, different fronts, different forms and different degrees of commit-

ment and participation. This means that all methods have their place, that all fronts of struggle are necessary, and that all degrees of participation are important. It is, therefore, an inclusive, anti-vanguardist and collective conception. The problem of the revolution [note the lower case] goes from being a problem of *The* Organization, of *The* Method, and of *The* Caudillo [note the capital letters], to becoming a problem that concerns all those who see that revolution as necessary and possible. In the realization of this revolution, all are important. The second point refers to the objective or aim of that revolution. It is not a question of the conquest of power or the deployment (by peaceful or violent means) of a new social system from the top down, but of something that occurs prior to one or the other. It is about building the anteroom of the new world, a space where, with equal rights and obligations, the different political forces contest for the support of the majority of society [...] The third point deals with the characteristics not of the revolution, but of its outcome. The resulting space, the new political relations, must comply with three conditions: democracy, freedom, and justice. (Subcomandante Insurgente Marcos, 1995)

That popular revolution is a process in which there is no fragmentation of consciousness between the revolutionary and society, and there is no single revolutionary path or form imposed by the organization. It is the people who change their own lives from one day to the next, in whatever manner they deem necessary, by means of their collective democratic decisions. In other words, it is a process that is not dominated by a higher power. This alone is "a revolution that makes revolution possible" (Subcomandante Insurgente Marcos, 1995).

Previously, I mentioned the tendency of radical movements in the 21st century to abandon the idea of organization, or, if they do not totally abandon it, to distance themselves from it in various practical and theoretical ways. But when we look at the Zapatista and Kurdish movements, the idea of organization and organizing remains quite central. Organizing is the fundamental basis for the struggle, in order to sustain concrete advances and push for new ones. "But what we have seen is resistance: knowing how to organize it and having organization first. Of course, there cannot be just resistance and rebellion if there is no organization. It's helped us a lot to organize those two weapons of the struggle, let's say that it opens the mind wider, gives us a way of seeing" (Moisés, 2015, p. 139).

But this is not the old-style organization: it is neither centralized nor hierarchical. The people involved in the movement are appointed by the community and commit themselves to fulfill the obligatory responsibilities assigned to them for a period of time. In other words, it is not left up to the pure volunteerism of self-appointed activists. The revolutionary attitude of the people lies in their fulfillment of the obligatory tasks determined by the community assembly of which they are a part, such as organizing a party for the community, or filling a position in the Good Government Juntas or in the autonomous municipalities. This means another way of doing politics: the communal politics that defines being Zapatista. As Subcomandante Moisés says, "It's not Zapatista merely to talk about Zapatismo, but only if you work collectively with the organized peoples" (Subcomandante Insurgente Moisés, 2015). For the duration of their rotation in community-service, a Zapatista does not receive a salary (only daily food rations) and does not leave their home or community. Not accepting the community mandate means abandoning the struggle and leaving the movement. In other words, refusing a collective work assigned by the assembly means giving up being in the struggle. Being in the movement is voluntary, of course, but as long as one is inside there are obligations, or, more to the point, the struggle is well ordered enough to challenge the capitalist order in the daily life of the community. The existence of these sustained roles implies the reproduction of a new way of life, the organized people sustaining their rebellion against the system that denies them everything. Consequently, they must accept the burdens that the struggle demands of them.

Although both movements are movements of negation—as they are self-affirming of their identities but not identitarian—neither the Chiapas nor the Rojava experience can be considered separate from their roots in the traditional Left. These are deep and fundamental roots that continue to determine the process of these revolutions. At the same time, both movements have managed to rebuild their organizational structure and their thinking around the struggle through a radical critique of the traditional Left. Organization and organizing, vital in both revolutions, do retain the traces of the traditional Left's hierarchical structures, but they have also been able to create new organizational structures that assume the forms resistance takes when it is led by free peoples. And beyond this, they have transcended hierarchy and passive resistance in their project of building autonomy. The basis of this form of organization is how it navigates the contradictions between verticalism and horizontalism, military structure and civil structure, rebellion and autonomy. According to Tischler, one of the fundamental points that differentiates Zapatismo from any other revolutionary organization is that they have learned how to shift between spontaneous disobedience and specific forms of organization. The Zapatistas act in the midst of the contradiction between verticalism, defined by a politico-military structure, and the power of autonomy of Indigenous communities as a form of struggle against capital, as well as between the power and dignity of various forms of resistance organization in different social and geographical areas (Tischler, 2011, p. 135).

Of course, this is not a pre-determined and pre-defined process; it is not without its contradictions. And both movements have questioned some of their own structures and points of view on the long road of their struggles. With time, they have rejected some and preserved others. Therefore, their acts of deconstruction must always be understood alongside their acts of reconstruction. They are constantly critiquing, dismantling and rebuilding their methods, institutions and social practices.

Remember, spontaneous movements involving millions of people have failed to complement the immediate struggle by failing to build a lasting popular base. Legions of people flow into the streets without then proceeding to build a space for long-term participation, and these movements disappear like foam. After the great popular rebellions, few are the voices who continue to protest, and fewer still are those who acknowledge that what needs to be done is to build a power that is counter-to-and-beyond the hegemonic system. The Zapatista and Kurdish movements not only involve millions of people, but have also been able to create these spaces and mechanisms of participation, so that the people themselves can be the protagonists of the revolution. They have built popular revolutions. And I would argue that the crucial element that has allowed them to do so is their tradition of mutual control and criticism between the politico-military structure and the civilian structure of the revolutionary movement.

In his fundamental book from the early 2000s, Öcalan discusses the transformation of the PKK under the new paradigm of struggle that emerged at the turn of the century. He defines this mutual exchange of critiques between the organization and the people as a relationship of dialectical transformation:

> If concrete transformations proved very difficult in the experience of the PKK, this is mainly due to the social terrain where that transformation has been desired. If the organizational structure has democratic characteristics, it's to be expected that many influences coming from the social terrain will penetrate the organization and affect the recently molded individual within it, turning this individual into an extension of themselves. Now, in a situation where these new social characteristics have no effect on the organization, where it remains insensitive to broad social

changes, the inevitable result will be that the organization will become isolated from society. But on the other hand, an organizational structure might convert itself into little more than a reflection of this social extension which has reached into it—and in this case, the organization will break, or at any rate it will become no different from the society it seeks to change. Thus, a balanced and desirable change necessarily involves synthesizing the effects of revolutionary change on both the social terrain and the organization itself, leading to a higher and richer political formation. The dialectical process whereby a revolutionary organization and the society it seeks to change transform one another must occur in this way. (Öcalan, 2004, p. 349)

In the Kurdish Movement, the mechanisms that help establish processes of mutual dialogue, mutual change and mutual recognition, both between and within the revolutionary organization and society, go by various names: criticism-self-criticism, platform, *tekmil* and report.[6] Since the transformation of the PKK's structure and goals in the struggle, these have become indispensable elements for the revolutionary process. They make it possible to establish a process of horizontal dialogue between the organization's militants and the people, to eliminate the subject-object distinction between the organization and society. Moreover, analogous methods among the Zapatistas—which they refer to as interpelar (to challenge) and vigilar (to maintain vigilance)—allow these organizations, although structurally contradictory, to exist and function together.

What ultimately results is a state of mind and a harmony between the politico-military organization and the civilian organizations, in which neither is stronger nor superior to the other, except at particular moments when the revolution demands it. In those moments, someone might take a leading role; but the institutions are sufficiently robust that their presence does not represent a threat to the balance between these two poles of the movement. This stability shows us that the revolution was built synchronously between these subjects, rather than imposed by the organization upon the people. We must keep in mind that these mechanisms exist not only to help us listen to each other, but also to produce recognition and a shared strategy—and by this mutual act, to ensure the continuity of the revolution. They learned this, too, by experimenting. As Subcomandate Moisés says:

6 For a detailed description of the process of *tekmil*, which, though it claims a line of descent from the infamous Maoist self-criticism or "struggle session," has evolved in a significantly more democratic and pluralistic direction that largely prevents the sort of purity-purges with which the latter is associated. See Tekoşîna Anarşîst, "Tekmil: A Tool For Collective Reflection" (3 May 2022) on the Anarchist Library. – *Translator's note*

That is why I've been saying, as the *compas* outlined in their exposition, that even if we are Indigenous people who are in power, if [the] people are not organized to watch over their government, we are just going to be better rats [than the ones who came before] because the poor Indigenous people there have seen what happens to those who come into office, and that, that is what happens to us. So, it's no use simply trusting ourselves, we have to organize ourselves to watch over ourselves [*organizarnos para vigilarnos*], which is why we say that it must be the people who have the final say on everything. (Moisés, 2015, p. 164)

The transformation of the daily life of society is possible only if capitalist social relations are replaced by relations based on community, solidarity and mutual aid—and these are recreated all the time through the construction of community networks in difficult conditions. In this sense, it is important to understand how autonomy is built. It is not enough just to build a replacement for the state by way of collective self-government. We must also collectivize all vital relations.

According to Étienne Balibar:

[W]hen the revolution unmasks and dismantles a certain form of domination (monarchical, aristocratic), it also exposes another, which in a certain sense is more fundamental: the domination of private property and capitalist accumulation. As a consequence, the revolutionary demand I recalled a moment ago, that of keeping the revolutionary process going so that it is not reversed in a restoration of the "old" order, becomes a demand to push the revolution beyond the "bourgeois limits" themselves, or to start a second revolution from within the "womb" of the first. (Balibar, 2018)

In this sense, it is important that both movements structure the economy so as to achieve the primacy of use-value, as against capitalist relations, which are characterized by the domination of exchange-value. They have, to the greatest extent possible, eliminated the use of money in their internal relations, except when it is absolutely necessary. Instead of private property, they organize more and more spaces of collective production. And through cooperatives, collective work and community spaces, they strengthen communal social relations for the long haul. These institutions radically differentiate the autonomy they have woven from the surrounding capitalist social relations. That they are also building common services, such as education, health and security, based on use-value, allows many autonomous structures to move together and create a revolutionary harmony.

The dynamic that decisively shapes both movements is the central role that women play in the process of struggle and autonomy. And not only with their presence—in both Zapatismo and the Kurdish struggle, women have managed to build their own perspective and the principle of women's self-determination into the very fabric of the movement.

Women have always been strong figures in the Zapatista movement, although they do not have their own organizational structure. But, tendentially, they strive for it. The fact that self-organization has been frequently discussed in the meetings of *mujeres que luchan* (women who fight) is a sign that women's decisions will be a determining factor in the autonomy of the Zapatistas in the future. In the case of Kurdish women, this has been going on for a long time and, today, in Rojava, a women's revolution is occurring that takes the concept of autonomy beyond geographical or territorial limits; it is a women's autonomy that, in parallel, concretizes an autonomy of the peoples (Dirik, 2022).

Wherever women organize themselves, a powerful force is created that throws the patriarchal pact into crisis—not only in society at large, but also specifically within mixed organizations (organizations with both men and women). The presence of women in the revolutionary struggle constantly pushes the movement towards the transformation of everyday patriarchal social relations. The mixed organization is thus reinvented and regenerated, becoming less patriarchal in turn. Women's organizing suppresses and dilutes men's contests for power within the organizational structure.

It could be said that women's organizations—their independent spaces for organizing within mixed organizations—are the most important factor in keeping the movement dynamic as an antagonistic existence. However, women do not organize against internal and external patriarchy in order to become the privileged group of the revolution. What they do when they organize is disarrange the patriarchal pact, which is the ultimate source of the power asymmetries in the macho Left and a partial source of the repeated errors that have brought revolutions to collapse. Women in struggle break these mechanisms of historic repetition and make problems visible, not to solve them, but to displace and reformulate them with a female gaze. Therefore, the struggle they carry out against patriarchy is not only for the benefit of women, it is for the liberation of gender, that is, for the benefit all of society.

These anti-capitalist movements do not understand the system they are struggling against to exist on a merely local scale. On the contrary, they believe that the struggle against capitalism should be an international struggle, just like the struggle against patriarchy. They establish relations with small political groups and collectives in many parts of the world, with the idea of strengthening one another through mutual aid. For example, today there are networks of support and solidarity with the Zapatistas in many countries around the world.

These solidarity networks mobilize for various purposes. When the Mexican state attacks and provokes in the regions where the Zapatista Army of National Liberation (EZLN) is organized, these networks organize protests and marches or send observers to Chiapas. And their use is not limited to strictly political actions: these networks are also the points from which Zapatista coffee arrives through cooperatives and solidarity trade. Through the export of coffee, the Zapatista cooperatives support the foreign collectives with a cut of the proceeds and help build their economic strength. Meanwhile, the collectives support the Zapatistas so that their coffee finds a fair price abroad. In other words, they build international mutual support. The secret behind the presence of Zapatista coffee on every continent is the network of international mutual aid created against the hegemony of monopoly-capitalist trade.

Similarly, the Kurdish Movement emphasizes that the revolution cannot take place only in Rojava, or even just in the lands that we Kurds call Kurdistan. For if the revolution remains only in one geographic area, it will not grow and will ultimately fail. It is frequently argued that only the revolution that has effects beyond one's own land—one that internationalizes, that meets and unites with other revolutions—can succeed. Holloway (2010) refers to this as the "meeting of cracks." This is not just an expression. The Kurdish Movement, which has mobilized the Kurdish diaspora to join other revolutionary struggles since the 1990s, has an organization that spans the globe and has turned its own territory into a meeting point for revolutionary internationalists, especially after the Kobanê resistance against ISIS.

The transformation of the PKK through various ruptures

Mutual recognition

The physical break with the Turkish Left, and the shift to defending the idea of national liberation around the national question, led to a debate between the Turkish Left and the Kurdish Left that has been ongoing for years. According to the Turkish Left, the Kurds betrayed the struggle for socialism and revolution; they shifted right, away from class struggle. It is very interesting to note that this attitude of the Turkish Left groups—that they are the revolutionary big brother and guide of the ethnic minorities—continued until the Rojava Revolution and its communal experiments were internationalized. This conflict, and the contradictory attitude it has engendered, are important for understanding the ideological development of the Kurdish Movement.

The PKK, founded within the framework of criticisms and accusations made by the Turkish Left and the political debates of that time, was born with contradictions that have determined its own history. Öcalan, who defines the organization he founded as the party of the Kurdistan working class, expresses the contradiction they experienced right from the outset regarding the name they gave to the organization, the Kurdistan Workers' Party, and affirms that taking this name meant "saving the honor."

> During the group period, we were known as the Kurdistan Revolutionaries. We dared to give ourselves a real name, but only until five years after we were born as a group. The crazy, exciting path, which started on Newroz in 1973, outside the Çubuk Dam in Ankara, and led us to take the name Kurdistan Workers' Party (PKK) in the village of Fis in the Lice district of Diyarbakır on November 27, 1978, made us assume that we saved our honor. Could there be a greater goal? After all, the modern organization of the modern class was established. (Öcalan, 2012, p. 270)

The party defined itself as a Marxist-Leninist party of the working class. However, the struggle did not aim to build a dictatorship of the proletariat, but rather a people's dictatorship in Kurdistan:

> The goal of the PKK is to liberate the Kurdish people from the imperialist and colonialist system, to establish a people's democratic dictatorship in an independent and unified Kurdistan and, finally, to build a classless society in an epoch of growing decadent imperialisms and rising proletarian revolutions.
>
> The struggle for the national liberation of Kurdistan, led by the PKK, is an integral part of the world socialist revolution, from which socialist countries, national liberation movements and working-class movements have emerged greatly strengthened. (PKK, 1978)

Cemil Bayık, when commenting on this period, states that they did not want to be called nationalists, but they had not been able to separate themselves from the national reality (Akkaya, Ateşten Tarih, 2005). What is meant by the concept of "national reality" that many PKK members mention when commenting on the organizational stage is never explained. However, when we look at the Kurdish society of the period, we see that the working class is not sociologically formed. Social relations are established by feudal and tribal dynamics with a peasantry (Beşikçi,1970; Sönmez, 1992). In this sense, it is understood that the revolutionary grammar of the leftist university students, which focused on the proletariat, was insufficient to express the social relations and reality of this period. It was, I suppose, this contradiction that the founding cadres felt.

> In Kurdistan there were similar cases to those of the working class. The existence of a bourgeoisie was felt. The phenomena were considered sufficient for the measurement of reality. But it would not be correct to say that we were sure. It had been an acceptance of principles. As such, I/ we were not completely closed to the natural flow of life in the dogmatic style. This side of us was going to disperse and would have generated our difference (Öcalan, 2012, p. 272).

In fact, the young people of the party, who had left the university and dispersed to various parts of Kurdistan, would discover the real social contradiction and their own contradiction with grassroots work. Therefore, it is not surprising that the first armed struggle (the attack on Hilvan in 1984) was against the landlords, not the colonial state. This initial physical encounter with the community constituted a process of mutual recognition between the Kurdish community and the PKK, and forced the PKK to abandon the revolutionary grammar of the traditional Left. This contradiction and coercion induced the process of negative dialectics, and the revolutionary experience began to determine politics. The Kurdish Movement expresses this as "we are learning from our practice." This made it possible to establish horizontal relations, which transformed the PKK from a vanguard organization into a popular movement, and led to the questioning of the subject-object distinction of the traditional idea of revolution, according to which the political is understood to be superior to society, or society subordinate to the political.

The original and new revolutionary grammar they established from their own experience was made possible by the transformation of the PKK into, as they put it, a "movement of self-criticism," a movement of negation.

Rejecting the construction of a Kurdish state

The Kurdish struggle never intended to seize power over the existing state, mainly because it is a struggle against the colonialist states. And, although initially its objective was to establish its own Kurdish state, the experience of struggle resulted in abandoning and rejecting that objective along the way.

The emergence of ideological defeat, expressed by Öcalan as the process of generating its difference, became clearer and more decisive for the struggle after the collapse of real socialism. At the Fifth Party Congress in 1995, a decision was made to remove the hammer and sickle, the symbols of socialism, from the PKK flag, and the experience of real socialism was widely criticized for fetishizing the state. The idea of party and state were challenged, but not completely abandoned. Rather, the state and the party were defined as a means of transition to socialism, not as the absolute goal of socialism:

> As we know, Lenin has a theory of revolution. He has the determination of "the break is in the weakest link" in the theory of the anti-imperialist revolution. He has precise views on the pioneer party and its battle tactics, on insurrection and guerrilla warfare. In addition, there is the theory of the dictatorship of the proletariat. Lenin conceptualized them, programmed them and, at the same time, organized them under the leadership of a party. He even led the latter towards nationalization. In the later period (especially with Stalin and those who followed), this was done to develop the state. What Stalin did was develop the socialist state. This situation advanced so far that it was handled in such a one-dimensional way that ideology almost disappeared from politics, even in economics. The party, as an ideological and moral force, disappeared in the idea of the state; they extinguished it. Moreover, the party can be extinguished as well as the state. Marx and Engels also realize this. The state is required at the beginning, but it must be extinguished; the same is true of the party, but only after it realizes its goal. The party and also the state are a means of transition. (PKK 5. Kongresine Sunulan Politik Rapor, 1995, p. 57)

"Class, party, state; all of these are figures of synthesis" (Tischler, 2011, p. 121), whereby socialist forms of these figures are superseded by movements and require radical breaks. "The principle of national self-determination," presented by Lenin, dictated that national liberation movements and socialists should focus on the creation of the nation-state. Those who did not act in this direction were even accused of not being socialists. For this reason, as Öcalan said, the PKK remained stuck in national statism, even though Kurdish existence was not debated (2016, p. 10). Therefore, the transformation of the PKK also meant transforming the idea of the party and the understanding of the party, solely with the aim of establishing a state:

> To be a state-oriented party or to establish a party in order to have a state must be seen as the most fundamental mistake; the correct position is to

renounce the idea of this kind of party with self-criticism. Both nationalization and the ideals of freedom and equality cannot be carried together. One requires overcoming the other. (Öcalan, 2004, p. 352)

This idea was expressed in the "declaration of reconstruction" published in 2005, 10 years after the 5th Congress, in which the PKK abandoned the goal of nation-state building. The reconstruction declaration refers to a radical break with the Leninist line. In this sense, the Kurdish Movement reinterpreted the principle of national self-determination and defined a new goal of struggle by deciding to build autonomy instead of the nation-state. This also meant the negation of the basic cell of the state, the power, and, from there, it concentrated on building the capacity to create, to sustain and to struggle. Today, the Kurdish Movement refuses to take power. Instead, it mobilizes according to an organizational model shaped by a network of councils that allow the people to become the subject of the decision-making process, ensuring the principle of self-determination emerging from autonomy.

This new goal of struggle, which was conceptualized as democratic confederalism, required a new organizational structure. In this sense, the movement has been ideologically and structurally reconstructed, and is organized according to the structure of the Kurdistan Communities Union (*Koma Ciwakên Kurdistan,* KCK) instead of following the classic Leninist party organization.

The Kurdish Movement, although still called the Kurdistan Workers' Party (PKK), is no longer a classic Leninist party. On the contrary, today it is organized as the KCK in the four regions of Kurdistan, with a confederalist structure, in accordance with democratic confederalism. In other words, it is a confederalist movement made up of many organizations. The new organizational structure is more complex: the military, political and civilian sectors are intertwined and serve as mechanisms of mutual control. That is, the model in which the organizational structure was formed by a single type of vanguard was rejected. The most important characteristic of this new form of organization is that the armed sector cannot take political power and cannot govern. This means that neither Subcomandante Moisés of the EZLN nor Comandante Mazlum Kobani of the YPG, who represent the military organizations, can be president in any civilian space. There is no state power that has been generated or taken in the revolutions of the Kurdish and Zapatista peoples. The people appoint certain individuals and entrust them with the tasks needed for the organization of autonomy.

The Kurdish Movement, whose goal since 2003 has been democratic confederalism, has been realizing this goal in Rojava and, in the last five years, in northern and eastern Syria as well. Before the experience of autonomy in Rojava, the Kurdish Movement had scattered and fragmented experiences in Bakur, Kurdistan-Turkey. After the liberation of Rojava, when the movement started to politically and militarily control the territory, it had the opportunity to build the autonomy project fully, with the dimensions of democratic confederalism: politics, justice, economy, education, health, self-defense, ecology, diplomacy, culture, society, gender and youth. But, as we will see in more detail, in Rojava, the Kurdish Movement and its political proposal are not yet fully accepted by society. This is primarily because although autonomy is defined as a system in which all peoples, that is, different ethnicities, can be part of it, sufficient peace among the peoples of Syria has not yet been reached. Above all, the insecurity created by the war and the uncertain future of the Kurdish Movement in Rojava, generate mistrust in society.

In addition, the Rojava community refuses to participate in the organization of autonomy because in the past they were oppressed by the Syrian state. It is very difficult for them to accept that the Kurds (and other peoples of Syria) can make decisions about their own lives; the idea seems absurdly utopian. For many, even if there were a risk of death, it would be easier for them to take up arms and join the war than to attend an assembly. It should be kept in mind that Kurdish society lives a reality in which the Kurdish Movement remains a movement centered on a single leader, Abdullah Öcalan, and, due to the ongoing war, the military structure is becoming more and more determinant. These are the elements that feed the contradictions and tendencies in the Rojava Revolution that we will analyze in the following sections.

The Kurdish struggle against capitalism

Like other rebel movements in many parts of the world, the Kurdish Movement has not narrowly defined itself as an anti-capitalist movement. However, that does not mean that it is not. The Kurdish Movement, especially in its approach to the idea of autonomy, has an anti-capitalist perspective. Moreover, it is a movement whose unfolding practices disrupt the dynamics of capitalist accumulation. From its daily practice, it generates an important critical knowledge of capitalism and how to overcome it.

The movement has expressed its opposition to capitalism since its modern inception and has analyzed it, especially in Öcalan's writings, as a relevant dimension of democratic autonomy. It has organized the economy following the principles of communitarian life and the subjectification of women as a goal under construction. The movement, which through a critique of capitalism had previously assumed a class-centered Marxist perspective, has established its own critical language since it sowed autonomy. We will see in detail how it understands capitalism and how it puts forward its own perspective on anti-capitalism. For the moment, I want to underline that the movement does not understand capitalism only from a political economy perspective. Rather, it is analyzing it in terms of state, patriarchal and capitalist systems as a whole. Put simply, according to Öcalan, the negation of capitalism has the same meaning as the negation of the nation-state: "The nation-state is the instrument of power for the domination of capitalist modernity over the economy, based on maximum profit. Without this tool, maximum profit and capital accumulation is not realized" (Öcalan, 2012, p. 464).

The negation of one is not possible without the negation of the other. And the negation of both is not possible without the negation of patriarchy. But how to establish an anti-capitalist system? This remains controversial, just like the question of the state. Breaking the relations of capitalist domination and building non-capitalist social relations is a more difficult process than that of creating a non-state polity. According to the Kurdish Movement's critique, the October Revolution was transformed into "state capitalism" and that is why it failed. The relations of capitalist domination could not be broken, as was also the case in most other revolutions. For this reason, political autonomy is insufficient to guarantee communal social life and non-capitalist relations in Kurdistan and elsewhere in the world.

While the proposed model of cooperatives, the creation of a collective communal life and the socialization of property have the potential to create serious cracks in capitalism, they also present limitations. How these limitations will be overcome in the Rojava Revolution is the most important question in this book. It has been the most debated issue in the course of revolutions throughout history, but an answer has yet to found. The only answer is to recognize that there is no answer, that is, there is no recipe, as is also the case in revolution. We need to learn from experience.

In the Kurdish Movement, when it comes to the establishment of new structures, it is considered that in Kurdistan society, community relations are hidden in the social memory of the tribe and maintain the forms they had in the clans.[7] They are democratic structures that have been preserved in spite of capitalism and the nation-state. Although these structures have been seriously damaged by the nation-state process, they are considered the main reference points of an anti-capitalist system. It is important to remember that under capitalism, women

---

7 For a more detailed about the concepts "tribal" and "tribalism" in Kurdistan and Middle East studies see Mohammadpour and Soleimani, "Interrogating the tribal: the aporia of 'tribalism' in the sociological study of the Middle East," *The British Journal of Sociology*, 2019.

were never able to become the subjects of decisions. The movement states that the communitarian mentality of women is the most vibrant social segment and, therefore, considers women pioneers in the struggle against capitalism. Consequently, anti-capitalist autonomy and communal economy are defined as a woman-centered autonomy and economy.

Rejecting patriarchal power

Öcalan points out that patriarchy is "the basis and the main womb of hierarchical and class society" (Öcalan, 2007, p. 25). Thus, the Kurdish Movement believes that, if a revolution aims to destroy class and power relations, it must eliminate patriarchy; otherwise, power and class will be reinstitutionalized on the basis of patriarchal terrain.

Today, in the Kurdish Movement, there are women who mobilize and organize together with men in what they call "general organization," while, in parallel, there are those who organize with women only in the women's movement of Kurdistan, in what they themselves call "original organization." This unified, but at the same time separate organization—in the civil, political and military fields— is based on the practice of rupture that started with the separation of women at the beginning of 1992. Then, the women's movement defined its practice as the "theory of rupture," which refers, in essence, to the rupture with patriarchy, treated by Kurdish women as physical and mental rupture (Jineoloji Academy, 2016, p. 11). Mental rupture refers to the fact that women are confronting slavery themselves and, in order to achieve gender liberation, they must reflect on their patriarchal mentality, shaped by the long history of patriarchy. Physical rupture takes place outside the organization and mixed spaces and seeks to create original organization and women spaces where women can discover their gaze, establish their modes of discussion and make feminine decisions. In this sense, physical rupture could mean a step towards mental rupture. However, since there is no rupture, as understood by separatist feminism (Frye, 1983), the discussion always implies a return to mixed spaces, but with feminine consciousness and strength. The first physical rupture, which occurred in 1992, involved the creation of battle brigades founded by the guerrilla women who criticized the PKK for being patriarchal. However, this break did not mean the creation of a separate organization, or separating from the mixed organization, but rather forming, at the same time, their own organization. Even Kurdish women are, in this sense, far from embracing the separatist idea.

The women's movement expresses the need to work hard to strengthen women's own spaces, because women's enslavement and obedience still run very deep. Kongra-Star (Northern Syrian Women's Congress) was founded in 2016 in northern Syria, where self-defense constitutes a fundamental principle to defend, develop and enhance the values of an ethical and democratic society. It should be noted that self-defense includes all spheres of life, not only military (Kongra Star, 2016, p. 3). From self-organization, they seek a return to being the subject of life and destroying patriarchy, through the use of the power they have acquired in their own spaces. The woman who does not recognize her ability to do for herself remains in the mixed spaces, that is, she remains a slave, because the experience of women in the PKK has shown that all mixed spaces are patriarchal, even if they are socialist. That is why women understand and feel the need to put mixed spaces in crisis and to create their own spaces in order to undo patriarchy and become, once again, a source of collective strength to recreate and redesign the mixed spaces, the mixed organizations, among them.

We know that women have been an important revolutionary force in all historical revolutions, such as the Paris Commune, the October Revolution and the Cuban Revolution, but they did not achieve their liberation as women. After the revolution, women returned to their homes, and patriarchy persisted, even in the most socialist revolutions. The Kurdistan women's liberation movement interprets this as what brought all revolutions to an end—they were socialist revolutions, not anti-patriarchal. The Kurdish struggle is loudly proclaiming that, in order not to repeat that failure, their revolution has accepted the leadership of women and that the struggle against patriarchy is the most fundamental struggle in all fields. The *ideology of women's liberation*, proclaimed in 1998, stated that:

> The story of the loss of freedom is at the same time the story of how women lost their position and disappeared from history [...] If we want to give true meaning to words like equality, freedom, democracy and socialism, which we so often employ, we must analyze and shatter the old web of relationships that has been woven around women. (Öcalan, 2013, pp. 10-11)

What is referred to here as "loss" is the loss of the decisive role women played in society. In order to understand this loss and, indirectly, the loss of society, a science of women is necessary. This is part of the process of mental rupture and is conceptualized as *jineolojî*. Mental emancipation can only be achieved by observing the historical and current experiences of women's struggle and transforming everyday life, so that women regain their central position in life and nature. However, the revolution for women's liberation is expressed not as a revolution for equality (equal public rights for women and men), but as a revolution for gender emancipation. In other words, women consider revolution as a phenomenon that aims to liberate not only women, but all sexes, that is, society as a whole, because they believe that the enslavement of men follows that of women (Öcalan, 2013, p. 9). Gender emancipation, through a struggle that occurs simultaneously, separately and in common, would ensure the emancipation of society.

The fact that Kurdish women act as a separate movement within the Kurdish Movement points to a more important antagonistic existence in the liberation movement. In fact, the oral history of the Kurdish Movement shows that, many times, women have saved the struggle from collapse. It is no coincidence that the women's movement was organized in the 1990s. As a political leader, Öcalan managed to capture the phenomenon of power in its weakest and most visible aspect by emphasizing the power relations between men and women, that is, patriarchal power, to respond to the power struggle among the PKK men. When women began to question the relations of domination between male and female guerrillas in the PKK, they became a destructive and antagonistic force to all forms of power.

Although the movement and Öcalan believe that the process of self-criticism that took place after the collapse of the experience of real socialism led to the negation of the state, that is, the negation of the idea of taking power, I believe this occurred once women pushed the movement to question the gender issue, that is, the movement's patriarchal relations.

The intellectual reflection on women's freedom elaborated by Kurdish women, whose philosophical and historical background is much broader than what I have described here, has made it possible to create an experience of real autonomy for women in Rojava since 2016. Kongra-Star plays an active role in organizing women in all areas of life: education, culture and art, economy, self-defense, social affairs, conflict resolution and justice, local governments, press and media, ecology and diplomacy (Kongra Star, 2016, p. 3). Women organizing into committees in all these areas within Kongra-Star build their communes, assemblies, cooperatives and academies. They thus create their own autonomous spaces, their decision-making mechanisms, their collective ways of working and their political training in *jineolojî*. Creating a women's commune where there is a mixed commune, and setting up a women's assembly where there is a mixed assembly, is the central axis of women's social organization. From a negative antagonism by which they put in crisis the mixed spaces while creating their own spaces, they are becoming a source of collective strength. Organized participation in mixed areas empowers women within the overall autonomy of Rojava. In other words, women who organize their own spaces participate at the same time in all mixed spaces, as well as in the mechanisms of co-presidency, joint spokesperson-ship and the 50% quota. In addition, they have an effective veto in all mixed spaces: this ensures that every collective decision taken in Rojava becomes, first of all, a decision of women and then of society as a whole. Also, Kongra-Star follows the principles of plurality and the democratic nation, includes women of all ethnici-ties and religions (Kongra Star, 2016, p. 5).

Towards autonomy

Having developed a very broad and heterogeneous popular base, and having expe-rienced its fair share of discussions, criticisms, ruptures and denials, the Kurdish Movement eventually succeeded in directing its struggle towards the idea of revo-lutionary autonomy.

Two important pillars allowed the struggle for autonomy to become a new utopian horizon, both for the Kurdish Movement and for other movements around the world.

The first is a crisis in the theories and practices of revolution that we have inherited from the last century. The Kurdish Movement has pointed out that real socialism failed to transcend the state and capitalism because its idea of revolution had become embedded in the seizure of state power and the establishment of a new "proletarian" power-structure. No matter the means by which the self-ap-pointed "revolutionary subject" achieved this power, they always considered it justified and legitimate—and so revolutionary practice became, no less than the old regime of power, the negation of society through violence and social pressure. The Kurdish Movement, like all those who continued to desire a new world in the wake of the 20th century, needed a new idea and a new revolutionary practice—a struggle for what the Zapatistas, on the other side of the world, were beginning to call autonomy.

The other main reason the movement found itself gravitating towards the idea of autonomy was the discovery that the crisis of the revolution was directly related to the crisis of the state. The study of the origins of the state, going back to the Sumerians of the Bronze Age Near East, led the movement to the conclusion that the Kurdish state itself could not provide the Kurds with social emancipa-tion, since, on the contrary, it is the state itself that dominates society. Therefore, for the Kurds, the politics of autonomy is the negation of the state; and through this slogan, the Kurdish struggle began to jointly question the state, patriarchy and capitalism as an interconnected structure of exploitation and oppression. Kurdish society has been discussing and practicing proposed versions of radically democratic autonomy since 2003 and, in the last ten years, has enriched and developed this idea with the experience of the Rojava Revolution. Therefore, we must analyze the perspective and experience of democratic confederalism in Rojava in order to understand the Kurdish Movement and how it is overcoming the crisis of the revolution and the contradictions of the present through its ongoing process of struggle.

CHAPTER 2

The Common History of Resistance

Hesen Salih's personal history

Upon awakening one morning in June 1963, the Kurds of Rojava discovered them-selves to be invisible. Hesen Salih, from the town of Serêkanîyê, was the first to notice. When he went to the Population Bureau to register his newborn son, the staff neither saw nor heard him. Yet he was speaking with people. Thinking that maybe it was a mistake, Hesen Salih walked between all the desks and through all the offices of the building. No one from behind their stations even looked at him. He returned home to tell his relatives and neighbors what had happened. The news spread.

After several attempts, they realized that state institutions and city officials simply did not see Kurds. Doubt crept in. The Kurdish people had become invisible from one moment to the next, as if in some strange fairytale. Asking, reaching out for each other, their bodies touched. And there they stood, and there their voices were heard.

People went out into the streets and searched for each other. Those with acquain-tances in other cities passed on news and informed them of what was going on. Even Kurds from outside Serêkanîyê came to bear witness to the event.

The nature of this peculiar case of invisibility revealed itself soon enough. Officers and soldiers paid Hesen Salih a house visit. He invited them in and offered them tea. With the kettle still boiling they slipped him a piece of paper, on which it was written that Mr. Salih and his family were no longer Syrian citizens and could no longer own property—hence, their land would be confiscated. His right to speak turned to deafening silence under the soldiers' guns.

When what happened in the Salih house spread throughout the city, it became clear that Kurds had disappeared from state records. Half were now registered as ajnabi *(foreigners), and the other half as* maktoumin *(illegals). The same story repeated itself in the Kurdish towns of Dêrik, Qamishlo, Amûdê, Hesekê, Dirbêsiyê, Girkê Legê,...*

At first, there was hope that the error would be amended, since Kurds had fought for and helped found the state; but the ruling Ba'athist regime declared there was to be only "One Language, One Nation." Kurdish political organizers were arrested;

Kurdish military personnel, including those of the highest rank, were discharged; Kurdish workers in the public sector were fired. Hundreds of thousands of Kurds were stripped of their identities. Hard days lay ahead.

Hesen Salih lost his job as a tea vendor at a government office, so he started singing at weddings and special events. But Ba'athist sanctions extended even to the Kurdish language, banning speaking, writing, or singing in Kurmanji, Sorani, or any other dialect. All the names of Kurdish municipalities were replaced by Arabic ones.

Hesen Salih's new line of work got him arrested. He was detained in Serêkaniyê for two weeks, then taken to Aleppo, where he was held for one month in an underground detention center before being moved to a prison outside city limits for another five months. Six and a half months after his initial arrest—for singing in his mother tongue—Hesen Salih went to the bus terminal to return home. Except he could not buy tickets because he had no identification. After spending that day and night on the street, he managed to pay the fare thanks to a fellow Kurd's kindness.

Now out, Hesen Salih spread the word about a state project called the Arab Belt. He recounted what Kurdish political prisoners told him while inside: that an Arab soldier named Talib El Hilal, who had served as a police chief in Hesekê Governorate, was planning an ethnic cleansing of Kurds in the region.

In the proceeding years, everything Hesen Salih had said came to pass. The region was now ruled by the regime. Kurds, already separated from their relatives by the Syrian-Turkish border, were forcibly moved behind a second border further south. Arab tribes from Raqqa and Aleppo settled in Kurdish border towns, from Dêrik all the way to Serîkaniyê. Two million hectares of land were stolen from Kurds; half was divided amongst Arab tribes, the other half amongst soldiers.

Beyond displacement, Kurds lost the right to continue or even receive an education. Everything, from traveling and finding a job, to getting married or divorced, became difficult. Those who disobeyed and resisted this plan were subjected to martial law judgments, arrested and, sometimes, disappeared. A long period of silence descended upon Rojava.

The Kurdish people staged the first major uprising against the Ba'athist regime in 2004. It was a watershed moment. Hesen Salih, then 71 years old, took part in breaking the silence. The freedom struggle continued uninterrupted until the declaration of autonomy in 2012. Ten days later, Hesen Salih could not get out of bed. He asked his grandson, Rahşan, for a glass of water. With Rahşan's help, he sat up and drank. At the age of 79, Hesen Salih, who spent most of his life in prison, spoke his last words before quietly closing his eyes: "My eyes will not be left behind. Nobody can destroy the Kurds."

Hesen's personal story[1] summarizes the Kurdish people's history in the Middle East. Although this history has been experienced differently across Kurdistan, the shared goal of its four colonizers has been to undermine and crush the Kurdish people. In turn, a spirit of resistance has been forged to fight back against such politics of destruction.

Rojava's collective history of resistance

This section focuses specifically on Rojava, the smallest and most sparsely inhabited region of Kurdistan. The formation of the Middle Eastern nation-states resulted in the fragmentation and colonization of Kurdistan. Through resistance, Kurds have countered this attack on their very existence.

Before outlining the course of this struggle, it is imperative to first recognize that Rojava's resistance is part of the collective history of the Kurdish people at large. My analysis is limited to Kurds; but other Middle Eastern peoples have also been subjected to exclusionary programs based on ethnicity and religion, leading to their own resistance movements. For example, the Syrian civil war was primarily driven by Sunni Muslims rising up against the Alawite dominated Ba'ath government. But as mentioned in the last chapter, Kurds have produced various strategies, ideologies and modes of struggle. The construction of autonomy and democratic confederalism is our focus because, of all the paths Kurdish politics has taken over the years, it alone has elevated the Kurdish Movement beyond a purely identitarian struggle and toward a theoretical and practical transformation unlike any other in the region.

Imposing the state in Syria

The Sykes-Picot Agreement was signed in secret on May 16, 1916. In the wake of the First World War, it aimed to divide the lands of the Ottoman Empire—especially those where Kurds historically lived and which they called Kurdistan—between France and Great Britain. The people who lived there were divvied up between the Persian and Ottoman Empires until the region was separated into its four modern nation-states, within whose borders they live to this day. With that, the Kurds had become an international colony.

Although some minor changes were made to this surreptitious arrangement with the 1923 Treaty of Lausanne, the colonization and fragmentation of Kurdistan were ultimately imposed and legitimated by the Western great powers. Portions of the Kurdish region were proclaimed—with natural and national

---

1 As written by Deniz Bilgin (2018).

justifications—to be territories of the newly independent Turkey, Iraq, Iran and Syria. But along with Jordan and Palestine, the Iraqi state accepted the British Mandate, while Syria and Lebanon fell under the French one. The latter lasted from 1921 to 1946, fragmenting Syrian territory into five administrative regions on the basis of social, ethnic and sectarian differences. And so, to the "national" borders drawn by the imperialist partition were added yet more artificial borders within the "nations." France supported and subsequently created a Christian elite class, the Druze (Arabic: *durūzī*)[2] and Alawi Arabs (*nusairi*),[3] at the expense of the majority Sunni Muslim population. It should be noted, however, that despite the divisions between ethnic and religious groups, popular uprisings against the French government nevertheless took place, fueled by increased taxes and agrarian policies that benefited the urban upper classes (Provence, 2005, pp. 27-29). The legacy of this inequity rages on today. It has led to the consolidation of long-standing sectarian conflicts and group hostilities, which are the driving forces behind the Syrian civil war.

Syrian intellectuals agree that the construction of an "ideal Syria" was made impossible by the French Mandate. Particularly damaging were its use of resettlement policies in a divide-and-conquer strategy, its granting independence to Lebanon, and its concession of Alexandretta to Turkey (Altuğ, 2018, pp. 72-73). Furthermore, the Sykes-Picot Agreement stipulated that Syria would be granted independence within five years, but France never followed through with this promise. France's failure to withdraw from the region led to an increase in pro-independence discourse and the emergence of Arab nationalism. During World War II, the Allies repeatedly promised Syrian independence, but only under pressure of riots and rebellions and British intervention did the last French troops finally depart the region on April 15, 1946. Two days later, the independent Republic of Syria was declared (Knapp, 2017, p.70).

Nonetheless, the power vacuum left behind by France led to successive coups d'état: over 20 governments and four constitutional amendments came and went. The Ba'ath Party put an ostensible end to such political instability in 1963. With regard to this long interregnum Knapp writes:

2 The Druze (Arabic: durūzī دُرُزِيّ plural: durūz دُرُوز) are a religious minority inhabiting mainly Syria, Lebanon, Jordan and Israel. There are small communities of Druze migrants in other countries. They speak Arabic and the language of the country where they reside. There are about one million Druze in the world, the vast majority of whom reside in the Middle East. The Druze call themselves Ahl al-Tawhīd, "people of one God" (monotheists). The origin of the name "Druze" is disputed and is usually attributed to the Ismaili Muhammad al-Darazi, one of the earliest prophets of the religion, who died in 1021 and is considered a heretic by the Druze today. In public, some Druze claim to be Muslims, while others claim not to be.

3 The former Syrian president, Hafez Assad, and his son, Bashar Assad, are also Nassiris. The followers of Ibn Nusayr were called Nusairi. Nusairids or Arab Alewites (Arabic: نصيرية Al-Nusayrīyah or علوية Al-Alawīya), along with the provinces of Latakia, Baniyas and Tartus in Syria, also live in Lebanon and in cities in Turkey, such as Hatay, Adana and Mersin. It should be noted that the term "Nusairi" or "Nusayri" has a negative connotation, so the Alawites, at least in Syria, do not use it for self-designation.

The old elites remained in power, but more Syrians, through military careers or education, were rising into the middle class ... In the country-side, a growing challenge to the conservative landowners led to a flowering of socialist and communist movements, but also nationalist and religious ones. (Knapp, 2017, p. 71)

Gilberto Conde points to two main political and ideological lines taking shape in Arab countries at the time: One was in favor of military pacts with the West; the other would end up allying with the other pole of global politics, the Soviet Union. But Syria, like Egypt, would ally with the Soviets on Non-Aligned princi-ples, ruling out the establishment of foreign military bases on its territory(Conde, 2013, p. 56).

Throughout this period, the various regional conflicts created by the impe-rialist powers (the United States, Great Britain, the Soviet Union and Israel) ended up strengthening tendencies towards pan-Arabism across the Middle East, including in Syria. In 1958, the United Arab Republic (UAR,1958–1961) was formed between Egypt and Syria under the leadership of Gamal Abdul Nasser (Conde, 2013, p. 60). As its very name suggests, the UAR was presented as an opportunity for all Arab countries to break away from local elites and unite in a great pan-Arab nation (Knapp, 2017, p. 72). However, Nasser's repressive policies, economic expropriation, and attempts to shut down all political organizations—including the Ba'ath Party and the trade unions—generated serious unrest among both the Syrian people and the elite. This finally devolved into the Syrian army staging a coup in 1961 with the support of the kingdoms of Jordan and Saudi Arabia; Syria then left the Arab League. Still, as Anne Sofie Schøtt notes, the ideas of pan-Arabism and Arab socialism were not abandoned by the Syrian Arabs but merely expressed by other means, for example, through the Ba'ath Party (Schøtt, 2017, p. 7).

The Ba'ath movement (Arabic for "resurrection") was established as a party in Damascus in 1940 and eventually took over the Syrian government through a military coup in 1963. From 1970 on, the Ba'athists established a one-party regime by changing the law so only their party could participate in elections. Since then, the Assad family has remained firmly in power. After the United States overthrew the government of Iraq in 2003, the Assads came to be widely seen as the main representatives of Ba'athism in the Middle East. Bashar al-Assad, who is in power today, is the son of Hafez al-Assad, who seized power in the original military coup.

In consolidating its power base, the Ba'ath Party established close relations with the Soviet Union and, today, with Russia. It was under Ba'athism that the process of forming the nation-state in Syria finally culminated. The regime combined ideas of pan-Arabism and socialism under the slogan "Unity, Freedom, Socialism." Throughout this process of national consolidation, both in Syria and in neighboring Iraq, a key policy goal was the assimilation of all ethnic and religious minorities into an Arabic identity—in order to make it the unique and dominant identity.

From an ethnic minority's point of view, this was by now par for the course in Middle Eastern politics. The names and end goals of the regime might change from country to country, but in Syria no less than in Turkey (with its Kemalist regime) and Iran (with its Mollā regime), this policy of forced ethnic integration has been the same. The group most seriously affected by such ethno-nationalism has been the Kurdish people—colonized by the Arab, Persian and Turkish nation-states alike.

The Kurdish struggle under colonial policies
A history of peoples, not nation-states

It is difficult to describe the history of colonization suffered by the Kurdish people or the conditions of oppression they still experience today, due to their afore-mentioned fragmentation and their position as an interstate colony without any recognized political status (Beşikçi, 1990). And although the forms of exploitation and oppression Kurds have experienced in different parts of colonized Kurdistan are similar enough, the subjectivities produced by these experiences vary significantly.

It should be noted from the outset that relatively little of the scholarly literature on Kurds even mentions that Kurdistan is a colony. Ismail Beşikçi was the first sociologist to point this out in academia (Beşikçi, 1990). Gülistan Yarkın—who discusses whether North Kurdistan (Bakur) is a colony of Turkey in her article on the denial of truth and the Northern Kurdistan colony—collates most of the "İnkâr Edilen Hakikat: Sömürge Kuzey Kürdistan(Denial of the Truth: The Kurdistan-North Colony)"—collates most of the basic reasons why academic studies refuse to acknowledge this reality:

> Today, discussing colonialism can still be seen as a "radical," "unscientific," and "politically extreme" endeavor. The most important reasons for this are the following: the deep influence of the official state ideology's denialism (ignorance) on intellectuals; the lack of legal recognition of Northern Kurdistan as a colony in the Turkish Constitution and in the international arena; this, despite the existence of confidential Turkish

state documents exposed in the 1990s, in which the state defines the "Orient" (Northern Kurdistan) as a *müstemleke* (colony), clearly stating that it would establish colonial administration in the region; the fact that such documents were not deemed relevant enough to be noted in publications across the social sciences; the prohibition in Turkey of discussing the colonial status of the region, both on campus and in academic and scientific journals; and finally, the existence of strong pressures on freedom of expression imposed through imprisonments and investigations by organs of the national security apparatus. (Yarkın, 2019)

Yarkın also stresses how in the 1980s and 1990s the Kurdish Movement incorporated the "Kurdistan as a colony" thesis into its platform, only then to abandon it in the 2000s. Classical anti-colonialism eventually gave rise to a discourse that is defined against the idea of the nation-state, based on the concepts of "democratic confederalism," the "democratic republic," the "common homeland," in which, finally, "Turkification" (becoming a Turk) plays an important role (Yarkın, 2019). Yarkın tries to show that Northern Kurdistan is a colony of Turkey, based on references from both the literature of colonialism and official documents of the Republic of Turkey. Mehmet Bayrak, another important researcher in this field who has had access to many official documents of the Turkish state, also claims that in many of its internal debates and policies it considers Northern Kurdistan to be its colony (Bayrak,1994, 2009, 2013).

In this respect, I agree with these authors in considering Kurdistan as a colony. But I also disagree with their reading of the past, in which the colonial state is effectively treated as the sole subject of history. Ultimately, such a view tends to treat the colonizing country's agency as unlimited and all-encompassing, while depicting the people it colonizes as incapable of being anything but victims. A narrative that says only nation-states can make history will only ever read history through the lens of their actions; it will flatten and homogenize the diverse peoples of these societies, seeing them only as colonial subjects or, for that matter, as mere objects of the violence exercised by states.

I prefer to see the colonial history of Kurdistan as the history of Kurdistan's resistance—a struggle rooted in the subjectivity of the Kurds living under the pressure of the four nation-states. Looking at history in this way allows us to see a movement that transcends each of the individual states in question and crisscrosses the artificial borders between them. This is also why the Kurdish struggle cannot be read only as a struggle against colonialism. It has gone beyond this, becoming a struggle for emancipation and social transformation. What we hear so often is true: the fate of the Kurds in Rojava will be determined by how Kurds position themselves in other parts of Kurdistan. For example, when the canton of Kobane was surrounded by ISIS, Kurds taking to the streets in Bakur and Europe ensured international intervention against this organization. This is a sign for those who study the movement: when resistance transcends borders, it opens a window onto a better understanding of its continuity.

Therefore, one cannot tell the story of the Kurds of Rojava—or even the personal story of Hesen Salih—without also tracing the rebellious existence of the Kurds across the Middle East. In this rebellion lays the very possibility of the Middle East's own emancipation—and through it, that of the world. That said, for all the revolutionary potential that has always existed within Rojava (indeed, because of this), it should be noted that ours is not a story without contradictions or conflicts. Likewise, in Deniz Bilgin's story, Hesen Salih did not live a life without contradictions. But these, then, are precisely what we must trace. For if the life of Hesen Salih represents the crisis of the Syrian state, it might also account for the crisis of the dominant system as such. The same goes for the history of the Kurdish Movement.

History of resistance in Rojava

The resistance struggle, whose historical flow I shall attempt to explain, has thousands of details, which makes it impossible to describe the entirety of its distinct subjectivity. So, in order to understand Rojava, we must explore the events, rebellions and movements that are most important to the collective history of the region's inhabitants. Many of these events were described in the interviews I conducted with movement participants and other locals in the area. Thus, the following historical research has largely followed the oral history of the peoples of northern Syria.

The Xoybûn movement

For all the work that went into the formation of nation-states and the establishment of national borders after the fragmentation of the Ottoman Empire following the First World War, the great powers failed in the end to divide the Kurds. The Kurds in the west (Rojava, in Syria) have always had a close relationship with the Kurds in the north (Bakur, in Turkey). The early years of the Republic of Turkey, especially, witnessed many Kurdish rebellions against the Kemalist ideology. Many of these revolts were suppressed through state plans to ethnically cleanse the region, such as the *Islahat Planı* (Rehabilitation Plan), with the rebel leaders killed shortly thereafter. The most important of these revolts was the Sheikh

Said rebellion in 1925, which spread to all Kurdish regions of Turkey. Mehmet Bayrak (2019) emphasizes that, though it went down in history under the name of the sheikh, it was in fact organized by the *Kurdistan Azadi Cemati* (Kurdistan Freedom Community), an organization founded by a group of Kurdish intellectuals from Istanbul, as well as some landowners and sheikhs (Kurdish: *şex*) from the Kurdish provinces. The rebellion was suppressed by the Turkish state, which bombed the cities, captured Sheikh Said in 1925, and executed him along with 48 other rebels.

Many of the surviving Kurds who had participated in this revolt crossed the Syrian border into Rojava. In 1927, they established a group called Xoybûn[4] (Kurdish for "to be"), known as the first Kurdish national organization in Syria. Jodi Tejel points out that up to this point, family relations and local, religious or tribal ties had determined the social practices and way of life of the Kurds in northern Syria. "It was not until the arrival of Kurdish nationalist intellectuals, formerly based in Istanbul, that the idea of a Kurdish national group took on some reality among a small minority of the Kurdish population in Syria" (Tejel, 2015, p. 20). Martin van Bruinessen, in his work *"Ağa, Şeyh, Devlet,"* also emphasizes that the way Kurds identified themselves under the old Ottoman national system had been determined by familial tribal ties rather than ethnic identity (Bruinessen, 2003). The purpose of the Xoybûn movement was to eliminate these vertical tribal relations and mobilize Kurds around the idea of a national Kurdish community connected by horizontal ties (Schøtt, 2017, p. 5).

It was in Syria, during the French Mandate, that the Kurds were first identified as a minority—as a distinct nation, an ethnic group. However, the formation of the most fundamental Kurdish national consciousness came as a result of rejected identities, forbidden languages, and massacres under the monist policies of the new ethnic nation-states. Celadet Ali Bedirxan, the first leader of Xoybûn, had been tolerated by the French. In addition to publishing the magazines *Hawar*[5] and *Ronahî*—important for the formation of the Kurds' cultural and literary memory—he helped to standardize the Kurdish language by creating its first Latin alphabet and making the first grammatical studies of the Kurmanji dialect. At the same time, Xoybûn supported armed struggle against the Turkish state through the rebellions of Mount Ararat (1928–1931), which lasted for five years. During this time, a Kurdish National Gathering was held on Mount Ararat, a national government was established, and Ağrı (the name of the mountain in Turkish) was

---

4 There are different ways of writing the name of this organization: Xoybûn (in Kurdish), Khoybun or Hoybun (in Turkish). The place where the organization was founded today is located in Lebanon.

5 In addition to Celadat Bedirhan, his brother Kâmuran Bedirhan, Osman Sabri, Nureddin Zaza, Cegerxwin and Kadri Can were among the writers of *Hawar*. The magazine published 57 issues until 1943, when it ceased publication.

declared the independent province of Kurdistan. Notably, there was continuity between this and previous revolts, a history stretching across the Syrian–Turkish border. As Sedat Ulugana puts it:

> All the resistance between 1923 and 1938 in Northern Kurdistan was interconnected. It is a tradition, like the beads of a rosary. The Koçgiri rebellion of 1921 is somewhat separate from these resistances, but it was the one that intellectually inspired the Sheikh Said movement. Seyitxan, Seyitxane Kerr, Alican, Ferzande, who participated in the resistance of Sheikh Said—that is, in the Azadi community, in 1925—also fought on Mount Ararat. They are the people who, in a way, organized the Zilan resistance. So, the following can be said: those who started the resistance on Ararat were the surviving fighters of the Sheikh Said resistance. There is such a link. While the fire of rebellion was extinguished in the triangle of Genç, Lice, Palu, the same fire was lit on Mount Ararat or Zilan. (Ulugana, 2019)

The five-year rebellion on Mount Ararat led to the Turkish state sending thousands of soldiers to the region and air bombing the villages and valleys. In his book *Ağrı Kürt Direnişi ve Zilan Katliamı* (1926–1931), Ulugana describes the Ağrı resistance through eyewitness testimonies, claiming that the state response constituted a form of genocide:

> Now nearly 95 years old, Hacı Şebab Kandemir says of that day, "More than 15,000 women, children and old people were tied together and subjected to Gatling gun fire. Children in the bellies of pregnant women were bayoneted. Crops were burned, concrete was poured into water wells." Hacı Şebab Kandemir was just a child in those days, "We escaped through the forest next to the village. We thought we were safe, that everything was over. But we were wrong; it had all just begun." (Ulugana, 2010)

In the course of the uprising—which lasted until 1931, involving some 606 settlements—more than 1,200 houses were forcibly evacuated by the government, and about 15,000 people were killed along with the Kurdish rebels and their families. During this massacre, the subject of many Kurdish folk tales, the Zilan River (Geliyê Zîlan) is said to have bled. Meanwhile, in Turkey, newspapers of the time and even comic magazines announced the killings with glee. The cartoon included below shows a tombstone placed on Mount Ararat; in Turkish it reads: "Here lies your imaginary Kurdistan." It would not go unanswered. The photograph that

Dönemin Türk basını 'çizmelerini giymişti.'
1930 yılının Eylül'ünde Milliyet, yukarıdaki
karikatürle kalkışmanın kanla bastırılmasını
sevinçle duyuruyor. "Hayali Kürdistan burada
gömülüdür" diyordu yanılacağını bile bile...

follows shows a tombstone placed by the PKK on Mount Ararat years later, which reads in Turkish: "Here lies your imaginary colonialism."

After the suppression of the rebellion on Mount Ararat/Ağrı by the Turkish state, Xoybûn withdrew to the Rojava region in Syria. It is often claimed that, from this point on, Xoybûn became an organization that conducted more cultural and linguistic activities than political ones (Schøtt, 2017, p. 6).

Towards autonomy in Cezîre

Cezîre (Arabic: Jazeera, French: Jazira), which today is an autonomous region of Rojava and northern Syria, means "the island" in Arabic. Geographically, it refers to the fertile lands of Mesopotamia, which lie between the Tigris and Euphrates rivers. This region has always retained its own subjectivity, even in the face of Syria's state-formation process. It has also proven a source and an arena of political

and economic conflict, due not only to the fertility of its land but also its copious fossil fuel resources. When talking about Cezîre, the people of the region say there is "black gold below, yellow gold above," that is, plenty of oil and wheat.

The uprisings and massacres in Northern Kurdistan (Bakur) resulted in Kurdish insurgents moving into Rojava. Indeed, the initial establishment of Xoybûn and many other factors led the Kurds of Rojava to make an official request for autonomy to the French Mandate government in 1929:

> Regardless of any differences of race and religion, all the residents mentioned below—tribal chiefs, farmers, merchants, landowners—want to have a say in their precious homeland (*patrie*). They demand from noble France and the League of Nations (*Cemiyet-i Akvam*), which holds in its hands the destiny of all the peoples, self-government (*auto-nomie locale*) for the following reasons: Cezîre (*Haute Djezireh*) was not part of Syria in any period of history. [...] During the period when the region (*contrée*) was under Turkish rule, it was not under the orders of the feudal lords of Damascus (*seigneur*), but under the banners of Diyarbakır and Mardin. The residents of Cezîre are Christians, Kurds and Arabs, and these groups have nothing in common with Damascus (request for autonomy from the chiefs and seigneurs of Jazira, April 5, 1936). (Altuğ, 2018, p. 88)

As mentioned above, France formalized the autonomous activities of these groups by supporting other religious minorities against the Sunnis in Syria. The Kurds' demands were mainly based on language and culture. They made requests, such as education in their mother tongue, the appointment of Kurdish rulers in Kurdish regions, and the establishment of Kurdish as an official language in these regions (Özkaya, 2007). However, under the French Mandate, the government rejected these demands for Kurdish autonomy. Many researchers have put forth different reasons to explain this decision. Nelida Fuccaro claims that the French authorities rejected the request of the Kurds because it did not consider them to have the status of a religious minority, like Alawis and Druze (Fuccaro, 2005, p. 252). According to the author, they also rejected the demand for autonomy because the Kurds did not constitute a majority living in a specific region—they were, after all, scattered all over the northern border of Syria and in the main cities (Fuccaro, 2005, p. 252). Özkaya, on the other hand, emphasizes the French-English conflict in the region and believes that the French wanted to prevent a Kurdish formation that would benefit Britain. Even so, he believes that the real reason was that the Kurds were, in the last analysis, too divided and powerless to make political and cultural demands (Özkaya, 2007, p. 94). For him, the Kurds' weakness can be explained as follows:

> The Syrian Kurds were not strong enough to effectively defend their demands at the time. Several reasons lay at the root of these weaknesses: first, the Kurds were not economically strong; almost all of them lived in rural areas and supported their lives in agriculture. Secondly, the Kurds in Syria were scattered geographically. And the last reason was that they were fragmented internally. The fact that the Kurds were more rooted to their tribes than to their ethnic identities, and the conflicts between the tribes, prevented them from uniting. (Özkaya, 2007, pp. 93-94)

But if we analyze the Kurds' struggles for autonomy over the years in different countries, it becomes clear that the most important reason for rejecting their demands was that their autonomy in one country concerned neighboring countries as well. For France, giving autonomy to the Kurds in Syria meant turning against Turkey, which in that period lived in fear of Kurdish revolts. To legitimize Kurdish demands would be seen as meddling in Turkey's internal affairs, so the French avoided it. The fear of "the neighbour's sensitivity" is, even today, the main argument against supporting the autonomy of the Kurds across the Middle East and in the broader international arena. In addition, France was probably worried about creating a new problem with important sectors of the Arab population of Syria—particularly the Druze, who had already rebelled in 1925 when Syria was divided into five sub-states.

Many authors agree that although the French Mandate government did not grant the right of autonomy to the Kurds, it tolerated their cultural activities (Tejel, 2015; Fuccaro, 2005; Schøtt, 2017; Özkaya:2007). The existence of Xoybûn would be the most important evidence in this regard. In fact, Xoybûn continued to conduct its cultural studies until 1946 and only ended its activities once the French Mandate government withdrew from Syria.

The Amûdê Cinema fire of 1960

Amûdê is one of the smallest settlements in Rojava and, as I found out, is locally famous for its many lunatics. On hearing this gossip and without knowing its causes, I could not help but chuckle: only in Kurdistan would some settlement become famous for its madmen.

My perception changed after visiting a cooperative in Amûdê for my fieldwork. There it was explained to me that "the Amûdê madness" is directly related to a little-known historical event called the Amûdê Cinema massacre, which caused the deaths of 283 children in 1960. In fact, although there is hardly any official information about this tragedy—nor did I manage to find very many sources—it is certain from what I did find that the Amûdê massacre is one of the most important events for understanding Kurdish collective memory and the ways it lends strength to the struggle in Rojava.

The usual narrative is as follows:

In the town of Amudê in Rojava, students were taken to the cinema on a compulsory basis, following the instructions of elementary school principals. Although the cinema had capacity for 120 people, 500 children were led into a room that used to be a stable. Two soldiers, waiting at the door, padlocked it from the outside. The movie being screened for the children was *Midnight Accusation*, an Egyptian film about the Algerian War of Independence. At the time, the war of independence against the French occupation in Algeria was ongoing, and the screening of the film was intended to support Algeria. A fire started in the middle of the screen shortly after the film began. The teachers told the children not to get up, even as they themselves fled the cinema. The fire grew and before long the screaming started; the children began to flee towards the door and crush each other. Despite their screams and howls, the soldiers at the door refused to open it. As the fire spread and engulfed the wooden building, people ran to the cinema screaming. As Mixemedê Seîd Axa sat drinking coffee, Dilşa, his sister, came running to inform him of what was happening. When Dilşa said, "There is a fire in the cinema, and your two sons, Hekim and Lokman, are also inside, and the soldiers are not letting anyone in," Mixemedê Seîd Axa ran to the cinema, took out his gun, killed the two soldiers waiting at the door, broke it down, and went inside. He began to save the children two by two. As the fire spread, his sister Dilşa shouted and said, "Don't go in anymore, your children are out here, you'll die." But Mixemedê Seîd Axa replied, "All Kurdish children are my children, I will go in until there is not a child left inside." He went in and became trapped. The cinema collapsed on them all. Mihemedê Seîd Axa died along with 283 children. Most of the bodies were unrecognizable, not even the bones of some of them were found. After the incident, officials said, "There is nothing to do, it's fate," and explained that the fire was caused by a technical failure. (BasNews, 2018)

The United Arab State did not conduct an investigation after the fire. The Syrian state, reconstituted in 1961, did not conduct an investigation either. Indeed, just as when the Turkish state called the bombing by F-16 planes of the villagers of Roboskî in 2011 an "accident," the Syrian state too claimed that the burning of the Amûdê Cinema was an accident. And just as in Roboskî, the Ba'athist regime banned any memorial to the Amûdê massacre. So, they say that people in this town became crazy for not having been able to overcome their grief.

Following Rojava's Declaration of Autonomy in 2012, a monument park was created in tribute to the children who died in the Amûdê Cinema. And the Rojava Film Commune (Komîna Fîlm a Rojava), which organizes an international film festival starting on November 13 every year, keeps this memory alive by highlighting the Ba'athist regime's policy on the Kurds (Rojava International Film Festival, 2019).

The 1962 census depriving Kurds of citizenship

The most important feature distinguishing Kurds in Syria from those elsewhere is that many are not even entitled to basic citizenship. In 1962, the Syrian state conducted a census specifically targeting Kurds, asking them to prove that they were officially registered as living in Syria before 1945. More than 120,000 people could not prove this status with any official document—even if they were listed in the census—and their citizenship was stripped. The new government revoked their IDs and issued them a red paper marking them *ajnabi* (singular: *ajnabi*, plural: *ajanib*), Arabic for "foreigner."

Those who did not participate in the 1962 census were registered as *maktoumin*, meaning undocumented or invisible persons. In the following years, about 75,000 people—second- and third-generation Syrian Kurds, whose parents had been registered as *ajnabi*—continued to be registered as *maktoumin*, not citizens. Many Kurdish children born after this census were also registered as

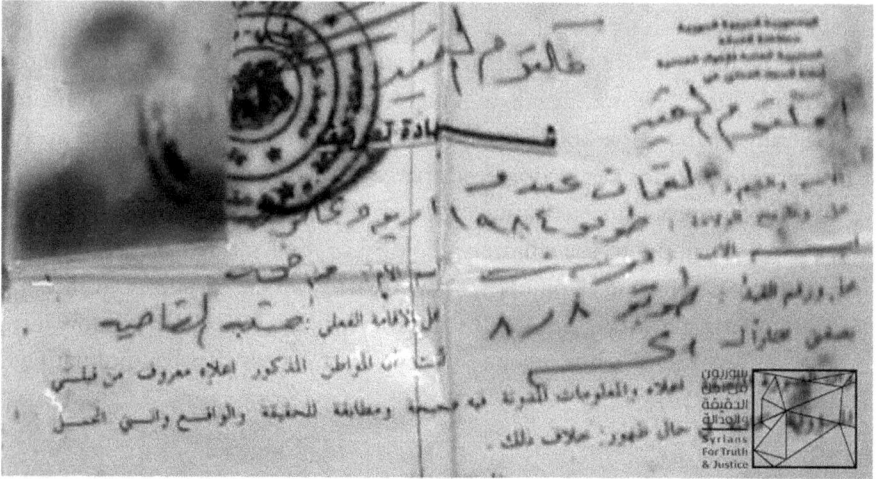

maktoum/maktouma or *maktoumin* (singular male/singular female and plural). Kurdish children become *maktoumin* when one of the following three conditions is met: if they are children of Syrian-born Kurdish "foreigners" who marry women who are Syrian citizens; if one of their parents is a "foreigner" and the other *maktoum*; or if both parents are *maktoumin* (HRW, 1996, p. 3).

The Danish National ID Center explains this rather complicated situation with the help of the table below.

Husband	Wife	Registration of marriage	Status of the children
Citizen	Citizen	Yes	Citizens
Ajnabi	Ajnabia	Yes	Ajanib
Maktoum	Maktouma	No	Maktoumin
Citizen	Ajnabia	With special permission	Citizens
Ajnabi	Citizen	With special permission, the wife keeps her original register number and is still considered single	Maktoumin. Ajanib if the marriage is registered
Ajnabi	Maktouma	No	Maktoumin. Ajanib if entered in father's family register
Maktoum	Citizen	No	Maktoumin
Maktoum	Ajnabia	No	Maktoumin

Table 1: Marriage registration and status of the children (Danish National ID Center, Stateless Kurds in Syria: Maktoumin and Ajanib, 2019)

Although it is not known exactly how many people hold this status, a report published in 1996 by Human Rights Watch states that people who were stripped of their citizenship and registered as *ajnabi* and *maktoum* represent some 20% of the estimated total Kurdish population in Syria (HRW, 1996, p. 3). According to Kurdish sources, almost 200,000 to 225,000 people were registered as *ajnabi* and *maktoumin* when the revolution began. The report published by the Danish National ID Center on January 16, 2019 states that in 2011, in Hesekê province alone, the number of *ajanib* and *maktoumin* categorized as stateless totaled 300,000 (Center, 2019). During my field stay in Rojava, I was even told that after a while Kurds simply stopped registering their children; besides their being deprived of citizenship, registering them with the government as *ajanib* or *maktoumin* would only cause them to be criminalized and discriminated against even further. Despite all this, Bingöl states that throughout this period of disenfranchisement Kurds continued to be recruited into the Syrian army (Bingöl, 2005, pp. 40-41). This is not surprising given that the military is one of the most important institutions of ethnic assimilation in the state.

Those who have lost their right to citizenship and have been left undocumented are also deprived of their most basic civil rights, such as the right to travel, to marry legally or to pursue an education. For example, a *maktoum* child requires formal approval from government officials just to go to school, an approval often granted only through arbitrary or corrupt practices. Moreover, even if they are accepted into school, they will not be given a degree and consequently, not be able to pursue university studies and careers. Practically no rights—from the acquisition of property or a passport to voting in elections—are within reach for those Kurds who have been banned as citizens.

> Since Syrian Kurds did not—and do not—have citizenship of another country, they are stateless under international law. They have been issued special red identity cards by the Ministry of Interior and, under a discriminatory state policy, are denied many of the rights enjoyed by other Syrians, such as the right to vote, the right to own property and the right to have marriages legally recognized. They are not entitled to passports and therefore cannot exercise the internationally guaranteed right to freedom of movement and to leave and return legally to their own country [Syria]. (HRW, 1996, p. 3)

State employees whose citizenship was stripped in this way were dismissed from their jobs and could not find another official job because they had no legal identity. Instead, they were forced to work for very low wages in jobs they could only find illegally. This meant, of course, that such Kurds had no labor rights either, because—contrary to the common practice of states towards unregistered "foreigners"—those not considered Syrian citizens were not deported, but rather forced to stay in their places, becoming a perpetual source of cheap and precarious labor for the Syrian state and capitalist class.

Although there are various rumors about the reason for this practice, the Syrian government responded to Human Rights Watch's request for information as follows:

> In early 1945, Kurds began to infiltrate the province of Hesekê. They arrived separately and in groups from neighboring countries, especially Turkey, illegally crossing the border between Ras al-Ain and al-Malikiyya. They gradually and illegally settled in the region along the border in major population centers, such as Dirbasiyya, Amoudeh, Qamishli, Qahtaniyya, and Malikiyya, until they began to constitute the majority of the population in some of these centers, e.g., Amoudeh and Malikiyya. Many of these Kurds were able to register illegally in the Syrian civil registries. They were also able to obtain Syrian identity documents by various means, with the help of relatives and members of their tribes. They did so with the intention of settling and acquiring property, especially after the enactment of the land reform law, in order to benefit from land redistribution. (HRW, 1996, p. 37)

In other words, according to the Syrian state, the purpose of this census was to identify non-Syrian Kurds who illegally entered the country from other parts of Kurdistan in an attempt to benefit from the great gains of Ba'athism. However, a simple glance at the historical record does not support this argument: among those who lost their citizenship were people like Osman Sabri, a prominent nationalist and poet originally from Damascus, born in Hesekê in 1906; and, even more importantly, the nationally respected Nizam al-Din brothers—Abd al-Baqi, who was an important politician between 1949 and 1957 and even served as a minister, and Tevfik, who became chief of staff of the armed forces in 1956–1957 (McDowall, 2004, p. 624).

What does this whole debate mean for the Kurds themselves? Because after all, for them there was no such thing as a border before the formation of the relevant nation-states. Even if it were true that some Syrian Kurds came from Turkey, their descendants were born and raised in the lands of Syria. Shouldn't they have the right to nationality? The real problem is that the situation of the Kurds cannot be understood as long as it is read within the framework of national identities and the borders that define these identities. McDowall states that many Kurds from various provinces of Turkey were unemployed as a result of the mechanization of agriculture starting in the 1950s, forcing them to migrate across the border to Rojava with the help of their tribes. Özkaya explains that the main reason for this is that the borders, relatively well-controlled during the period of the French Mandate, could not be maintained during the first years of the independent period (Özkaya, 2007, p. 96).

Leaving aside the debate of whether or not the Kurds as a whole were "originally" from Syria, the November 1963 report prepared by the Hesekê police chief, Lieutenant Muhammed Talab Hilal, clearly reveals that the practice of stripping the Kurds of citizenship was merely the first step in a much more ominous state policy.

Hilal explains his position as follows:

In Jazeera they are ringing emergency bells, they are urging the Arab conscience to save this region, to cleanse it of all these bad people who are the disgrace of history—because Jazeera, by virtue of its geographical location, offers all sources of income and wealth, as do other provinces of the Arab lands. [...] The Kurdish question, around which today the Kurds are organizing, is only a tumor that has developed in the body of the Arab nation. The only solution to this is to eliminate them. (McDowall, 2004, p. 625)

He proposed the following 12-point plan to accomplish this:

I   Displace Kurds from their lands;
II   Deprive them of their right to education;
III   Expatriate any fugitives to Turkey;
IV   Deprive them of access to employment;
V   Initiate an anti-Kurdish propaganda campaign;
VI   Displace Kurdish imams, and replace them with Arab ones;
VII   Pursue a "divide-and-conquer" strategy, stoking divisions within the Kurdish community;
VIII   Relocate Arabs into Kurdish regions;
IX   Establish an Arab Belt along the frontier with Turkey;
X   Establish collective farms for Arab farmers;
XI   Deny the right to vote or start a business to non-Arabs;
XII   Refuse to accept as Syrian citizens any non-Arabs who wish to live in the region.

(McDowall, 2004, p. 625)

The next period consisted of implementing these policies one by one. The main objective of the Syrian state was to make the presence of the Kurds invisible, at least in the official records; to strip them of all their rights in the state and in the social sphere; and, in doing so, to convert them into slaves or cheap labor, while at the same time preventing them from leaving Syria. I consider the main goal of this policy to have been ensuring their dispossession. This process of stripping the Kurds of their citizenship rights would only deepen in subsequent years as a result of the so-called Arab Belt policy.

The Arab Belt: the dispossession of the Kurds

The demographic policy, called the Arab Belt (*al-hizam al-'arabi* in Arabic), essentially aims to empty the Kurdish settlements and replace them with an Arab population, in order to break the geographic contiguity of Kurdish populations in Syria and prevent them from gathering and organizing politically. The plan also applies to the entire border of northern Syria, from Afrîn to Dêrik, to prevent Kurds from crossing the Rojava border into or through other parts of Kurdistan.

The Arab Belt as a political project is based on a report prepared by Lieutenant Muhammed Talab Hilal, the police chief of Hesekê. According to his plan, the Belt would be created along the Turkish border, extending into Iraq and then across the region from the Iraqi border to Tal Kuchik; this would represent 10 to 15 kilometers from the northern border to the south and 375 kilometers in length. The plan suggested that approximately 140,000 Kurds living in 332 villages would be displaced, and that Euphrates Bedouin Arabs—who had themselves been displaced from the filling of the Hafez Al-Assad Lake, formed in 1994 after the construction of the Tabqa Dam—would populate those villages (McDowall, 2004, pp. 624-625). Border towns such as Qamishlo in the Arab Belt area, which mostly consist of villages and rural areas, were excluded from the plan. The project envisioned a radical demographic change: the Arabization of the region where the Kurds live (Gökcan, 2018, p. 172) and the gradual fading of the remaining Kurds into the Arab identity.

It is notable that in the wake of the Arab Belt policy, both peoples, Arabs and Kurds alike, were each in their own way displaced by the state; the Kurds were left landless, while the Arabs became workers in a land they did not know. Despite this, of course, the Arabs seemed at the time to be the final "beneficiaries" of this policy. And in a world where ethnic groups too often turn against each other rather than their common oppressor, it seemed all too natural for the Kurds to think so. But decades later, the revolution in Rojava would show both Kurds and Arabs that the Belt was neither natural nor just, but rather a policy of state domination, and that to break this domination it was necessary to build a new mentality where neither group had any hostility towards the other.

The Kurds use the word *makhmuri* to refer to the displaced Arabs brought from Tabqa and Raqqa for the purpose of settling on Kurdish-owned land. At the onset of the Syrian civil war, many of the Kurds who were displaced and became landless thought they could get their land back after Kurdish forces declared regional autonomy. They hoped that the *makhmuri* Arabs would be expelled and the land would be returned to its original owners. However, it soon became clear that neither the Kurdish revolutionary forces nor the Self-Administration would support this idea in their policies. On the contrary, they refused to expel the Arabs from the region. The autonomous government accepted and defined the reality of the *makhmuri* as a social problem that was on the table to be solved. After the revolution, through the practice of establishing what Öcalan's theories call democratic nation,[6] a strong social and political compact was achieved among the peoples of Rojava that has prevented the makhmuri from remaining a contributing factor to large-scale social conflict.

In 1965, the Ba'athist regime legalized the Arab Belt plan by official decree, however, the conditions for its realization only matured with the coup d'état at the end of 1970. The government of Hafez Al-Assad that came to power on the heels of that coup d'état began to fully implement the plan in 1973. Before this, the 1967 Syrian-Israeli War had directed the attention of the Syrian state mainly towards the center in Damascus and out towards the Gulf. McDowall attributes the delay in the plan's implementation to the fact that land redistribution remained incomplete due to Kurdish resistance (McDowall, 2004, p. 626). Indeed, according to news reports disseminated by the Rudaw news agency (based on eyewitness testimonies), dozens of Kurds who resisted during this period were arrested and subject to violence (Rûdaw, 2016). According to the Land Committee (*Komite Axarî*), who I interviewed in Rojava, although there was some resistance at the time, it was not particularly powerful, and the resulting revolts did not achieve results because the Kurds at that point were very disorganized (interview with *Comite Axarî*, 2018). That said, these state policies would create an important political and social base for later political organizing. It should be noted here that it is in fact quite difficult to find official sources speaking directly about the Arab Belt and explaining the development of the rebellion against it, because the state implemented it under another name: "model villages."

At the end of 1970, Hafez Al-Assad, the Minister of Defense and Commander of the Air Force, seized power in a coup called the Corrective Movement (*Tashih*),

---

6 See the 'democratic nation as a form of struggle, self-management and common life' of this book, p. 156 (check the page)

which opened a new chapter in Syrian political history (Özkaya, 2007, p. 97). The Ba'athist party came to power in their own coup in 1963; but in 1966, intra-party politics had led to a second coup by a different faction. In 1970, Hafez Al-Assad carried out a coup against his own party to correct the previous coup in 1966. In doing so, he effectively turned the Ba'athist regime into a one-leader dictatorship.

Hafez Al-Assad completed the long-planned land redistribution program and set Syria on a path of agricultural industrialization. His first action in office was to rename the Arab Belt project and implement it:

> The government began implementing the resettlement plan in the early 1970s, but under a new terminological cover: the "Arab Belt" was replaced by the "Plan to Establish Model State Farms in Jazeera Province." Under this new justification, the government would build "model farming villages" in the Kurdish region and populate them with Arabs. The government expropriated from Kurdish landowners the land on which it constructed these "model farms," either under the pretext of land reform or because the owners were Kurds who had been stripped of citizenship in 1962 for failure to prove residency in that year's census. In 1975, the government resettled some 4,000 Arab families on 41 "model farms" whose land had been flooded by the construction of the Tabqa Dam on the Euphrates, in the very heart of the Kurdish region. The government suspended the Arab Belt project in 1976, but never dismantled the model villages or returned the displaced Kurds their land. (HRW, 2009, pp. 10-11)

Rendering the Kurds stateless by taking away their citizenship also aided in the confiscation of their land as "state property." The Arab Belt, established through the displacement and dispossession of at least 60,000 Kurdish families until the end of 1975, was followed by the suppression of Kurdish identity and culture in many areas of social life. The use of the Kurdish language was banned in public institutions, schools and hospitals. All kinds of bans were imposed on the dissemination of Kurdish printed or oral material; even singing and listening to Kurdish was forbidden. Newroz, the New Year's festival that Kurds and Persians celebrate on March 21, was also banned. It was impossible to register children under Kurdish names. All Kurdish villages, towns and streets were renamed and Arabized. Altuğ claims that Kurdish villages were named after Palestinian villages occupied by Israel (Altuğ, 2019).

Similar policies were carried out under not only the Arabization policy in Syria but also the Turkification policy in Turkey. Any action against the government was considered terrorist activity, on the pretense that organizing politically, establishing a dissident party, or taking direct action meant dividing the state. Of course, as Yasin Duman pointed out and as we have seen, it was not just the Kurds who were affected by the Syrian Arab Belt policy but also the Arab *makhmuri*—they had to migrate to another region where they faced new problems and were also victims of the government's policies. As a result, the Arabs who settled in a predominantly Kurdish region faced a possible conflict with the Kurds. This is why they were armed by the regime to protect themselves (Duman, 2016, pp. 71-72). However, it should be noted that many of them played a complicit role in the ethnic cleansing as paramilitaries.

Until 2004, the Hafez Al-Assad administration pursued and completed the establishment of a Syrian national culture based on Arab identity exclusively, without facing any serious Kurdish resistance. In fact, from 1976 on, despite all the ongoing bans and repression he imposed upon the Kurds in Syria, Al-Assad, playing the Kurdish card, actually supported the Kurdish movements in Iraq and Turkey—a testament to his contradictory relations with these neighboring countries (Özkaya, 2007, p. 98).

The crossing of Abdullah Öcalan into Rojava and the experience of the Bekaa Valley

The PKK—which held its founding meeting in Fis village, Lice (Diyarbakır municipality in Turkey) in 1978—predicted that there was going to be a military coup in Turkey. With the arrests that occurred following the capture of Şahin Dönmez, one of the organization's main cadres, they realized that the internal structure of the PKK had been deciphered and had fallen into the hands of the Turkish state (Karayılan, 2011, p. 106).

However, on July 4, 1979, more than a year before the coup—the military coup in Turkey did indeed occur on September 12, 1980—, Öcalan crossed the border from Suruç, Bakur (Turkish Kurdistan) and arrived in Rojava (Syrian Kurdistan), with the help of a family from Kobanê. Murat Karayılan, a PKK militant and commander, states that Öcalan, as the leader of the organization, had only two options in this period: go to the mountains or leave Turkey. He thinks that the decision was made for Öcalan to leave the country for two reasons. First, the PKK, though it was preparing for the armed struggle, was not yet trained in any real guerrilla and military tactics. Second, they were aware that a war against the Turkish state could not be pursued if they did not first establish serious foreign relations with other movements and struggles abroad (Karayılan, 2011, p. 106).

Ahmet Hamdi Akkaya thinks that the departure of the PKK's leader from Turkey allowed the Kurdish struggle to survive the 1980 coup (Akkaya, 2015). That coup crushed the Left and all opposition movements in Turkey; many leftist political leaders were captured and executed; thousands of people were disappeared into state custody; prisons became torture centers; and people were totally oppressed (Amnesty International, 1989). The state took unimaginable actions in the Kurdish provinces. Murder and kidnapping became systematic. Thousands of people were collectively killed in acid pits. The state of emergency, which was maintained in the western (Turkish) provinces and only suspended a few years after the coup, continued unabated until 2002 in the Kurdish provinces (Hafıza Merkezi, 2020).

Öcalan stayed in Kobanê for some time but his main objective was to reach the Bekaa Valley. When he arrived in Damascus, around the end of 1979 or early 1980, he became associated with the Democratic Front for the Liberation of Palestine (*Al-Jabha al-Dimuqratiya Li-Tahrir Filastin*, or in English, the DFLP) through the Democratic Left Party of Syrian Kurdistan (the *Partiya Çepa Demokrata Kurdî* or PÇDKS). After a few meetings, he reached an agreement with the DFLP to set up a PKK militant group that would receive armed training in the *Hevre* Camp in the *Bekaa* Valley—an area that, at the time, was in Syrian regime territory. This partnership with the Palestinians was the first internationalist relationship in the history of the PKK and would prove of great importance in the international relations it would establish in the future. Although no attention is drawn to this aspect, the internationalization of the PKK constituted a fundamental phase in its transformation from a national liberation movement into an anti-capitalist movement. The first PKK group, which departed from Bakur, arrived at the DFLP's Camp Hevre before the military coup of September 12, 1980 (Schmidinger, 2016, p. 91). In 1982, the PKK group had its first experiences of war fighting for the defense of Palestine. But the Palestinians soon closed their camps in this area when the Bekaa Valley came under direct Syrian control in 1985. The PKK, meanwhile, had launched the war against Turkey with the Batman-Eruh raid in 1984.

In addition, this period saw the re-emergence of the conflict between Syria and Turkey over the region called Hatay (in Turkey) or Alexandretta (in Syria). This was a historical border dispute between the two nation-states dating back to their foundation, whose revival was provoked by the fact that Turkey left Syria without water with the construction of a new dam on the Euphrates River for their Southeast Anatolian Development Project (*Güneydoğu Anadolu Projesi* or GAP). Coupled with this, Turkey was supporting the Muslim Brotherhood organization (*Cem'iyyetü'l-İhvânü'l-Müslimîn*) against the Ba'athist regime. These intrigues led the Syrian state to allow the PKK to use the Bekaa Valley after 1986, and the Hevre Camp became the main site for PKK training until 1992.

It has been alleged that the Syrian regime supported the PKK's actions against Turkey and that Öcalan, in turn, pledged that the PKK would not establish a relationship with the Syrian Kurds (Schmidinger, 2016, p. 91); it is even said that the PKK itself adopted the legend so central to the propaganda of the Syrian state, which claims that "in Syria you do not find Kurds who are originally from Syria, you find refugee Kurds who came from Turkey" (McDowall, 2004, p. 632). However, there is no official statement from the PKK on this matter. And in the first interview Öcalan gave to a Turkish journalist, Mehmet Ali Birand, in 1988, when asked if the PKK had relations inside Syria, he only replied, "Only at the level of families" and said that they had no direct relation with the Syrian regime. He added that the Syrian state was very sensitive about the security of the Syrian–Turkish border, so the PKK did not use that border to cross to Turkey (Öcalan, İşte Apo, işte PKK, 1988).

The fact that the PKK was a Marxist-Leninist oriented organization made it ideologically very popular among the Kurdish youth in Damascus in the 1980s. Accounts from people in Rojava claim that in this period Öcalan visited Kurdish families in Syria one by one, that he stayed there until 1998, and that he assigned cadres to organize the people secretly. It should be noted that many young people in Rojava have always been affiliated with the PKK. "Thus, over time, the field of those who followed Öcalan's ideas became the main Kurdish political option in Syria" (Conde, 2017, p. 60). The cadres who were formed and trained by the PKK were sent to the battlefield in Turkey; many of them returned to the Rojava countryside decades later when the revolution began and established the YPG (the *Yekîteyên Parastina Gel* or People's Defense Units) and YPJ (the *Yekîteyên Parastina Jin* or Women's Defense Units). Likewise, and despite being in hiding, from this period on the PKK led the organization of the popular rebellions—or *serhildan*—in Rojava. For example, although it was banned in 1986, hundreds of thousands of people came out that year to celebrate Newroz; the regime's soldiers opened fire on the celebrants and one person was killed. The funeral became a great demonstration of revolt and spread to every city with a large Kurdish population. In Afrîn, the Syrian regime arrested dozens of people. After decades of repression against Kurdish culture, the Newroz celebration acquired a political dimension and became a day of resistance and rebellion for the Kurdish struggle.

The Bekaa experience does not just explain how the PKK developed in a military sense. I would emphasize that this experience led the Kurdish Movement to encounter many other revolutionary movements that were being trained in the Palestinian camps at the same time, among them the Nicaraguan Sandinistas, the Greek communists, and the Colombian Indigenous people. This dynamic pushed a nationalist movement into becoming an internationalist movement—a moment which, in my opinion, was decisive in the ruptures and radical changes of the Kurdish struggle's long-term ideological transformation.

Furthermore, instead of the war tactics it had used in Turkish Kurdistan, the movement in Syrian Kurdistan began to focus more on mass organization and built up its social acceptance among the general population. This allowed it to become more deeply rooted in Rojava until, particularly in Syria, it would become the main symbol of the regional struggle for the emancipation of the Kurds.

These aspects of the movement's history are important for understanding how and why the Kurdish revolutionary movement seemed to have appeared so suddenly in Rojava when the Syrian war started in 2011—not to mention how it was so quickly accepted by the local society. Appearances can be deceiving. In fact, one must understand how all the activities of the PKK in the Bekaa Valley and throughout Syria over the course of decades led the Kurdish struggle to become a dynamic rather than static social movement, one which could break with the grammar and practices of the leftist canon while also building up a revolution that was merely waiting for its time to come.

The spark of revolution:
Serhildana Qamishlo (the Qamishlo Revolt)

Hafez al-Assad died in 2000 after 30 years in power. He left the country to his youngest son, Bashar al-Assad, who at the time was studying in Great Britain. As Bashar al-Assad was very young and inexperienced, the Ba'athist Party cadres did not fully accept him. Therefore, it was important for the new president to cultivate public support. Indeed, odd as it seems now, in the first years of his rule Bashar was seen as a progressive: he carried out a series of reforms that increased cultural and political freedoms, especially for minorities, and thousands of political prisoners were released in the context of these early appeals. He also established informal dialogues with several Kurdish parties. Taking advantage of this atmosphere of change, the Democratic Union Party (the *Partiya Yekîtiya Demokratik* or PYD) was established in 2003 as part of the larger KCK umbrella of political parties seeking to establish democratic confederalism.

Meanwhile, the long running Kurdish Peshmerga (insurgent) struggle achieved regional autonomy in Iraq in 2003, thanks to the overthrow of Saddam Hussein and the support of the United States. The autonomy of the Iraqi Kurds would inspire serious social movements elsewhere as well, as it was the first concrete achievement of Kurdish struggles in the Middle East. Kurds were potentially well primed to revolt elsewhere. The social process was set in motion. In the late 1990s and early 2000s, part of Turkey became the scene of popular revolts (*serhildana gel*). The PKK became a popular movement during this period, and its influence provoked an undeniable social mobilization. A few leading cadres were enough to start large popular revolts. The people of Rojava were also influenced by the growing mobilization of the Kurdish people. The fuse was set; all that was needed was a match to light it.

On March 12, 2004, in Qamishlo, Syria, a scuffle broke out between fans of an Arab soccer team from Deir-ezzor and the Kurdish home team. This marked the beginning of the uprising in Rojava, which would continue thereafter. It is alleged that the fans of the Arab team, al-Fatwa, started shouting pro-Saddam slogans against the Kurds to provoke them, and that the Kurds responded in kind with pro-Kurdish slogans. The match had not yet started when a group of al-Fatwa youth, armed with guns and chains, entered the stadium to attack the Kurdish fans. The regime's police forces allegedly opened fire on the Kurds, in support of the Arab group (Ayboğa, Flach, & Knapp, 2017, p. 109). Eight Kurds and four Arabs were reported killed in the initial clashes.

The next day, at the Kurds' funeral in Qamishlo, the coffins were draped with the Kurdistan flag and pictures of Assad were burned. Later, the Syrian state tried to violently suppress the demonstrations, deploying army troops to the region (Özkaya, 2007, p. 104). This insurrection lasted for days, spreading throughout Rojava and even to other districts where Kurds lived, in places like Damascus and Aleppo. International solidarity soon followed. The government of Iraqi Kurdistan emphasized national identity and solidarity among Kurds by announcing that it would accept Kurdish refugees whose lives were threatened by the Syrian state. In Diyarbakır, Turkey, the Kurds of Bakur issued a press release in which they declared themselves to be a part of the Qamishlo rebellion (*serhildana Qamishlo*) and called on the people to continue fighting through democratic means until they achieved freedom. Tejel states that, for the first time in modern Syrian history, the Qamishlo revolt spread throughout the country, strengthening the symbolic unity of Syrian Kurdistan (Rojava) (Özkaya, 2007, p. 104).

The Syrian armed forces intervened heavily in this revolt. All exits to the province of Hesekê and the borders with Iraq and Turkey were closed, prohibiting entry and exit to the city of Qamishlo. Additional army units were sent to all cities where marches and protests were taking place, and the state declared a curfew in all Kurdish provinces. Some 2,000 people, mostly Kurds, were arrested. Although the exact number is unknown, dozens were killed. A few months later, the government sent a letter to all Kurdish parties operating illegally, stating that their activities were banned because they did not have a license (Özkaya, 2007,

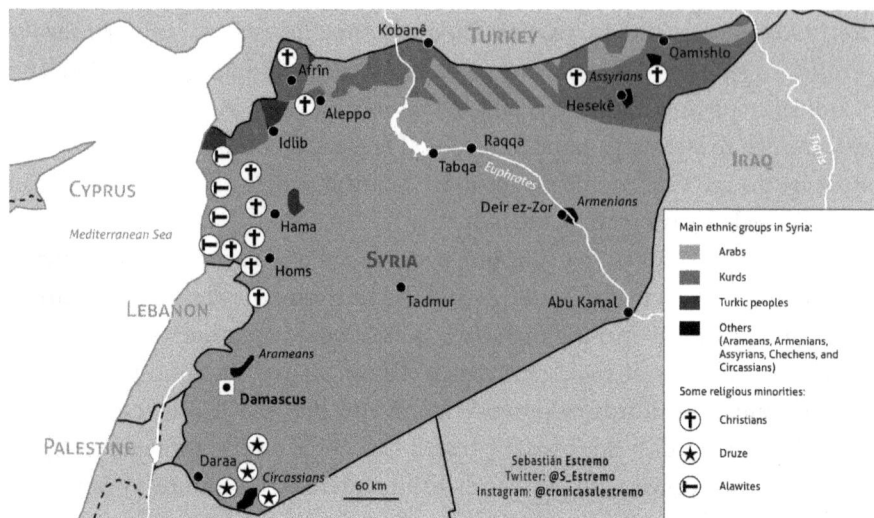

Ethnic and religious composition of Syria (2010)

p. 104). All the activities of the PYD were banned, and dozens of its social leaders were imprisoned. Subsequently, an international consensus was established between Ankara, Baghdad, Damascus and Tehran on the need to coordinate to control the Kurdish question (International Crisis Group, 2014).

Although the uprising of the Kurds in Qamishlo in 2004 ended with a lot of violence and political repression, it was an important popular mobilization. In the words of those who participated in these mobilizations, it was an epochal moment: "the first spark of revolution and autonomy for Rojava was ignited" (Yunis, 2019).

These fragments of the past constitute key aspects of the history of resistance in Rojava. Undoubtedly, history, and especially the history of resistance of colonized peoples, is much broader than any one narrative can capture. Nonetheless, I have seen fit to mention these particular fragments for three main reasons. First, to demonstrate the continuity of the Kurdish people's struggle, despite the numerous successive state-building projects that sought to wipe them out. Secondly, to underline that revolution does not arise spontaneously, but is the result of a long social process of rebellion and resistance that build upon one another to develop revolutionary consciousness. And finally, I believe these fragments of history are very important to understanding the historical and emotional reference points of the Kurdish revolutionary subjects who are building autonomy in Rojava today.

CHAPTER 3

Rojava's Autonomy as a Movement

In the first chapter, I discussed how the Kurdish Movement came to the idea of autonomy through a process of transformation that it had been undergoing since 1978, and defined it as the main objective of the struggle after 2003. The Kurdish Movement responded to the ideological ruptures by effecting changes and transformations based on an analysis of its own experience and that of other struggles around the world, leading to changes in its path.

Firstly, the movement turned away from the idea of the nation-state, prompted, in large part, by the USSR's fetishization of the state with its model of socialism. Later, the movement turned away from the very idea of power, analyzing patriarchal relations on the basis of the gender contradictions discerned within the freedom movement.[1] Since then, autonomy has gained strength in political discourse, not only within the Kurdish struggle, but also among many other movements in the 20th century, becoming a concept in which different political practices have place and meaning. Many theories and politics defined as Marxist, anarchist, syndicalist, feminist, ecologist, "assemblyist," and so on discuss autonomy. However, social movements, national liberation struggles and Indigenous movements create a variety of autonomous practices, using tools and applying organizational mechanisms to exercise autonomy from below (masses), as part of their own life and based on their own subjectivity. In this regard, we can say that autonomy refers not only to a series of theoretical debates, but also, and above all, to the practices that arise every day in different parts of the world and from the political and theoretical debates that enrich these practices. The Kurdish struggle and its search for autonomy is one such example.

The search for autonomy in the Kurdish struggle

Autonomy is a concept with several meanings, since it expresses practices of struggle that occur and continue under different conditions, as well as within different intellectual discussions. These meanings and ways of understanding are diverse and can be quite complex. In fact, similar practices are often expressed

---

1 To learn more about this political transformation, consult the work by Abdullah Öcalan, *Bir Halkı Savunmak*, Weşanên Serxwebûn, 2004, p. 135.

in different theoretical debates. In the introduction to *Pensar las autonomías [Thinking on Autonomy]*, which attempts to systematize these discussions of autonomous practices, different ways of understanding autonomy are analyzed: as a way of doing politics, as diversity, power and possibility, as prefiguration or as an emancipatory horizon (JRA, 201: 10-11).

When we observe the debates on the Kurds and autonomy in the political and academic world, we see that what the Kurds define as autonomy is not taken into account, nor is the criticism they employ to develop this idea, nor the place from which they wish to build it, nor how they politicize the practice of autonomy through their subjectivities. In conventional academic circles, the debate on autonomy is treated as if it were a sterile issue and merely a matter of politics. It is viewed from a Eurocentric perspective, in a unidirectional manner, as a right recognized by sovereign states. The debate on the autonomy of the Kurds is often caught up in discussions of war, dialogue, peace and cultural rights, without taking into account the practices of their struggle, the ruptures and contradictions or the autonomous practices of life that communities have been building over their prolonged resistance.

In particular, the concept of autonomy in Bakur (Kurdistan-Turkey), where it has been most debated and socialized, and has been most asserted as the main political demand of the struggle, is caught up in the context I have just mentioned. As such, Kurdish members of parliament, mayors, political parties and platforms, as well as human rights organizations, NGOs and others, who advocate autonomy in the legal political sphere, attempt to legitimize the Kurds' quest for autonomy on the basis of the European Charter of Local Self Government or in the United Nations Declaration on the Rights of Indigenous Peoples. From the perspective of these instruments, autonomy should be negotiated between the PKK and the state. In other words, the definition and the demand for autonomy are addressed on the basis of a legal regulation or constitutional amendment in which the state recognizes the local rights of identity and culture. Cuma Çiçek, who has written several books on Kurdish autonomy, notes that there is no consensus among the Kurds in Turkey on the definition of autonomy (Çiçek, 2015). In fact, the Kurdish Movement in Turkey, supported by neighborhood assemblies, cooperatives and academies, has engaged in some autonomous practices, but these were quite fragmented and deemed illegal by the Turkish state, consequently the movement did not construct a common idea of autonomy.

Since 2003, there has been a contrast between the discourse on autonomy and the practice of autonomy.

Despite having adopted the project of libertarian municipalities advocated by Murray Bookchin,[2] whom Öcalan has called his teacher, the practice of municipalities in Kurdish cities, in Bakur, was far from that. Although the Kurdish people know that the movement defends and seeks autonomy, it is still unclear what the content and practice of that autonomy would be. In my opinion, there are two main reasons for this (in addition to personal interpretations and the political pressure generated by this contradiction). One is that the idea and possibility of achieving a "Kurdish state" is still very present in the mindset of most Kurds, and the other, closely linked to the first, is that the debate on the autonomy of political subjects is still very much inclined to adopt the dominant perspective, that is, the persistent concern for legitimization and negotiation with nation-states.

The fact that Iraqi Kurdistan became a federated autonomous region after 2003 has not necessarily enriched the discussions on autonomy. From the beginning, both the Peshmerga movement and the PDK (Kurdistan Democratic Party of Iraq—Partîya Demokrata Kurdistan a Irak) advocated for an independent Kurdistan based on the nation-state model; that is why, eventually, this partial autonomy led to an independent Kurdistan from a state perspective. The debate surrounding the self-government of Iraqi Kurdistan was approached mainly from the perspective of independence, of how to move from a federation to a nation-state, and how this transition would bring about transformation in the oil-producing regions.

Perhaps, with the declaration of de facto autonomy in Rojava in 2012, it has started to become clear, for the first time, what the Kurdish Movement is talking about when it speaks of autonomy. Instead of basing itself on tertiary or secondary sources, the Kurdish Movement started to explain the idea of autonomy as the subject of the process, creating its own tools and its own experience of time and temporality. Furthermore, the international attention that emerged after the Kobanê struggle created the conditions for the movement to be heard. In Rojava, with the creation of the armed women's defense units (YPJ), the Kurdish Movement reached a popularity it had never seen before, and many people are now open to hearing about it. The Kurds' struggle, especially against the Islamic State, began to be seen as a "reasonable" struggle by a wider public. However, given that many people became aware of the existence of such a struggle for the

---

2 Bookchin was born in 1921 into a Jewish family in New York. During his childhood, he joined the communist youth organization. During the Second World War, he abandoned Stalinism for Trotskyism and later became an anarchist. In the 1980s, he distanced himself from anarchism in order to defend the power of citizen assemblies or the revolutionary project of "libertarian municipalism." Bookchin's perspective on local government as part of an ecological perspective is called "social ecology." Bookchin also uses social ecology to refer to "eco-anarchist" projects. In 2004, Öcalan wrote a letter to Bookchin, through his lawyers, commenting that he wanted to think more deeply about the reality of the Middle East and expressed his desire to have a discussion with him. In the same letter, Öcalan described himself as a student of Bookchin. That meeting never took place due to Bookchin's health problems, but the correspondence between the two continued until Bookchin's death.

first time and that the Kurds were at the beginning of a comprehensive practice of autonomy, the narrative shifted to a focus on describing the movement's political perspective or transformation.

To date, it is difficult to find in-depth field research on how autonomy is organized and practiced in Rojava. Field data and observations are not subject to critical analysis due to an idealized image of Rojava. The narrative is without contradictions and conflicts and, consequently, does not consider other possibilities. Many studies on Rojava's autonomy, generally conducted from an external gaze, focus on legal and military debates, and summarize the idea of autonomy in terms of national and international recognition. The dominant view is that autonomy is not sufficiently developed due to the conditions of war; from this idealized perspective of autonomy, it is asserted that for autonomy to develop, a post-war context is necessary in which the authorities of Rojava are recognized by the Syrian state.

Although it is true that the conditions of war greatly affect the practice of autonomy, to conclude that it has not yet developed is a limited view. From this perspective, autonomy is seen as occurring only in one territory (Rojava and northern Syria) and as starting at a specific moment (the declaration of the Autonomous Government of 2014). However, the historical background of the struggle I mentioned in Chapter 1, and the way in which it is playing out in Rojava, show that the idea and practice of autonomy emerged from the Kurdish struggles themselves and has persisted throughout their history.

The ongoing struggle, led by the PKK since 1978, has coincided with a maturing in the thinking about autonomy. The conversion into a popular movement, which started with the organization of the party, gave rise to the process that produced the idea of autonomy. From my point of view, the form of the struggle and resistance is the first practice of Kurdish autonomy, because it transcends and transforms time and space (as borders that divide and define) and is not static or defined. As such, the experience of Rojava cannot be fully understood if it is not seen as part of the Kurdish Movement's struggle for transformation and as a social and geographical point reached by that transformation. On the other hand, the recent practice of autonomy in Rojava has destroyed previous ideas and definitions of autonomy, both for the Kurdish Movement and for the Kurds themselves. A fresh outlook is needed to understand the authenticity of Rojava within the context of the debate on autonomy. There is also a need to listen to the local people and see how they engage in these debates in their everyday life.

In the literature on popular struggles, the most important starting point of nearly all debates on autonomy is the right to national self-determination. This principle was discussed by Kautsky and Rosa Luxemburg in relation to the Polish question during the Second International. Later, Lenin formulated it as the right of the oppressed nation to political independence, to secede and establish its own nation-state (Lenin, 1968). The Kurdish Movement, as I mentioned, justified its separation from the Turkish Left on the basis of this principle and defined the party of the proletariat as its tool of struggle, the armed struggle as its form of struggle, and the construction of an independent state as its objective of struggle. However, in the declaration of democratic confederalism, Öcalan asserted that Lenin's formulation was wrong and that for the Kurdish Movement to understand the right to self-determination as the establishment of a state was a fatal error. Moreover, the most serious error in this understanding of self-determination is that the freedom of society can only be achieved through the mediation of the state (Bilim Aydınlanma Komitesi, 2009, p. 47).

Consequently, the idea emerged that this right should not be denied but rather reinterpreted by the debates on autonomy. Democratic autonomy and/or democratic confederalism are a new and different interpretation of the right to national self-determination, one in which the starting point for current-day discussions is autonomy, understood as the right to self-determination of communities rather than of nations. Francisco López Bárcenas, in his article on Indigenous autonomies in Latin America, expresses this with the concept of "free determination":

> The first version of free determination gives rise to sovereignty, the second to autonomy. Autonomy is the form that Indigenous movements have chosen to exercise their right to free determination, which is why autonomy is cited as a specific form of exercising free determination (Bárcenas, 2011, p. 78).

Bárcenas also states that Indigenous movements express this demand in different ways, such as: self-affirmation, self-definition, self-delimitation, and internal and external self-willingness (Bárcenas, 2011, p. 78). We can add to this list self-management, the Marxist concept that refers to the autonomy of the working class, which became prominent in the reclaimed factories in Argentina after the 2001 crisis and was used for the experience in Bakur in 2015. However, the declaration of the Şırnak People's Assembly shows that in the Kurdish struggle, the definition of self-management is a departure from the original Marxist meaning:

> We, as the Şırnak People's Assembly, cannot reject the state, but we cannot walk with the institutions of the state in this manner, as all the

institutions of the state in this city have lost their legitimacy for us. In this regard, no designated state will be able to govern us. Afterwards, we will build our lives upon a democratic basis, sustained in our self-management as a people. Then, we will make our democratic self-defense against all the attacks that will ensue. Subsequently, we will govern ourselves in our city. We will not allow others to lead. (Şirnak People's Assembly, Declaration of self-management, August 2015)

In this regard, in the announcement of self-menagement of the people's assemblies in Bakur between 2015 and 2016, in an area covering approximately 20 provinces, or in the democratic autonomy exercised in Rojava, the main demand was for the people to govern themselves. In other words, the basic meaning of democratic autonomy and/or democratic confederalism is expressed as the right of Kurdish society to determine its own destiny, that is, to decide on its individual and collective life. As Bárcenas underlines, even though there are many different ways of defining autonomy, they all have the same utopian project, and among their most significant demands are: to be peoples with full rights, with territories, natural resources, their own forms of organization and political representation before state bodies, the exercise of internal justice based on their own law, conservation and development of their cultures and the elaboration and implementation of their own development plans (Bárcenas, 2011, p. 68). Thus, in terms of the Kurdish struggle, the idea of autonomy or self-government is the method, the struggle and the language of resistance to oppose the monist policies of nation-states.

The first element that must be understood about the Kurdish struggle is that the possibility of self-government does not constitute a right demanded from the state; on the contrary, it is an alternative form of organization against the state system. In this way, as is the case in many experiences of autonomy, the question of the state is at the heart of Kurdish autonomy, because through democratic autonomy it seeks to build an alternative to its current form. The question of the state is fundamental to understanding and constructing autonomy, as autonomy presupposes a break with the state. As Mabel Thwaites Rey states, "but we are also convinced that the nation-state category still retains a centrality that is very difficult to ignore in thinking about collective action" (Thwaites, 2004, p. 59). From this standpoint, there is a dichotomous relationship between the state and autonomy. It is not a dichotomy in which without one there is no other; but rather a dichotomy in which one cannot be discussed without discussing the other.

In the debates about autonomy and the state, two main approaches emerge. The first posits that autonomy can be achieved by transforming and reforming the state. This approach does not envision the disappearance of the state, but rather affirms it as an asymmetrical relationship/structure that opens space for autonomy and even recognizes the right to it. The second approach, which I will consider, rejects the state, denying it as an institution of power; it must be eliminated for social emancipation to be possible. The negation of power also requires the negation of capitalism in the daily life of communities. That is why we can say that autonomies with a negative approach are anti-capitalist autonomies. This approach, developed by theorists of open Marxism, libertarian Marxism, councilism and anarcho-syndicalism, considers autonomy as a form of struggle and as a model of radical social organization aimed at achieving collective freedom. Examples of this include the Zapatista experience in Chiapas and many other instances of Latin American Indigenous popular resistance. It is an approach that view autonomy as anti-state and anti-capitalist.

To these approaches can be added Kurdish autonomy in Rojava, which, being anti-patriarchal and putting gender liberation at the center of its construction, enriches the debate on autonomy with the proposal and practice of democratic confederalism. Democratic confederalism is both a political project and the Kurdish Movement's theoretical attempt to make sense of the world and its own struggle. And even though Öcalan elaborated on the project in many of his writings, I do not consider the project finished, determined or fixed. On the contrary, I believe that the Kurdish struggle is being built through the experience of the autonomy of Rojava. I also believe that by discussing their practice of daily life, the people offer fundamental reflections and make contributions to the debates on autonomy as they go about creating autonomous ways of life. In the following section, I will briefly consider the concept of democratic confederalism, and then explain the practices of building democratic autonomy that have been implemented in Rojava over ten years of revolution.

Weaving autonomies: democratic confederalism

Although the concept of democratic confederalism was first used by Öcalan in 2005, we find its theoretical synthesis in the various political defenses he presented before the court on the island of Imrali, where he was after 1999. During this time, Öcalan elaborated two main arguments in his countless defenses, political perspectives and documents. One pertained to building a new political objective and project to replace the real socialism that had collapsed. The other pertained to rebuilding the symbolic and emotional world of Kurdish society because, especially in the 1990s, the struggle gave rise to a popular movement and the people had united in the struggle for a nation-state of their own. Öcalan and the PKK reinterpreted that objective as a fetishization of the state that would not lead the struggle beyond capitalism.

Starting from this critique and consciousness, they had to change the meaning of the struggle without disrupting the unity of the Kurdish people. In other words, the idea of a united and independent socialist state of Kurdistan fell apart after real socialism was thought to have collapsed because it has been sustained by power and the state. However, while the idea had collapsed, the popular movement was nevertheless growing independently. This contrast required the start of a new phase, a new form of struggle. The struggle against capitalism could no longer be carried out with the concepts and ideas of the previous century. The struggle for national liberation had to be reconstructed such that it would not lead to building a Kurdish state, and this had to be explained to the people. For this reason, Öcalan played the role of a leader and strove to reinterpret the history of the Middle East and the Kurds. His reinterpretation asserted, on the one hand, that the identity of the Kurds had deep roots and they constituted one of the oldest nations in the Middle East, and, on the other hand, they had never become a state organization and therefore had retained democratic elements that would allow them to think beyond the nation-state. That possibility would open the door to democratic confederalism. Öcalan's reinterpretation is both negative and affirmative because, while affirming Kurdish identity, it denies the nationalism that is part of this identity. In this regard, he poses a new form of struggle that rejects both nation-state and nationalism.

A multitude of political, social and philosophical movements and thoughts influenced Öcalan and the Kurdish Movement from the outset. However, in the new trajectory of the 1990s, Öcalan's approach to the works of Fernand Braudel, Immanuel Wallerstein and, lastly, Murray Bookchin, turned the political break into an intellectual break with the Marxist-Leninist pattern. For example, Öcalan addressed the emergence of hierarchical society, one of Bookchin's central pillars of analysis (Bookchin, 2013), as a cornerstone to understanding the Middle East. In his book Sümer Rahip Devletinden Demokratik Uygarlığa *(From the Sumerian Priestly State to Democratic Civilization)*, which he submitted to the European Court of Human Rights (ECHR), Öcalan states that the first known hierarchical and class society was founded by the Sumerians[3] and that, on the path toward

---

3 The Sumerians of southern Mesopotamia, south of present-day Iraq, who lived between 4000 and 2000 B.C., were a polytheistic civilization, with 35 city-states organized around priest-kings. What is known about the Sumerians, obtained from the cuneiform tablets they left behind, is that they were advanced in many areas. The Sumerian mythology described on these tablets, dealing especially with mythical stories and struggles between gods, are primary sources in the analysis of the history of Sumerian civilization (Samuel Noah Kramer, Sumerian Mythology, 1961, Library of Alexandria; Harriet E. W. Crawford, Sumer and the Sumerians, Cambridge University Press, 1991). Although the Sumerians, who made many innovations, were not the only community in this period, the most important feature that distinguished them was the establishment of the first known political and economic system in history. The ziggurats (pyramid-shaped temples), considered the place of God on

their freedom, the Kurds could not aim to achieve a state, because the state is the oldest and deepest existing hierarchical relationship in the Middle East (Öcalan, 2001).

On this basis, the Kurdish Movement emphasized that the main social contradiction—which, following Marxist canon, was previously expressed as class contradiction—is essentially the contradiction between the state and society (Bilim Aydinlanma Komitesi, 2009, p. 9). Therefore, it is crucial to defend society against the state (Karasu, 2017). The Kurdish Movement argues that the nation-state, fetishized as the current model of the state since the French Revolution, is the political instrument of capitalism (Bilim Aydinlanma Komitesi, 2009, p. 17), it divides society into classes and establishes power (Karasu, 2017). Contrary to the Marxist perspective adopted in the past, the development of capitalism began simultaneously with the development of the state. Striving to establish a state became synonymous with building capitalism (Andok, 2017). According to Öcalan, the social system organized by the Sumerians around ziggurats was the first form of state institutionalization:

> Albeit there are many features that can define civilization, its decisive characteristic is that the human being, driven towards efficiency rather than consumption, becomes a surplus product giving way to the enslavement of property. The idea of the Sumerians was that the ziggurat would operate as the place that would play the role of temples and, at the same time, of collective business and social production. These centers, which are the representatives of the system of heaven on Earth and of the identity of society, and which acquire a sacred significance, are the prototypes of temples, assemblies, business centers and military headquarters, educational and cultural centers that will develop throughout civilization; that is, they are the main womb of the institutionalization of the state. The invention called state, i.e., the ziggurats, would, at the beginning, be declared sacred by the priests, ideologues of that time, for their surplus productivity; they would also dominate the human mind as representatives of heaven on Earth through the sacred order, and would be promoted as the most advanced source of authority. (Öcalan, 2001, pp. 25-26)

In other words, according to Öcalan, the state was first formed through the primary accumulation that took place through the ziggurat system, in which humanity was converted into property.

---

earth, were symbolic spaces in which society was defined and separated into social layers.

In the 1990s, having transformed into a popular movement, the PKK and the liberation movement were interested, in general, in the gender contradiction that arose with the participation of women in the PKK. Öcalan felt the need to explain the origins, not only of the state, but also of the conflict between men and women, which was decisive in Kurdish society. Upon his reading of history based on mythology, he claims that the establishment of a hierarchical and class society by the Sumerians and its evolution into a state system under the authority of their priests was made possible by the creation of patriarchy. Öcalan, who defined pre-Sumerian society as a natural society—Bookchin spoke of an organic society (2013, pp. 117-137)—pointed out that in this period, social life woven around women was dominant; their characterization as goddesses showed them as leaders of society. With the development of Sumerian society, women lost their role in the organization of society and social relations. Thus began the institutionalization of patriarchy,[4] which led to the enslavement of women and their exclusion from the social structure, turning them into sexual objects and, ultimately, the "queen of commodities" of the capitalist system, as defined by Öcalan (Jineoloji Academy, 2016, p. 149).

These analyses, based on the origin of patriarchy and the state, which can be summarized very briefly in this way, were identified as the new axes of the Kurdish struggle: the struggle against the state, patriarchy and capitalism. A new form of struggle aimed at fundamentally abolishing the hierarchical systems. These three main axes seem to be decisive for the construction of democratic confederalism in Rojava today.

In order to understand democratic confederalism, another important aspect must be mentioned: Öcalan's bilateral understanding of history. On the one hand, he examines how sovereignty, hierarchy, patriarchy and the system of exploitation developed, that is, how humanity lost its freedom. On the other hand, parallel to this history of domination, he invites us to understand the history of those who resist, who oppose, who are not nationalized, who constantly break out of these systems of domination, rebel or fight for freedom. According to Öcalan, the historical reading of this antagonistic dichotomy can be imagined as two parallel but opposite rivers; on the one hand, the river of sovereignty, that is, the line of capitalist civilization; on the other, the river of freedom, that is, the line of demo-

---

4 When male gods—in the role of father, brother or son—begin to appear alongside the goddesses, the social relations of the natural society are transformed. According to Öcalan, the period in which the goddess Inanna was in a balanced power relationship with her brother Enki, but at the same time fought, is followed by the period when the female goddesses were erased from the arena of history by the cunning of the male gods. Thus, the moment when patriarchy began to dominate is the time when the Sumerian goddess of love, Innanna, being deceived by her brother Enki, became the enemy of other goddesses. Öcalan reads this and describes it as a second sexual rupture. The first sexual rupture began with the Neolithic revolution carried out by women and continued until the Sumerians. The second sexual rupture, when the settlement of society transformed the division of labor between male hunters and female gatherers, caused men to begin to use the power they had yielded as hunters to dominate the household and women, as a form of counter-revolution.

cratic civilization (Öcalan, 2016). In some of his writings, he expressed this duality as capitalist modernity and democratic modernity.

> I am neither discovering nor inventing democratic modernity. Although I have something to say about reconstruction, I do not care much for it; or, better yet, what matters is elsewhere. It is this: Democratic modernity has been in a dilemma since official civilization was formed. There was a place and a time when it happened. What I am trying to do is to give this form of civilization (informal civilization, or however it may be called) what it deserves, that is, to develop remarkable explanations in its main sectors. It is, also, to know the basic mentality, its structuring and its society in life and, from there, to make definitions about what it is. (Öcalan, 2009, p. 215)

Öcalan states that these two social forms exist in an antagonistic dilemma and have a mutual determinism. His main point of departure is Rosa Luxemburg's thesis that "capitalism can only exist as part of the existence of non-capitalist societies"; he adds that, instead of only using this argument to define the capitalist period from the perspective of Marxism, the same can be used to look at all historical and social processes (Öcalan, 2009, p. 211). According to Öcalan, true history is the result of the struggle between the capitalist powers, which include the state, the monopoly of capital, the patriarchal system, and the democratic powers, made up of women, slaves, workers, all the exploited and oppressed social groups. This definition is based on the critique of Marx's assertion that "history is the history of class struggles"; according to Öcalan, the concept of class struggle is insufficient to describe historical conflict:

> In the systems of hierarchical and state society, the conflict between the democratic element and the adjoined power and war is the main political phenomenon. There is a permanent struggle between the democratic elements based on the mode of existence of society, communality, and the power and war group, which assumes hierarchy and state coverage. The motor of history is not a narrow class struggle in this sense, but a struggle between the mode of existence of the people (demos), including the class struggle, and the destructive power that feeds itself by attacking this mode of existence of the people. Societies are essentially based on these two forces. (Öcalan, 2004, p. 103)

In fact, here Öcalan expands on the concept of class and reconsiders the struggle, widening it to include a broader population. We must remember that class distinction, which was not yet evident in Kurdish society at the time of the founding of the PKK, could not encompass the concept of class struggle. When the struggle became a popular struggle, the question of who the revolutionary subject is had to be answered and redefined again, because it was no longer only workers or militants and partisans. How should the Kurdish landowners' support for the freedom struggle be interpreted or how would it be possible to join the Turkish working class when it supported the Turkish state's war against the Kurdish people? The reality on the ground was gutting the existing concepts. For this reason, the concept of class was abandoned, and the concept of people began to be used more confidently. However, this was not only a conceptual choice; it also determined the dynamics of the struggle. The discourse of popular struggle against hierarchy, instead of class struggle against capital, became the main discourse.

In this sense, Öcalan defines democratic confederalism as follows, expressing it as a "proposal":

> Democratic confederalism is the valid solution for the peoples of the Middle East and even for the whole world. Democratic confederalism is a non-state democratic national organization. Democratic confederation is a minority organization, a cultural organization, a religious organization, even a gender organization and other similar organizations. I define this as the organization of a democratic and cultural nation. It can exist in every village as a commune. It is a confederation of all cultural organizations, the unity of them. It must be taken as a line. I define it as the non-state democratic confederation. Democratic confederalism is very important; I recommend it not only for the Kurds, but also for the Middle East and even for the world. (Öcalan, 2005, pp. 117-118)

As this quote makes clear, Öcalan's most basic proposal is the reorganization of the social fabric, sustained by the commune, or what Bookchin refers to as ecocommunity, on a democratic basis (Bookchin, 2014). In the Newroz declaration of 2005, read to the public in Amed, democratic confederalism declared itself as follows:

> The democratic confederalism of Kurdistan is not a state system, but rather a non-state democratic system of the people. This system reflects the politics created by all sectors of the people, especially women and youth, who have freely created their own democratic organization in their own citizenship assemblies at the local level, on the basis of confederal, direct, free and equal citizenship. It is therefore based on the principle of

self-empowerment and self-sufficiency. It takes its power from the people and adopts self-efficacy in all sectors, including the economy. (Öcalan, Demokratik Konfederalizm, 2005, pp. 8-9)

Because Öcalan is the leader of the PKK and has a symbolic value for the Kurdish people, the proposal became a political project and an objective in the ensuing years. As mentioned above, the PKK restructured its organizational model at its ninth Congress, called the "Reconstruction Congress." Instead of a "party" structuring and seeking to establish a state and assert power and war/violence, it switched to the KCK system (*Koma Ciwakên Kurdistan* – Unity of Kurdistan Society), which is less centralized and based on organization in the form of democratic autonomies in all parts of Kurdistan. In this sense, the PKK was created in a confederal structure as part of many KCK organizations, becoming an organization of the latter. It was also stated that society would be reorganized on the basis of democratic confederalism.

> As you know, it has been on our reconstruction agenda for a year. For a period, within the framework of change and transformation, Önder Apo[5] has developed a new paradigm, a paradigm of democratic, ecological society, of gender emancipation. The creation of a democratic and ecological society was established as a strategic objective. The major difference with the previous objective is that it is based on science, getting rid of the influence of dogmatism. The main difference of the new PKK is here. On these principles it develops a new school, perspective and paradigm. A revolution based on three pillars: the democratic, ecological and gender revolution. It is based on a democratic system, free of state, power and hierarchy. Instead of the nation state, it sees democratic confederalism as a strategy in and of itself. On this basis, it wants to create a new society. Its purpose is a new democratic ecological society. The new PKK is being reconstructed as an ideological and philosophical force for these purposes. (PKK, 2005, pp. 11-12)

In other words, both Öcalan and the PKK are committed to leading the Kurdish struggle on the road to freedom with a new purpose and manner, and call for the people to continue and fight for the goal of democratic confederalism instead of a Kurdish nation-state. Founded under the name of the Reconstruction Congress of the PKK, the KCK refers to the new organizational structure (democratic

---

5 In Turkish, *Önder* means "leader" and Önder Apo means "the leader Abdullah Öcalan." However, when the PKK says "leader" it does not refer to Öcalan as a person, but to the role he fulfills together with other leaders of the PKK. This means that Öcalan's leadership is symbolic. In recent years, members of the PKK have started to use the word *Rêber* which is Kurdish for "guider of the way."

confederalist structure) that I emphasized in the first part of this chapter; it includes the ideological, political, self-defense, social, economic and autonomous organization of youth and women. For this restructuring, called democratic trans-formation, it was stated that all civil society outside official state society should implement its own democratic organization, that is, organize its political and social autonomy. Furthermore, in establishing the model of democratic organi-zation, it was stated that the politically oriented democratic party should position itself as the ideological, theoretical and administrative coordinator of the demo-cratic society (PKK, 2005, p. 66).

The party structure was not abandoned, but the hierarchical and vanguard form of the party was criticized. The PKK would remain as a party, but it would be restructured on the basis of democratic confederalism, which required a radical transformation and self-critical formation. The Kurdish movement was creating a completely new organizational model; within this system, the movement envisaged general people congresses, people assemblies in cities and provinces, communes in neighborhoods and villages, cooperatives, non-governmental orga-nizations, human rights organizations and libertarian municipalities.

For this purpose, the Democratic Society Congress (*Koma Ciwaka Demo-cratic*—DTK) was established in 2007 in Bakur-Amed. On July 14, 2011, the Congress, akin to the idea of democratic confederalism, declared the democratic autonomy of Kurdistan in Turkey. Democratic autonomy was defined in the Declaration of Democratic Autonomy, read by Aysel Tuğluk, the first woman co-president of the Democratic Society Party (DTP-Demokratik Toplum Partisi):

> Democratic autonomy is the natural life system of all societies. Demo-cratic autonomy is neither destroying a state nor building a new state. Nor is it a state system. It is the system of people's participation in the self-management of their own territory, which is not a country. It is an expression of the fact that all sectors of society, especially women and youth, have created their own democratic organization, and that they conduct politics in their own assemblies on the basis of direct participa-tion and free and equal citizenship. It is therefore based on the principle of self-determination and self-sufficiency. Democratic autonomy is not the change of borders and symbols, but the new social contract itself, in which the values of the peoples of the region are accepted within the common boundaries and are among the common values. (DTK, 2011)

With this declaration, the Congress called upon the Kurdish people to participate in the process of autonomy building and explained to Turkish society that this was not an event that would divide or destroy the Turkish state. On the same day, the media reported that the PKK, and not the Congress, had declared autonomy, therefore the content of the declaration was not up for debate, and it was categorized as "a terrorist action" that aimed to divide Turkey. In the ensuing process, the DTK established democratic autonomy building committees, based in Amed, that would build democratic autonomy "illegally" on the basis of "sectors of democratic confederalism." Having been on the economic committee established in 2012 and being part of this process allowed me to observe the process from the inside.

Certainly, several analyses of this process are possible, but I would like to point out two that, in my view, are important. One is the internal fragmentation of the Kurdish struggles that distinguished themselves from the Turkish socialist movement in the 1960s and converged on the basis of the idea that Kurdistan was colonized. The Kurdish struggles, which until then had only distinguished themselves for their socialist and nationalist approach, and that joined together with the aim of a united and independent Kurdish liberation struggle, radically and intensely separated once democratic confederalism was declared. The ideological conflict materialized in the tension between the "anti-state" solution and the "state" solution, or between the PKK-Apo line and the PDK-Barzani line. From my point of view, this separation clarified the anti-capitalist and capitalist struggle. Moreover, it created two extreme political directions for the Kurdish movements, and often pitted one against the other. Although it can clearly be seen that 20 years of liberal autonomy did not create any freedom for the people of Iraqi Kurdistan, the other reality is that the concrete realization of the Iraqi Kurdistan Regional Government, on the path toward the nation-state, on the basis of the politics of the PDK-Barzani, became a permanent emotional barrier to the full adoption of the idea of democratic confederalism by the Kurdish people.

The second point I want to underline is that although the PKK decided to give up its vanguard role as a result of self-criticism based on a restructuring of the understanding the party, this has taken time, as has clarifying the division between the political-civilian and political-military areas based on action and spoken word. Regarding the organization of social space, the first assemblies were formed from above and it took time for them to be extended to the base of the villages, since the participation of the people to elect their delegates was still limited. Furthermore, the way in which the assemblies operated has been controversial. The ban exercised by the state, which included the use of the word "autonomy," and the perception that those who participated in these assemblies did so as "members of a terrorist organization," created a very high-pressure atmosphere. For this reason, instead of waiting for the development of democratic and horizontal relations from below to strengthen the assemblies, the cadres designated as "leadership" continued with their vanguardist habits, thereby perpetuating the party structure. Often, in practice, the cadres dominated the assembly, imposing their political perspective, and acting as they would in the guerrilla meetings in the mountains, which are based on a military hierarchy.

Consequently, the Kurdish Movement has come to understand that the creation of democratic autonomy will take a long time, and, to achieve it, it first needs to reorganize social relations in order to create an experience of autonomy from below. This is why autonomy has become prominent within the discourse of the "new life" and the "new society." Of course, many contradictions arise from the internal dynamics of the struggle. However, it was observed that these two contradictory aspects, the tension between the desire for statehood and organizing autonomy, and the difficulty of the cadres in abandoning the vanguard role, have also been very decisive in the experience of autonomy in Rojava. This research does not predict the disappearance of these contradictions, because they exist not only among the Kurds, but also in almost all popular movements in struggle. However, this work observes the kind of tendencies and mechanisms that the Kurdish Movement is trying to develop to overcome these contradictions, particularly with the experience of Rojava.

While I will continue this discussion in the next section, one point that must first be addressed is how the Kurdish Movement treats and analyzes Middle Eastern society. The Kurdish Movement attempts to develop an anti-nationalist policy of common life in the Middle East by analyzing the fundamental conflict based on nationalities and religions.

The "democratic nation" as a form of struggle, self-management and common life

The Kurdish Movement developed an analysis of Middle Eastern society as shaped by the logic of the state, with class, ethnic and religious contradictions at its base:

> Although the social structure of the Middle East still retains the democratic-communal roots of natural society, tribalism, nationalism, religious dogmatism, conservatism and patriarchal familism dominate. All these problems represent the crisis in the Middle East and the rupture it has created in the overall system.

> All these problems are the product of the system of state power, particularly capitalist statism. The nationalist mentality and the nation-state model are directly responsible for this impasse in the Middle East. The

dominance of the nationalist mentality has led nations, tribes, religions and sects to war and mutual destruction. (Bilim Aydinlanma Komitesi, 2009, p. 24)

The idea is that, in order to achieve social emancipation and liberation in the Middle East, the above-mentioned conflicts must be analyzed and reformulated. The state disperses society through hostility and opposition, so society should be reintegrated on the basis of peace and solidarity. The Kurdish Movement does not see the Kurds as the only oppressed and exploited sector of society, but rather stresses that the whole society is oppressed and exploited by the state system. Therefore, instead of fragmenting and opposing ourselves, it is necessary to build a political system of struggle and coexistence. This understanding has prompted the Kurdish struggle to abandon the axis of national struggle, that is, the identity struggle. For this reason, Öcalan introduced the concept of democratic nation-hood as a policy that, it is hoped, will eliminate national hostilities, understanding that these are the determining factor in the creation of national identities in the Middle East. I want to focus on this concept because, today, autonomy in Rojava is often referred to as the system of a democratic nation and yet, based on the organization of autonomy, Rojava has created a practice of coexistence that goes beyond that concept.

The concept of democratic nation brings together a series of ideas proposed by Öcalan to overcome the artificial conflict and hostility experienced in the Middle East as a result of differences in national, religious and cultural identity (Öcalan, 2016). Each nation in the Middle East defines its national identity based on its hostility/opposition towards another nation, and this has resulted in a system of social control that is used by nation states. Thus, in the Middle East, lynching has become a culture, showing how deep and acute nationalism is in society (Belge and Günçikan, 2016). Lynching campaigns have become a social mechanism of fear implemented by the state and, based on it, society has also committed several massacres, emulating the actions of the state.[6]

The first factor generating conflict between different identities is ethnicity; the second is religion. Religious differences are as decisive as national identity in the fragmentation of society. For the dominant national identities—Arabs, Turks, Persians—the dominant religious perspective is Islam. Conflicts between Muslims, Christians, Assyrians, Êzîdîs[7] and different sects of Islam determine

---

6 The genocide of Armenians and the massacres of Alevis in Turkey are massacres carried out not only by the Turkish state; as it was against "non-Muslims," and Turkish society participated in these massacres. Many times, the speeches coming from the state led to lynching of Kurds, perpetrated by Turkish society.

7 Most Êzîdîs (in English, Yazidi; in Arabic, Yazidî or Yezidî) are Kurdish speakers and consider themselves ethnically Kurdish. The Êzîdîs are religiously distinct from the predominantly Sunni Kurdish population of Iraq. Êzîdîsm is an ancient faith with

the political existence of states as well as the social existence of society. The main
pillars on which the state is built, that is, the fundamental identities of the nation-
states are Arab Muslims or Sunni Arab Muslims; Turkish Muslims or Turkish
Sunni Muslims. For example, to understand the scale of oppression in Turkey, the
fundamental pillars of the Turkish state are Turkish, Muslim and Sunni identities; Alewi Turks have been excluded from all state institutions, and Alewi Kurds
have been exposed to direct violence by the state, first because they are Kurds and
second because they are Alewi. In the case of Syria, while Alewi Arabs constitute the basis of the Syrian state, Sunni Arabs have been excluded and exposed to
inequality. The Sunni Kurdish people experienced this exclusion and inequality
much more intensely, as I have already mentioned. For this reason, conflict and
war in the Middle East are permanent, and have become a social crime (societal-
cide) with proxy wars.

Asya Abdullah, who was the first co-president of the Kobane canton, says
that in Syria the Kurds were denied and ignored and could not participate in any
political activity. She explains how they experienced the politics of the nation-
state before autonomy was established:

> The economy was monopolized by the state. Society was subject to the
> policy of displacement. The aim was to displace the people of Rojava
> and assimilate them in the cities [...] Thus, society was faced with two
> choices: to not surrender or to live in assimilation and denial. Those who
> surrendered were assimilated; those who did not would have to resist the
> policy of the nation-state. Wars, massacres and events occurring in the
> region today are the result of the nation-state system. The nation-state is
> responsible for all of this. (Abdullah, 2014, pp. 104-105)

In this regard, we can say that the "democratic nation" is the concept through
which the Kurdish Movement is seeking to understand and analyze the Middle
East. However, in addition to being a concept, it is also a policy that proposes
transforming the Middle East. As long as it is a highly conflictive society, peace
and the coexistence of peoples form the basis for liberation and, thus, the tools for
the struggle for autonomy. According to Öcalan:

a rich oral tradition that integrates some Islamic beliefs with elements of Zoroastrianism, the ancient Persian religion, and
Mithraism, a mysterious religion originating in the eastern Mediterranean. The Êzidîs have inhabited the mountains of north-
western Iraq for centuries; the region is home to their sacred sites, shrines and ancestral villages. Outside of Shingal, the Êzidîs
are concentrated in areas north of Mosul and in Dohuk province. There are remnant communities in Turkey, Germany and
elsewhere. For the Êzidîs, land has a deep religious significance and they make pilgrimages to the holy Iraqi city of Lalesh. For
them, the peacock represents the shadow of God, they call it Tawusî Melek and, every year, on the first Wednesday following
April 13, they celebrate Çarşema Sor (Red Wednesday), the day when God ferments the world and life begins, that is, the
beginning of the year. For more information, see: https://www.nationalgeographic.com/news/2014/8/140809-iraq-yazidis-
minority-isil-religion-history/ .

For societies, the nation-state model is a trap of oppression and exploita-tion. The concept of the democratic nation inverts this definition. The notion of the democratic nation, which is not tied to strict political boundaries, monolingualism, culture, religion and interpretation of history, refers to common life in solidarity among plural, free and equal citizens and communities. The democratic nation is the nationaliza-tion of peoples without depending on power or the state. This mode of nationalization requires politicization. And not only politicization, but not having to be the state and power, showing that it is possible to nationalize with autonomous institutions of self-defense, economy, justice, diplomacy and culture. (Öcalan, Demokratik Ulus, 2016, p. 21)

The philosophical infrastructure of this concept proposed by Öcalan is based on Bookchin's "social ecology" argument. Bookchin defines social ecology as the dynamic unity of diversity (Bookchin, 2013, p. 95) and points out that, in order to understand it, one should not look at the details of differentiation but at the logic of difference (Bookchin, 2013, p. 104). In this sense, according to Öcalan, the ecology of Middle Eastern society was constructed by nation-states under the logic of hostility; the democratic nation, on the other hand, implies breaking with this logic and weaving in its place a logic of peace and coexistence. The demo-cratic nation foresees in Rojava the peoples organizing themselves and building autonomy together, against the disruptive understanding of the nation-state. In other words, national identities defined by the dominant logic are rejected and each nation redefines its identity on a democratic basis, in order, from there, to recreate its own social organization.

We can call this a common practice of self-definition. It is a practice because it involves self-definitions arising from discussions, meetings, collective work and common decision-making in assemblies, cooperatives, municipalities and the other autonomous structures. Although within the structure of autonomy the existence of every ethnic and religious identity is guaranteed by the politics of the democratic nation, over time the people who come together and carry out the aforementioned practices of action realize that what is vital and fundamental is not identity differences, but common organizational practices. Thus, in my interviews, when I asked whether Arabs, Assyrians or other ethnic and religious identities who participated in autonomy building in Rojava were discriminated against by Kurds within the structure of autonomy, the answers indicated that my question was still very traditional compared with the practice they had experienced. In this manner, the practice of Rojava shows that the democratic nation does not mean the democratization of the Kurdish nation, but rather sees the Kurds and other peoples of the Middle East uniting on the basis of democratic space and relations, overcoming their national identities. The democratic understanding of the nation is the negation and rejection of both the state and the identities defined by nation-states. The establishment of these democratic relations allows for the re-signification of identities shaped on the basis of the above-mentioned conflict. In Rojava, while ethnic identities, especially the Kurdish identity, are expressed more freely with symbols, marches, songs and protests, social relations are established under a new social space, with a new mentality. As Cemil Bayık states:

> This mentality, in addition to removing the idea that the nation is part of the state, does not see it as a bloodline formation. In other words, it does not consider being of the same ethnicity a condition for being a nation. Understanding the nation as a democratic nation puts at its center the society that has gathered around the democratic community culture. For this reason, it also defines itself as a "cultural nation." In this understanding of the nation, gender, religion, ideology or ethnicity are not taken into account; what is considered is how much they have been appropriated by the nature of human beings and by society, and how much they determine us morally and politically. In this way, all those who act in accordance with social nature are brought into the movement. Therefore, the revolution of Rojava is not only the revolution of the Kurds. Although the Kurds may be leading the way in this revolution, they are not doing so with a nationalist approach. The People's Assembly, the Kurdish Supreme Council, the speeches of "Democratic Syria, Autonomous Kurdistan" are the result of a diplomacy that attracts all peoples with their differences and with a mentality that understands that there is a heterogeneous nature to society. (Bayik, 2017, p. 23)

The democratic terrain of the nation that excludes the nation-state is the new terrain of social relations; it is the mentality of the democratic nation. For example, while redefining their relations with the Assyrians, Armenians, Turks and Arabs, the Kurds are also redefining themselves in some ways and, in doing so, organizing a new revolutionary practice, leading to the reestablishment of social relations between peoples and religions on the basis of democratic autonomy. Although the Kurds are leading this process, the democratic nation, understood as a fundamental policy adopted by the Kurdish Movement (often referred to by the Kurdish Movement as the philosophy of the democratic nation), ensures that the Kurds do not become a privileged or dominant group within democratic autonomy. With this, an autonomy based on the coexistence of peoples is foreseen, eliminating the hierarchy and privilege created by the nation-state to weaken and exert control over society.

The democratic nation, which is an important determinant in the deepening of autonomy in Rojava, requires each community to participate directly in the common assemblies from their autonomous organizations. Asya Abdullah expresses the democratic nation as the empowerment of society by uniting against the state:

> The model of Rojava embraces all cultures, languages, religions and different political currents. When all differences are united, society becomes stronger. Society is more successful when all its forces are united. The philosophy of the democratic nation helps society constitute itself in a free manner. Today, this model is practiced in Rojava; all nations living there share equal leadership. We all fight and we all serve society. This is a valuable achievement for society. (Abdullah, 2014, p. 106)

The practice of making decisions and living together is the core of the theory of the democratic nation, not borders and state laws. The democratic nation is a guide that shows how different communities can organize collectively and for themselves.

> Syria, like Rojava, is a country with a diverse social, ethnic and religious mosaic. Therefore, the centralized nation-state system cannot be the solution. The establishment of the democratic system is truly necessary to successfully resolve the crisis in Syria. The democratic nation is the best system for all the people of Syria. In practice, the society organized as a democratic nation is capable of directing its daily life, its organizations and its decision-making procedures. This system functions according to the needs of the society; such as the establishment of institutions, academies, assemblies, cooperatives and elections. For these reasons, the best system that truly serves the people freely is the democratic nation. And this system is practiced in Rojava. (Abdullah, 2014, p. 108)

The Co-President of the Autonomous Government of the Cezîre region affirms that the democratic nation, beyond the mechanism of participation, tries to generate the collective will and, in Rojava, all peoples have a voice in the decision-making process:

> [...] The Kurds had never been in a position of government and had never been rulers; governing was in the hands of a certain group only. However,

today, all the peoples living in northern Syria are present at all levels of self-government; all the peoples have the right to participate, whether in a city or a village; everyone who lives there must be in the autonomous organization. This is how the organization of each people was formed, and how the organization of Arabs, Assyrians and Kurds was formed [...] The people organized assemblies through their own decision and will and created the municipalities of the city. Each people's organizations participate in these spaces and, from there, they have come to realize that they can make collective decisions in the assemblies. They understood that they have a say in all decisions. This is an important difference, which means that they are in the administration. They realized that they have voice and will in the decisions made in the system of democratic autonomy. Society itself makes all the decisions. (Interview with Yunis, Co-President of the Autonomous Government of the Cezîre region, 2019)

As the Co-President of the Autonomous Government said, making decisions about one's own life and participating in decision-making processes is a new experience, not only for the Kurds, but for all peoples, and that is one of the components of the revolution in Rojava:

Not only Kurds, but all ethnic groups are experiencing this for the first time. It is the first time this is happening also for the Arabs. They have a voice and will, they can make decisions about themselves, everybody can express their views [...] all this was impossible before for the Kurds as well as for the Arabs. A decision was made from above and everyone had to obey. But now the decision comes from the community, all decisions are made together. The Arabs understood this, every nation can participate with its own culture and language, and this system protects their rights [...] by protecting religions as their rights. There is no process of exclusion that deprives people of their subjectivity. Cultures, nations, languages and religions can live together, and people understand that this is their richness. This ensures that all peoples are in the autonomous system. When communes and assemblies were being organized, many people from many communities, for example, Arab and Assyrian peoples, called us and asked us when we were going to go and organize their communes and assemblies or, for example, in the participation of military forces, many young people joined YPG and YPJ. For example, the Kurdish women and men in the resistance of Serîkanîyê defend the Arab people of Tilkoçer; people also see this courage, the people giving martyrs every day. They saw this reality of the revolution [...]. (Interview with Yunis, Co-President of the Autonomous Government of the Cezîre region, 2019)

An understanding of the democratic nation begins with considering society as a set of sectors; this requires recognizing the existence of each of these sectors in all institutions, fields and organizations of democratic autonomy. Thus, it accepts the Kurds as a social sector, as well as Arabs, Christians, Assyrians or Yazidis, women and youth. No institution, structure or organization can be created without the voice and physical presence of these sectors. The organization of each sector is considered a prerequisite. In this sense, any individual/community/sector that is organized and wants to make decisions about their own lives and their own social and cultural rights has a place in the organized institutions of democratic autonomy. Even if it is only an individual, it is desired that he or she be organized, that he or she adopt the thinking of democratic autonomy.

The most important difference between yesterday and today in Rojava and northern Syria, that is, the difference created by the revolution, is the establishment of collectivity and solidarity based on the commune, rather than hierarchy and hostility, in determining social relations. As Hevrin Khalaf said, this alone is a revolution for the Middle East:

We worked with Heval Gerdo from the first day of autonomous government. Many times, he would say "We started the struggle together and we will finish it together." He was our friend and a very good person. He was a very good person ethically. When we would talk about the terms of the democratic nation, I would always tell him, "You were our first friend to understand the democratic nation, even though it was not yet an explicit part of our political program." Because he understood and realized this; it was part of his nature. He came from the city of Tirbespîyê and, in this city, people were living together and in peace, so I was observing his nature in his relations with Arabs and Kurds, Muslims and Assyrians. He repeated many times, "Serok [Abdullah Öcalan's honorary title] made us aware of it, and we are also very comfortable with it. We did not know that as Assyrians we had such rights; we had forgotten them, but now we know our cultural and political rights, thanks to his prison writings." Gerdo always said that we must defend the project of democratic autonomy. He did it in a very calm way, but we worked together in the spirit of a democratic nation for more than four years. It really had the spirit of the democratic nation. If there is one good thing about this self-government, it is the unity of the people. An Assyrian works with the Kurds, a Kurd with the Arabs. This was not something we could have achieved easily. This alone is a revolution. (Interview with Khalaf, Co-President of the Economy Council, 2018).

The transformation mentioned by Hevrin was not perceived within the revolutionary debate until now. That is why the revolution in Rojava also redefines the meaning of revolution. As I discussed in Chapter 1, all revolutions in history have been based on the seizure of power and the changing of property, but the revolution in Rojava gave a new meaning to revolution, excluding these two senses. To understand this, I will take a closer look at the practice of autonomy in Rojava.

Times of autonomy

After the Qamishlo rebellion, Serhildana Qamishlo, in 2004, the Kurds continued to organize clandestinely and prepare for a new rebellion by holding meetings in family homes. In those years, with the Arab Spring, the Middle East witnessed intense revolts. The Kurds observed this process closely. The civil war, which began in Syria in 2011, and started out with the demand for political transformation, opened the door to a Kurdish Spring. The civil war conditions created a de facto situation that allowed the Kurdish Movement to enter the territory of Rojava and build the autonomy project it had long been fighting for. In 2012, after gaining control of key Kurdish territories in Syria, autonomy was declared. We can divide the recent history of autonomy in Rojava and northern Syria into three periods:

The first struggle is the internal struggle!
(July 2012 to January 23, 2014)

This period coincides with the first two years of the Rojava Revolution. It began when the Democratic Society Movement, TEV-DEM, a platform formed by the PYD and other Kurdish parties, and the self-defense forces, YPG/YPJ, expelled the Syrian state soldiers and seized state silos and buildings. It happened first in Kobanê and then in other regions densely populated by Kurds, such as Afrîn and Qamishlo. The student demonstrations of March 6, 2011, in Deraa, where the slogan "the people want the destruction of the regime" (*Ash-sha'b yurīd inhā' al-in-qisām*) appeared, dragged Syria into a civil war, which clearly showed that the Arab Spring was no longer so much of a "spring" (Taştekin, 2015). The demonstrations, which had started as a protest against the Assad regime, were replaced by the Sunni-Alawite sectarian conflict. Different armed organizations that called themselves opposition groups emerged in Syria, and in the second half of 2011 they merged and formed the so-called Free Syrian Army (*Al-Ŷayš as-Suri al-Ḥurr*). After withdrawing or being expelled from the regions where the Syrian Sunnis were a majority, the Baathist regime entrenched itself in Damascus. There had been a demographic shift as a result of the imposition of the "Arab Belt" (heritage of the Baathist regime) in Rojava, that is, "northern Syria" or "western Kurdistan," however, the Kurds remained the majority population there.

As the different warring factions of the civil war established themselves, the Kurds did not support the continuity of the Baathist government or the opposition groups that wanted to establish a new power with Sunni Arab roots and that went on to join the Syrian National Council (al-Majlis al-Watani al-Suri). Instead, they defended autonomy, which they called Xeta sêyemîn (third way strategy). As Conde states, even though some Kurdish organizations joined the demonstrations against the regime, it soon became clear that the Arab opposition, with few exceptions, was reluctant to include the Kurds' demands. Moreover, many of them were allied with the Turkish state against the Syrian state (Conde, 2017, p. 62).

This period was marked by debate and internal struggle around who represented the Syrian Kurds. In Syria, even today, there is tension in the relationship between the PYD (*Partiya Yekîtiya Demokrat*, or Democratic Union Party), representing the autonomous anti-state movement, and the ENKS (*Encûmena Niştimani ya Kurdi li Suriye*, or Kurdish National Council), representing the line of nationalism in favor of building a Kurdish state. As I mentioned above, in the history of the Kurdish struggles, this is an ongoing tension that is now been playing itself out in Rojava. The PYD has had social support since its foundation, in 2003, and has been acknowledged by the Kurdish community in Rojava because of its proximity to the PKK's ideology. The PYD has managed to bring about a concrete social project of autonomy that could solve the causes of wars of all peoples. Therefore, Kurdish society in Rojava regard the PYD as a possible solution. Unlike the PYD, the ENKS lacked a political project and never obtained social support. Moreover, it based its entire political discourse on its hostility towards the PKK, as did the Barzani Movement. For that reason, Kurdish society united around the revolutionary project. Thereafter, the Arab and Assyrian societies joined the project as well. As Taştekin states, the PYD was the only organization that was capable of mobilizing society. It took a structured stance in the face of the conflict and was able to control the situation in terms of self-defense (Taştekin, 2016, p. 120).

Thus, the Apoist Kurds[8] gained military and political control, led by the TEV-DEM (Democratic Society Movement),[9] which included the PYD, the Ideological Coalition Party and the anti-state organizations in the provinces where Kurds are a majority. There were no serious clashes with the Syrian armed forces; they were simply expelled. The administrative power of the government was taken over and given to local authorities, and the municipalities were liberated and declared autonomous municipalities. Despite this, although it has no power of sanction over the people of northern Syria, the Syrian government still preserves the image of the state with its physical presence. At a time when war was raging across Syria, the most important policy of the Kurdish forces in this period was to maintain social control in order to prevent the war from reaching Rojava. This was achieved, but only until 2014, when ISIS (the Islamic State) and Al-Nusra directed their attacks in Rojava against the Kurds. With the weakening of the state, and under the leadership of TEV-DEM, people quickly organized the first popular assemblies in the villages to discuss the third way strategy. The Assembly of the Peoples of Kurdistan-Rojava (MGRK – *Meclisa Gel a Rojavayê Kurdistánê*), the founding assembly that prepared the Rojava Social Contract (ANF, 2019), was created through an agreement among the local assemblies. The local assemblies did not appoint delegates or professional politicians to create this founding assembly; instead, they chose people who had always been politically organized and had suffered repression due to their political activities before the revolution. They were well-known figures from the times of underground political activity.

Defending autonomy! (January 2014 to December 2017)

With the establishment of the Legislative Assembly of the Rojava Democratic Autonomy Administration, which converged on January 6, 2014 in Amûdê, Rojava and authorized the Rojava Social Contract, a new stage began in northern Syria. Autonomous democratic governments (*Rêveberiya Xweseriya Demokratîk*) were declared in Cezîre on January 21, in Kobanê on January 27, and in Afrîn on January 29. It was announced that in Rojava autonomy would be organized in the form of cantons: three separate cantons and three autonomous governments. The co-presidency system was adopted in each autonomous canton (Afrîn, Kobanê, Cezîre).

8 Those who recognize Abdullah Öcalan as a leader and are aligned with his stance for the struggle.

9 The following parties united under TEV-DEM: PYD, Liberal Party, Kurdistan Communist Party, Democratic Peace Party, Patriotic Union of Kurdistan and Syrian Democratic Community. Other important components of TEV-DEM were the Yekitiya Star (Kongra Star) women's organization, established in 2004, youth organizations, traders' unions, trade unions and humanitarian organizations. Representing the social diversity in Rojava there were, in ethnic terms, Kurds, Arabs, Turkmen, Syrians, Chaldeans, Armenians and Chechens; and in religious terms, Sunnis, Alawis, Christians and Êzîdîs. It was also established that this social diversity could make joint decisions in the proposed organizational project.

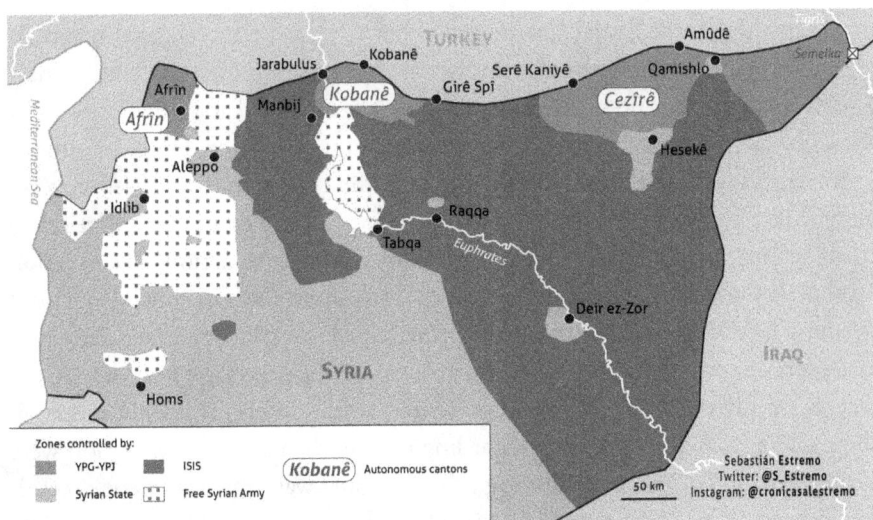

The autonomous cantons of Rojava in 2014

Through the popular assemblies, communes and committees that had been established prior to the declaration of autonomous governments, the TEV-DEM ensured local self-organization to address many societal needs: self-defense, security, health, education, municipal services, infrastructure and cleaning. The task carried out by the autonomous governments in this period was to form, strengthen and coordinate relations between peoples in spaces of civil society. The first autonomous governments were organized from above; the war situation and the displacement it caused prevented the co-presidents or administrative coordination body from being elected by the people or assemblies. Also, the people had not sufficiently discussed what methods they would use to elect them. Thus, the autonomous governments were formed by people in charge of the TEV-DEM and Kongra-Star (initially called Yekîtîya Star) who took an active role in organizing social areas. With the canton system, the committees were organized under the supervision of the cadres of TEV-DEM and the councils (*destaye*)[10] that had been created by the autonomous governments. Coordination groups were also built to organize the different areas of democratic autonomy.

10 The Self-Government Councils are: Foreign Affairs Council, Self-Defense Council, Internal Affairs Council, Justice Council, Local Governments and Municipalities Council, Finance Council, Social Affairs Council (a Council to provide jobs and workers), Education and Training Council, Agriculture Council, Electricity Council, Industry and Mining Council (Energy Council), Health Council, Trade and Economy Council, Martyr Families Council (Martyrs' Council), Enlightenment and Communication Council, Transportation Council, Youth and Sports Council, Tourism and Archaeology Council, Religious Affairs Council, Women's Council, Human Rights Council. In total, there are 20 councils; all function as executive councils within the TEV-DEM. (In Kurdish, the councils are called *destaye*, they are the autonomous hands of the government. *Destaye* is sometimes translated as "ministry," but I prefer to use the word "council").

Even though the Social Contract had been authorized, coordination could not be set up immediately. For some time, the two organizational systems, namely government and autonomous institutions on the one hand and organizations of the social area on the other, were disconnected from each other. The autonomous organization was developing rapidly through the creative power of self-government. More and more people's assemblies were held, and communes were being created. But because of the lack of a rhythm of collective action, the situation was becoming increasingly complicated. All civil and social spaces had been built by the TEV-DEM and Kongra-Star according to the principles of democratic confederalism, while the self-governments began to be organized according to the sectors through councils. While popular and autonomous organization was on the rise, conflicts and confusion regarding roles in the field of organization were also emerging. For instance, although the economy was organized as one sector, the Economy Council (*Destaye Aborî*), where the local political leaders of Rojava worked, and the Social Economy Committee (*Aborîya Civakî*), built by the cadres of the Kurdish Movement, formed a dual and sometimes parallel structure in the sector. My interviewees' accounts of this period indicate that, even when the Council and the Committee worked together, conflicting and multi-headed processes emerged from time to time. Likewise, the Women's Economy (*Aborîya Jin*) of Kongra-Star was also part of this complexity.

This process continued as a spontaneous quest for coordination until the end of 2016. In early 2017, the confusion of roles between the movement and the autonomous government, that is, between political cadres and local leaders, made it evident that the "local movement had failed to develop its own initiative, independent of the cadres" (interview with Khalaf, Co-President of the Economy Council, 2018) and the movement analyzed this as a notable danger to social emancipation in Rojava. This led the organization to restructure many sectors. Thus, in the social economy sector of the Autonomy it established the Rojava Social Economy Coordination body, which in early 2018 was renamed the General Coordination Body of the Social Economy of Northern Syria. This included the Self-Government Economy Council (*Destaye Aborî*), the Social Economy Committee (*Aborîya Civakî*) and the Women's Economy Committee (*Aborîya Jin*). This process can be described as a revolutionary and transformative quest for harmony. As I emphasized in Chapter 1, one of the most important characteristics of the Kurdish Movement is its ability to transform its organizational structures in order to build a popular revolution.

In 2004, the Islamic State of Iraq and Syria (ISIS) was founded following the U.S. invasion of Iraq in 2003. In 2014, after announcing that its organic relationship with the al-Nusra Front (*Cebhetü'n-Nusra*), with which it was previously partnered, had ended, ISIS no longer acknowledged al-Nusra Front as representative of the Islamic State in Syria. It then attacked the city of Mosul and the main Êzîdî (in English, Yazidi; in Arabic, Yazidî or Yezidî) city and sanctuary, Shingal. ISIS also announced that it would enter Syria to establish an Islamic state from Iraq to Europe. This is why it attacked Shingal and declared *jihad* (fight for Islam); it wanted to wipe out any force opposing the Islamic State. The brutal Êzîdî massacre occurred because the Peshmerga (Kurdish-Iraqi insurgents) did not defend the people from the ISIS attack. In order to stop the massacre and defend the people, PKK guerrillas came down from the mountains to Shingal. After the Shingal massacre, named by the Êzîdîs the *73 Farman*, in reference to the 73 times that the Êzîdî people have suffered massacres (Dinç, 2017), the Syrian civil war became an international war.

After being in the battlefield, ISIS spread like a plague: it carried out suicide attacks all over the world and videos of the organization's beheadings circulated, causing great fear among the international public. This led to the creation of an international coalition against ISIS in 2014, led by NATO and the U.S., and involving some 40 countries. Rapidly, ISIS became a dominant force in Syria; it advocated an anti-modernist line that was met with widespread support, especially among the Sunni-Muslim Arab community. The city of Raqqa was declared the capital of Jihad and Êzîdî women who had been kidnapped in Shingal were sold in its main square as "odalisques." After the liberation of Shingal by the PKK guerrillas in September 2014, ISIS gained access to Kobanê canton, directing its attacks against the Kurds. Thus, the Kurdish struggle in Syria became a war of honor, not just autonomy.

Kobanê: the Stalingrad of the Kurds

The Islamic State completely besieged Kobane on September 15, 2014. At that time, there was no land connection between the three autonomous cantons (Afrîn, Kobanê and Cezîre) and the Islamic State attacked Kobanê from three sides. During this time, the Turkish state closed the northern border. The city of Kobanê was completely isolated and it was impossible to get help from other cantons. The siege could only be broken by fighting from within. A group of YPG and YPJ resisted inside for a month. The action of Arîn Mîrkan, a female guerilla, turned the tide. On the night of October 5, she blew herself up under a tank to stop the Islamic State. On the same day, Turkish President Recep Tayyip Erdoğan stated in Gaziantep, right across the border from Kobanê, that "Kobanê has already fallen or will soon fall." Arîn's action was a call to resist Erdoğan's wish. The "sacrifice" of the female commander was not read as a military guerrilla attack, but as a self-criticism that decried the insufficiency of the current resistance. Arîn Mîrkan was stating that the YPG/YPJ's form of resistance had reached a dead end; it was no longer enough for only the guerrillas to resist. Her action sent a message: the fight should go beyond Kobanê.

That same night, the Kurds of Bakur rose up in a rebellion that was called the revolt of October 6-7 (*6-7 Ekim Serhildanı*) and spread the protests to all of Bakur and the Turkish metropolises. The protesters called for the creation of a humanitarian corridor and for the Turkish state to open the border. As the violence in Bakur escalated, Kurds in the diaspora in Europe occupied airports and embassies. The collective heart of the Kurds beat for Kobanê. When the PKK defined Kobanê as "the Stalingrad of the Kurds," hundreds of Kurdish men and women, adults and youth, crossed the border and went to Kobanê to join the fight. Motivation to fight rose up in all parts of Kurdistan. The resistance also spread around the world with the help of the image of the "Kurdish warrior of YPJ," which prompted internationalists from all over travel to Kurdistan or organize protests to support the Kobanê resistance.

When the peoples of the world spoke in favor of Kobanê, an international coalition was established against ISIS. It began bombing the points where the ISIS organization was located. The first move of the strategic agreement between Kurdish forces and the U.S. military was to bring helicopters with weapons to Kobanê. On the night of October 31, Turkey was forced to open Xabur customs, which had been closed for months, for the Peshmerga to officially cross into Kobanê. In this way, guerrilla brigades of the PKK (disguised under the Peshmerga flag) were able to enter Kobanê with heavy weaponry. Humanitarian corridors were created through civilian initiatives and, in the following days, the cantons of Cezîre and Kobanê established the first territorial contact through a humanitarian corridor. The resistance of Kobanê lasted 136 days.

On the morning of January 26, 2015, the YPG/YPJ announced that Kobanê had been liberated. While Kobanê's resistance strengthened autonomy, strategic and aid agreements had to be accepted in order to defend Kobanê, and this created a dependency chain. Rojava became a battleground between Russia and the United States. The Kurds would now build and defend the Autonomy in the cantons, but simultaneously, they would also fight against ISIS. The YPJ women considered the fight against ISIS an anti-patriarchal fight against the mentality that wanted to turn women in the Middle East into slaves and odalisques. Meanwhile, under the agreement signed with the International Coalition after the victory in Kobanê, the Coalition would provide weapons and technical assistance to the YPG and YPJ, and they would fight ISIS. The defeat suffered in Kobanê weakened ISIS. This was not only a military defeat, but also a psychological defeat for its militants—dying at the hands of women meant not being able to enter paradise.

Once Kobanê was liberated, the forces of the YPG/YPJ prioritized the unification of the cantons, not only in a political sense, but also in terms of a land connection. In 2015, the cantons of Cezîre and Kobanê were connected, while the Afrîn canton, located east of the Euphrates River, was never connected to the others. Simultaneous to this, the Turkish state had been engaged in a peace dialogue with the PKK, but, after the Kobanê victory, it accused the YPG/YPJ of being a terrorist organization and the dialogue with the PKK ceased.[11]

On October 10, 2015, a new armed force was created in Rojava, the Syrian Democratic Forces (QSD).[12] Two explanations have been put forth to explain its formation. First, the Kurds claimed that the struggle for autonomy had transcended Rojava, and they formed the QSD so that Arabs could also join the armed forces in the Arab areas that had been liberated. Second, the international coalition created the QSD to play along with the Turkish state and, at the same time, to continue collaborating with the Kurdish forces, since the QSD did not present itself as a Kurdish organization. Undoubtedly, each explanation provides part of the answer. Indeed, the YPG (People's Defenses Units) and the YPJ (Women's Defenses Units) have maintained their organizational autonomy but have also been an important component of the QSD. The YPG was made up of former guerrilla cadres who had participated in the PKK and who had gone to Rojava to establish the YPG when the revolution began. In contrast, the QSD was made up of Kurds, Arabs and Assyrians from Rojava who armed themselves for the self-defense of their villages and who acquired their first fighting experience in the Rojava Revolution. Even so, soon after, the Turkish state started its accusations again, claiming that the QSD was also an organization of the PKK and that the Coalition was misled.

Despite this, on December 10, 2016, the QSD launched operations on Raqqa, the center of ISIS, with the support of the United States. Rojda Felat, from the YPJ, was the commander of the operation, and stated that the first objective of the fight against ISIS was to free all women, especially Êzîdî women. After a long war, on October 17, 2017, the United States announced to the world that ISIS had been defeated in Raqqa. And the women of the YPJ hung a picture of Öcalan in Raqqa square, where ISIS had sold women in iron cages, and claimed

---

11 The dialogue between the Turkish state and the PKK was announced by Öcalan on Newroz Day (March 21) 2013 and lasted until March 2015. In this process, the Dolmabahçe Agreement was signed; it basically included the laying down of arms by the PKK and the signing of the peace agreement, but the process gave way to war again.

12 Syrian Democratic Forces is *Hêzên Sûriya Demokratîk* in Kurdish, and *al-Quwat al-Suriya al-Dimuqratiya* in Arabic, however, people orally use QSD in both languages, thus, I will also use this form.

YPJ militants celebrating the victory of the liberation of Raqqa.

that the victory of women against the patriarchal mentality in Raqqa was a gift to Abdullah Öcalan, the greatest companion of the women's struggle in the Middle East and of all women in the world (ANF, 2017).

This was not an image that the United States wanted to beam to the world, especially when it would continue its alliance with the QSD until the end of the 2018 to liberate Deir ez-Zor, the oil region controlled by ISIS.

The Autonomy's geography was also redefined during this period. With the Arab regions liberated, in 2017, the Rojava Autonomous Region changed its name to the Democratic Federation of Northern Syria. The Constituent Assembly, created under the principle of the democratic nation, declared the Democratic Federation of Northern Syria, with its Social Contract, aimed at establishing democratic governments in liberated places that were part of the autonomous governments. So, in July 2017, the Autonomy, previously organized into three cantons, was reorganized again into six cantons and three regions. The name change was a sign that the autonomous government was open to negotiating with the Syrian state. During this process, Russia proposed holding a dialogue between the autonomous government and the Syrian state (Reuters, 2019).

It should be mentioned that, from the first day of struggle, the autonomous territory was never delimited. This has repeatedly led to attempts to define its geography; even today, there is no established territorial definition and the war on the territory continues. This situation creates some difficulties in planning and being able to meet the collective needs of society, and also for the return of those who have been displaced by the attacks. Nonetheless, frequent territorial shifts have also produced societal shifts. This is one of the elements that keeps the Autonomy dynamic and open to change, precisely because of the political trans-formation. The constant change in the autonomous region has made Autonomy not solely an issue of the Kurds, as there was a need to create a space for all peoples living in this region to be involved in the Autonomy.

The newly liberated regions were predominantly Arab. This led to new political actors interacting in the Autonomy, including Arab tribes, sheikhs and leaders of Arab society as well as some Arab parties with broad support. Despite the variety of new political actors, there was no change in the discourse around autonomy; rather, the Arab actors adopted the thinking of the Kurdish Movement and agreed on some issues, and organized together. This allowed democratic autonomy to find a sociologically and politically more appropriate terrain for the Democratic Nation approach. Although from the beginning the Kurdish Movement talked about the paradigm and having a Democratic Nation, the social terrain was not very ethnically or religiously diverse. Arabs and Assyrians had remained at a symbolic level of representation. However, the territorial shift that took the revolution beyond Rojava turned the Democratic Nation theory into a reality, with a deeper and stronger practice of autonomy.

3.2.3. The institutionalization of autonomy!? (December 2017 to the present)

In this period, after defeating ISIS, the QSD achieved military control over the entire east of the Euphrates River. The "liberated zone" expanded along the Iraq border. The autonomous territory reached its natural borders, until it was occupied by the Turkish state and jihadists; first in Afrîn in 2018, and then Girêsipîyê and Serêkaniyê in 2019. It should be noted that although many new regions were organized according to the model of democratic autonomy, the cantonal practice does not include Raqqa.

With the defeat of Raqqa, the QSD and the International Coalition, represented by the United States, ended ISIS's territorial control, taking over the rural areas of Deir ez-Zor, Syria's largest oil region. The Euphrates River separates the city of Deir ez-Zor from its countryside, a desert with significant oil reserves. Deir ez-Zor, one of the main industrial cities in Syria, had been bombed by the Syrian regime forces to prevent its occupation by ISIS. This forced many civilians from the city to cross the Euphrates River and settle in the desert in tents. The desert had been under the military control of ISIS since 2013, because it was the organization's entry point into Syria. Especially after their defeat in Raqqa, all ISIS militants concentrated in this area.

I had the opportunity to travel to this area during my first visit to Rojava, before the beginning of the Deir ez-Zor operation. The women who secretly took me to their homes said they were expecting the YPJ to liberate the women there, as they had done in Raqqa. One of the women I spoke to had not left the courtyard of her house in three years. At that time, the only objective of the ISIS militants, who had become tougher on society, was to sell as much oil as possible.

The extensive oil reserves explain why the United States wanted to be there. But why did the QSD want to liberate that territory? I wondered about this while I observed the ISIS militants in Deir ez-Zor. I only understood on my second visit. It became clear that the QSD agreed to fight in Deir ez-Zor because it knew that it was not possible to build and defend autonomy in Rojava as long as it did not completely wipe out ISIS, which had been defeated everywhere after Kobanê. But U.S. objectives went much deeper.

The fact that the Kurdish-led democratic autonomy proposal was accepted by Syrian society proved that real autonomy was being built and was an unstoppable reality. That is why the United States decided to push the region towards autonomous policies, but without Öcalan and without the PKK, especially after the Raqqa image circulated. It sought to liberalize autonomy, because democratic autonomy rejects capitalist, statist and patriarchal relations, and this represented a crisis for the dominant system. On the surface, the United States' goal was to clear all the oil fields through a joint military operation with the QSD, using the combat skills of the Kurds. However, on a much deeper level, it was pursuing policies that would move Rojava away from radical autonomy, with the aim of integrating these areas into the chain of capitalist exploitation. Thus, the United States used the threat posed by the Turkish state to the Kurds to blackmail the Autonomy. By establishing an atmosphere of insecurity and constantly stating that they would withdraw their armed forces from northern Syria, they were putting the Kurds at risk of a Turkish invasion. In this way, they pushed the autonomous government into a "forced relationship" with the United States. Indeed, when Afrîn was invaded in early 2018, U.S. President Trump claimed that Afrîn was not among the regions of interest to the U.S. (because Afrîn is not an oilfield). A year later, in October 2019, the U.S. military withdrew, paving the way for the Turkish invasion of Serîkanîyê and Girêsipîye (*The New York Times*, 2019).

In addition, NGOs brought the "aid" policy framework into northern Syria. This makes people feel in debt to the institutions and causes them to identify themselves as "victims" of the war, prompting them to move away from the idea of organizing and seeing themselves as subjects of social and political transformation. This logic tries to create ideological and psychological breaches between the people and the movement, (or between the YPG and the PKK), in order to weaken the organizational power of autonomy.

The fact that in 2018 the United States backed the Turkish state in the invasion of the Afrîn canton, historically the oldest Kurdish territory in Rojava, constituted a first sign of this oppressive approach. When society embraced the project of autonomy against the occupation, the United States gave away the region of Serîkanîyê and Girêsipîyê as a "safe zone" to the Turks. That meant excluding the people from decision-making processes in order to turn society into a ruled community and to create a small tribal state, like southern Kurdistan, leaving power in the hands of a professional group of politicians. This opened the region to capitalist exploitation of all its resources, especially oil.

This is the policy, not only of the United States, but of all the capitalist states—the dominant actors—that have plans for the Middle East. They know very well that the state apparatus functions as a machine that destroys revolutionary processes and projects of social emancipation. They are very much aware that a stateless system, such as democratic autonomy in which society decides and creates its own conditions of daily life, can actually prevent the conditions of exploitation in the Middle East from building up. They clearly see that it will not be possible to develop capitalist relations if democratic autonomy is communalized and the idea of the state loses value in society. They know that the idea of autonomy without a state means dreams of hope for social emancipation for the whole Middle East and for the world. They are much more aware than we are that autonomy, which means self-determination of daily life, means popular revolution in the long run.

Rojava not only creates its own pace of emancipation, but it recreates and relives all the consequences of the defeated revolutions throughout the history of liberation as a present experience. The Barzani government has carried out a systematic embargo on Semalka, the only commercial customs crossing in the region, with the purpose of disciplining the Kurds of Rojava and causing economic instability. This is the approach of the PDK, which is favorable to establishing a nation-state. They are attempting to turn Rojava into a sub-colony of southern Kurdistan, which is already a colony in itself.

The counterinsurgency war makes it difficult for the Autonomy to escape the atmosphere of violence. Psychological and hegemonic war hang over the Kurdish struggle. It also encourages certain sectors of Rojava society that identify with nationalism and are against the liberation movement, such as the ENKS, to support the economic embargo. It also results in the domination of money in social relations through the NGOs and the creation of a common psychology of being subjugated, instead of having the psychology of struggling peoples. All these internal and external factors send a message to the peoples of Rojava and northern Syria: if you want to be autonomous, the only option is a statist, capitalist, patriarchal autonomy.

There is an important feature that differentiates the last two years from the first five years of the struggle: the combination of all the above-mentioned factors, along with the weakening of ISIS, had led to a tendency towards institutionalization, with the goal of institutionalizing autonomy in Rojava and northern Syria.

Institutionalization—a tendency to create established and defined institutions and bodies to keep power—is a logic that all social emancipation projects and revolutionary processes tend toward. Establishing a bureaucratic class as the administrator of these institutions involves a certain class being positioned above society. As it is based on a hierarchical relationship, it requires establishing a form of state. When this logic becomes dominant in a revolutionary process, it means that its transformative capacity is weakening in the face of a logic that understands revolution as the creation of a new (socialist) system of administration and power. In Rojava, although the logic of creating a socialist state or a new ruling class was rejected, external pressures and certain internal practices are generating a strong tendency towards institutionalization. A possible emergent state as a form of power exists in the Rojava Revolution and all revolutionary processes and this is a dangerous contradiction.

Of course, this is not a new situation. The Autonomy in Rojava and northern Syria has been facing this contradiction from the beginning and has been fighting it. The brutal systematic violence makes the situation complex and has resulted in the rise of practices that heighten the risk. In fact, restructuring autonomy in the form of a federation created the preconditions for this type of contradiction to emerge. Therefore, it is very important that, in addition to exploring the external dynamics, we look at the internal dynamics and pay attention to the revolutionary process. In the next section I will take a closer look at the practice of social and political organization, especially in assemblies and communes, in order to determine the organizational capacity of democratic autonomy to overcome these emerging contradictions and uncertainties and to understand how the Autonomy works.

The Democratic Federation of Northern Syria[13]

Article 47 of the Social Contract of the Democratic Federation of Northern Syria, adopted on December 29, 2016, states that the peoples and groups of the Democratic Federation of Northern Syria shall organize their free and democratic

---

13 Since November 2017, with the liberation of Deir ez-Zor, the name changed to Democratic Federation of Northern and Eastern Syria, but the same Social Contract is still in force.

social life on the basis of communes, social institutions, trade unions and assemblies. The democratic social system will be established and developed from these institutions (Social Contract of the Democratic Federation of Northern Syria, 2016). In other words, the mechanism that enables the people to make common decisions in the autonomous region of Rojava and northern Syria is the system of people's assemblies, which are formed by the communes across the region. This, in fact, simply reproduces the Rojava Social Contract. Thus, the first assembly is formed in the communes, which represent the smallest organizational unit of democratic autonomy. In the commune assembly there is no system of delegates; everyone is free to attend the assembly of the commune where they live. However, the municipal, provincial, cantonal and regional people's assemblies are made up of 60% of the delegates elected by the people living in the communes and 40% of the people elected by the social sectors. In addition, each assembly must ensure that 50% of those participating are women (Social Contract of the Democratic Federation of Northern Syria, 2016).

Under the Rojava Social Contract, each canton had its own self-government; and under the Federation system, the autonomous territory was organized into six cantons and three regions and the self-governments were formed at the regional level. For every two cantons there is one autonomous government. For example, the autonomous region of Cezîre is made up of the cantons of Hesekê and Qamishlo, which means that the operations of the autonomous government of Cezîre are centralized to cover these two cantons. The Social Contract states that the autonomous regions are legislative and executive in their region and that they will act as a federation in the Congress of Democratic Peoples.[14] In other words, the Congress will assume the role of the government of the Federation to coordinate the three autonomous regions (Afrîn, Firat, Cezîre). Previously, each canton had an autonomous government, but with the Federation system, the autonomous governments were reorganized at the regional level. Today, each autonomous government is assigned two cantons at the regional level, a major change to the system.

---

14 **Article 57 – The congress of democratic people** represents all the peoples living in the "Democratic Federalism of Northern Syria". It is a symbol of integration, fraternity, coexistence, and free democratic union of peoples in northern Syria. The conference includes Kurds, Arabs, Syriacs, Assyrians, Armenians, Turkmen, Circassians, and Chechens. From the doctrinal and cultural groups, it includes Muslims, Christians, and Êzîdîs. It considers the historical, demographic, geographic, religious, doctrinal, ethnic, and cultural structures and characteristics of all peoples and groups; and it is formed based on their demands and will (Social Contract of the Democratic Federation of Northern Syria, 2016).

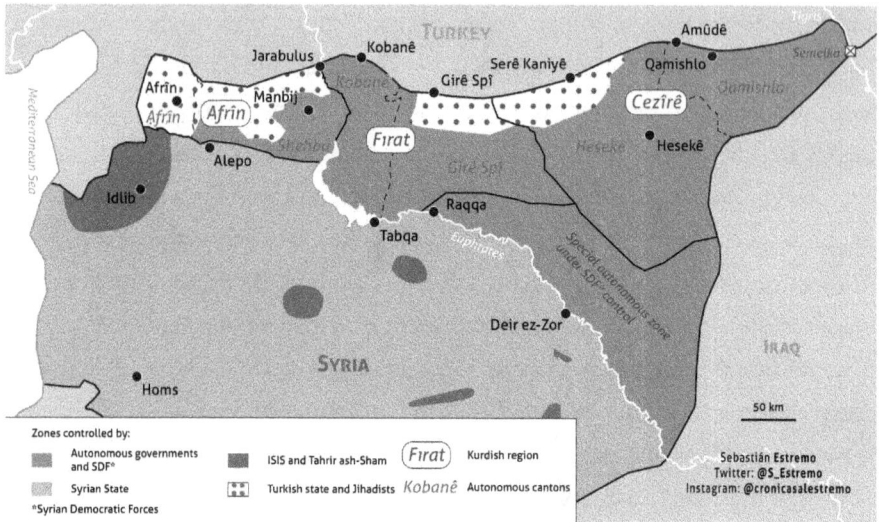

Regions of the Democratic Federation
of Northern and Eastern Syria in 2021

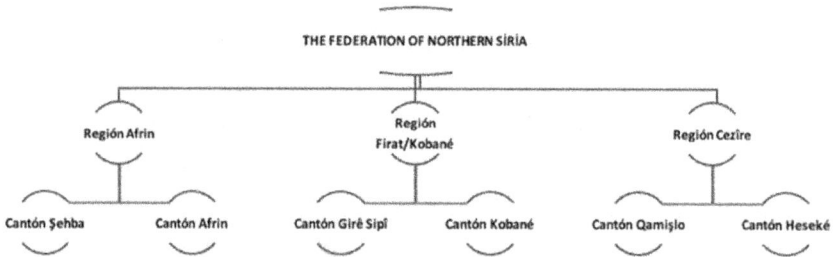

The Constituent Assembly of the Democratic Federation of Northern Syria defined a three-stage electoral calendar to construct this system; the regional electoral laws were passed on July 28, 2017. In line with this decision, the elections of the commune co-presidents were held on September 22, 2017; and the elections in the local assemblies of provinces and cantons were held on December 1, 2017. As a result, in the Cezîre region, 5,102 co-presidents were elected for 2,551 communes; in the Euphrates region, 1,698 co-presidents were elected for 849 communes; and in the Afrîn region, 830 people of different ethnicities, religions and ages were elected as co-presidents for 415 communes (ANF, 2018).

The third stage of the elections was to elect delegates to the Congress of Democratic Peoples and to the assemblies of the autonomous regions in January 2018, however, these elections could not take place due to the Turkish invasion of Afrîn canton on the January 20, 2018. Consequently, 60% of the delegates could not be elected by the villages, and were appointed instead through the TEV-DEM or Kongra-Star.

There were no major changes in the organization of the autonomy until 2017. The committees and people's assemblies, previously disconnected from each other, were linked through elections in the Federation system. This way of organizing introduced a key factor of institutionalization in that all financial and economic resources, which were previously independent, came under the control of the autonomous governments, which also became the only authority with the power to make decisions on how resources are spent. Thus, the communes, assemblies, municipalities or cantons have no "official" right over the distribution of the common wealth. Instead, a budget is assigned to each Council (*destaye*). Councils operate within each of the autonomous regions and under the autonomous governments. The Council budget is distributed among the organizations that comprise the sectors the Council is responsible for. In my interview with the co-spokespersons of the economic committee of the Hesekê canton, they stated that the committee has constantly had conflicts with the economic council of the Cezîre region, because they could not carry out decisions and projects approved at the economic assembly of the Hesekê canton. In this sense, they pointed out that the assembly is losing its meaning:

> **Co-spokeswoman:** Our resources depend on them; we can't get anything without telling them. For example, even if our car breaks down, we cannot send it for repair without their authorization. If we are given the resources, we actually do not need the economic council (*destaye aborî*), because we organize the whole sector of the economy; we coordinate with economic actors and institutions. The cadres are also with us. If our resources were autonomous as they were before, we would not need the *destaye*.

> **Co-spokesman:** We have taken the training of the cantonal system. In fact, after the sector committees were created in the cantonal assemblies, the councils were supposed to disappear. But they didn't; they have more power. This situation increases bureaucracy, we call it "routine" in Arabic. Let's say that, if the local actors depend on the committee, the committees depend on the council and the council depends on the executive assembly of the autonomous government, bureaucracy is unconsciously increased.

> **Co-spokeswoman:** That creates centralization...

Co-spokesman: So, our activity is slowing down... (interview with the economic committee of canton Hesekê, 2019)

As pointed out by the co-spokespersons, the transition from the autonomous cantons of Rojava to the Democratic Federation of Northern Syria and the centralization of resources show the tendency towards institutionalization, bureaucracy and centralization, rather than toward autonomous social organization. Previously, role conflict or task conflict was perceived as the result of the dominant mentality that had to be overcome by the revolution; that is, it was seen as a social reality that should be transformed into social struggle. Today, this conflict is not seen as a problem of the approach or mentality of those who participate in the autonomous spaces, but as a conflict between institutions; it is brought up as a corporate problem. The objective of improving inter-institutional relations, rather than social transformation, stands out as the main policy.

There is another contradictory practice that reinforces institutionalization, namely, all elected or appointed delegates to the assemblies of the autonomous governments, provinces, municipalities or cantons have, through the salary system, become a "ruling class." In the Federation system, the only elected people who do not have a salary are the co-presidents of the communes. According to my interviewees, this is why many co-presidents have resigned; they feel they have been treated unfairly, since many elected positions exist only "on paper" and do not perform their duties. All the delegates I interviewed said they did not know they would receive a salary when they were elected; only one said he knew he would receive "fund."

In Rojava and northern Syria, the concept of "fund" rather than "salary" is used. The term "fund" was used to refer to the money that the Kurdish Movement gave its cadres to satisfy some of their basic personal needs. The cadres do not have any private property or family or partnership relations. A cadre, somebody who participates in the organization as a professional militant, gives their whole life to the organization. They do not have a home of their own. They stay in homes with the community and, if security conditions in the community are inadequate, they stay irregularly in safe houses set up by the movement. These houses are also called "communes." No one has any personal objects, except for clothes; everyone has only what they wear. Although the people generally meet all the needs of the cadres on a communal basis, the movement gives them funds for certain personal needs, such as cigarettes, travel expenses, clothes, shoes, menstrual pads or hair dye etc. This money is sourced by the people's donations to the organization and contributions obtained from the activities of the organization.

Although they were not cadres of the movement, during the first years of the Rojava Revolution all those who participated in the processes of the social organization were included in the fund system. TEV-DEM and Kongra-Star started giving fund to people they defined as "local cadres" so that they could meet their needs and those of their families. These people spent all their time working for the organization of the people and the construction of democratic autonomy, just like the cadres the movement. These people had lost everything because of the war, so they were almost in the same situation as the cadres or maybe even worse, since they had families and children to support. That is why the cadres made the decision to give them funds.

However, the material situation was different, and the people to whom funds were given at that time are not the same as the ones elected today. The fund were disbursed on an as-needed basis; that is, no one was paid for participating in the social organization. The fund was given on the basis of solidarity and were not always monetary. At times, the movement helped people who were part of the revolutionary process by covering their basic needs, providing them with food or fuel for heating. In war conditions it has been difficult to sustain life and be part of the revolutionary process. However, people did not expect to be paid for organizing and fighting. It was the movement's cadres who included them in the existing mechanisms when they saw that people fighting for autonomy were having difficulties. Receiving fund was seen as "pitiful" by many people; during my first visit they usually told me of it in secret. Today, in the system created under the Federation, payment equivalent to the work performed is perceived as an obligation. In other words, it functions as a regular salary and creates a different class, even though it is still called a "fund."

When the people elected for the coordination of the autonomous organization perform these tasks on the basis of a monetary relationship, such positions begin to professionalize and become institutions of power. In order to avoid the construction of power in their communities, many communitarian movements in Latin America consider these tasks to be "community services":

> In indigenous communities, in all of Latin America I would say, the position, that is, what in our logic would be "holding power." is considered a service, right? A service to the community. Something that is done out of obligation. You are elected and you are obliged to exercise that office, because the concept is "the service." (Zibechi, 2017)

In the Zapatista Autonomy, in which "service" is rendered in accordance to the uses and customs of the communities in which it is organized, all community services are carried out as a personal obligation. They are rendered on a free and rotating basis: in all autonomous spaces—*Buen Gobierno* (Good Governance) Councils, municipalities or autonomous schools—those who are responsible consider their own service to be part of the deployment of autonomy, since exercising the position means, in itself, resisting and fighting. Community service is a form of concrete work (amtel in Tsotsil), that is, it is not abstract (kanal, in Tsotsil), because it is not performed for money. However, it should be noted that an important basis of this system, developed by the Zapatistas through collective work, is that they still live in the villages and maintain their livelihood through agriculture. The recovery of land and the collective work they have established on it allow the community to generate resources to meet certain basic needs of the people who hold community positions. In contrast, in Rojava, the collectivization of land and communal work for the whole society has not yet been achieved; the majority of the population lives in cities and lacks the tools that would allow them to sustain the material conditions of life. Therefore, to a certain extent, the existence of a "salary" is understandable. However, the risks come when "salary" is linked to "election", because it can generate a class of professional politicians.

The Kurdish Movement created political parties so that the Kurdish struggle could be represented in Turkey. It also supported their election in municipalities, Parliament, etc. This resulted in the formation of a class of politicians who placed themselves above the Kurdish society in Bakur. Between 2009 and 2015, several political parties with a Kurdish popular base were founded: the DTP (Democratic Society Party), the BDP (Peace and Democratic Party) and the HDP (People's Democratic Party). This generated a class of Kurdish politicians in Turkey, in the context of Turkey's transition process to the European Union and peace talks between the PKK and the Turkish government.

In summary, the practices of centralizing economic resources, creating a wage system and forming a ruling class after elections within the Federation system, namely, institutionalization, have generated a contradictory tendency with first four years of the revolution.

Organizing for the commons: the experience of communes and assemblies

The communes

In the Rojava Social Contract, the people's assemblies were not defined as an institution, but rather as the space where the people were to exercise self-management. In the first text, there was no mention of communes, but when referring to the Rojava system, it was common to highlight the communes as a practice. In other words, until the Federation was declared, the communes were not considered a formal institution but rather a common political practice. Finally, the Social Contract of the Democratic Federation of Northern Syria defined them within the law as the smallest organization in the social system. In article 48 of the contract, communes are defined as follows:

> The commune is the fundamental organizational form of direct democracy. The commune is a management and decision-making body with organizational and administrative boundaries. The commune functions as an independent assembly at all levels of decision-making. (Social Contract of the Democratic Federation of Northern Syria, 2016)

It is claimed that the epistemological origins of the word "commune" (in written Kurdish *komîn*) comes from the root *kom*, which means "to come together" or "community" in Kurdish (Abdullah Öcalan Sosyal Bilimler Akademisi, 2012, p.74). In the text entitled "Communal Democratic Economy," the outcome of discussions and research conducted in the mountain academy (guerrilla academies) based on Öcalan's readings, it is stated that the commune determines the organization of common life in all social areas. The commune is a space of social life based on communality, sharing, solidarity, equality and freedom. The features that make the commune possible are common spirit, willingness to live together, main purposes and objectives. They are the form of community that defines collective action and common behavior (Abdullah Öcalan Sosyal Bilimler Akademisi, 2012, p.74). Communes are considered a social lifestyle that happens in the "we" mindset. That "we" implies taking into account not only some communes, groups or communities, but the entire community, in which the monopolies of capital-power and their conscious collaborators are not included. If we speak about "the other" antagonistically to the "we" on a commune basis, it is emphasized that "the other" are only the statist civilization forces and those who consciously agree with them (Abdullah Öcalan Sosyal Bilimler Akademisi, 2012, pp. 75-76). In other words, the first condition of belonging to a commune is to reject any state system or state idea, because the state is a mechanism that fragments communality. People who voluntarily come together in communes do not create a hierarchy, even if there are differences among them. The members of the commune are communities that make common decisions about their lives and are political-moral organizations that do not need the state to make decisions about their lives.

In accordance with the principle of the democratic nation, the communes established in Rojava represent the first level of communal life and exist because of the natural character of communal life. In regards to organizing autonomously, in almost all villages and neighborhoods of Rojava, communes are the indispensable space where people with different ethnic identities, religious beliefs and political views come together. This is at the same time a sociohistorical phenomenon. In other words, the natural organizational structure of Rojava society is based on cultural and religious diversity. The communal council is formed with the participation of all those who live in the commune. For example, in the commune assembly I attended in Tirbespîye, I observed that there were Arabs (who in Cezîre are usually Muslims), Assyrians (who are usually Christians) and Kurds (who in Cezîre are usually Muslims, Christians or Êzîdîs). This is a phenomenon that occurs almost everywhere in Rojava. The Co-president of the autonomous government of Cezîre Region emphasized that even if there is only one Armenian in a village, the will of this Armenian should be present in the commune assembly; otherwise, the assembly cannot be established (interview with Yunis, Co-president of the autonomous government of Cezîre Region, 2019). In the urban areas of northern Syria, it is very difficult to find ethnically and religiously homogeneous communes.

However, the case of villages is different; historically, villages were built in a segregated way. There are villages that are Kurdish, Arab or Assyrian and ethnically and religiously homogeneous. Even so, it is still difficult to find politically homogeneous communes. This means that the democratic nation can be read as the coexistence of different political perspectives and as the production of decisions in which a specific ethnic and religious identity does not prevail. In other words, the society of Rojava and northern Syria is quite heterogeneous socially and politically.

We can argue that Öcalan's concept of the Democratic Nation is key to understanding the sociology of the Middle East. It also allows this natural plural existence of society to become a sociopolitical dynamic that enables decision-making processes about the "common" for the conditions of peace and reconciliation. It is worth noting that the Kurdish Movement defines politics as "making a political-moral decision about the common"; and that being "moral" means "respecting everyone's right to exist" (Bingöl, 2019).

The first communes in Rojava were formed after 2012. According to the Kurdish Movement, the construction of the first communes took place in the context of coordinating access to basic needs, including self-defense, bread, water, electricity, heating oil, health and garbage collection. The TEV-DEM started creating people's communes and the Women's Congress (Yekîtîya-Star)[15] started

---

15 At the beginning of the revolution, the Women's Congress had been called Yekitiya-Star; it later changed its name to Kongra-Star.

organizing women's communes. The fact that those who did not participate in the commune could not benefit from the defense service of the YPG/YPJ forces ensured that everyone participated in the commune in a "compulsory will" form and that all parts of society were quickly organized by communes and became acquainted with the idea and project of democratic autonomy. Although the exact number is unknown, hundreds of thousands of communes were built during this period. The first communes did not have a limit on the number of individuals participating, but they were limited to 50 to 170 houses or families. Taking into account that the average family size in Rojava is five members, each commune had between 250 and 850 members. According to 2017 Federation elections, there are 2,552 communes in the Cezîre region; 849 communes in the Firat(Euphrates) region and 415 communes in the Afrîn region.

Communes are created at the village level or at the street or neighborhood level in the cities. When a commune is formed in a village, everyone living in the village participates in the commune; the commune assembly is open to everyone to participate. The communes of the cities are formed following the divisions of the neighborhoods. Each neighborhood is constituted as a commune; but large neighborhoods, with many inhabitants, are divided into several communes according to streets. When there is a voluntary union of several communes geographically close to each other, the *komîngeh* (*commingeh*) is formed. The term *commingeh* is often used to refer to the common house or communal space shared by the communes. In addition, the existence of the commingeh shows the level of solidarity and collaboration between the co-spokespersons of many communes that coordinate with each other to meet the common needs of their region. In the case of certain specific needs, such as road construction or electricity production, mediated by cooperatives for generating electricity, communes that are close to each other come together. Collective production makes it easier to meet the needs at the *commingeh* level.

Communes choose their names at their first assembly. In Rojava, it has become a tradition to name the commune after its first *şehîd* (martyr), the first person they lost in the battle of the revolution. Each commune has two co-presidents and two co-spokesperson of the committees, which are organized harmoniously with the sectors of autonomy at the cantonal level. The commune coordination body, which is formed of two co-presidents and the co-spokesperson of the all committees, must resolve the collective needs of the commune in coordination with the governments and autonomous municipalities.

Depending on the needs of the inhabitants of neighborhoods or villages, the communes establish committees that are important to help solve the problems people face in their everyday lives. For instance, almost all communes have committees for education, economy, women, youth, peace and reconciliation and self-defense. The education committees organize training programs for commune members and neighbors in various fields, such as cultural awareness, coexistence, ecology and human rights. The economy committee is in charge of the commune's financial resources and expenses. (Duman, 2016, p.90)

The committee's main function is to organize and resolve collective needs directly as a community. The self-defense committee's main task is to form the people's self-defense forces under the *Hêzên Parastina Ciwakê* (HPC – People's Self-Defense Forces) and coordinate the military training activities provided by the YPG/YPJ to ensure that all people are able to use weapons and defend themselves. The economic committee's main task is to ensure that the commune's basic food needs are met and to organize a social economy through cooperatives.

As in all areas of the Rojava Autonomy, the communes also take into account gender equality in the system of co-representation. In the communes, equal participation in ethnic and religious terms is also sought. This means that a man and a woman are elected as co-presidency, and these co-presidents must represent cultural diversity, e.g., Arab-Kurdish or Kurdish-Assyrian.

Once all the houses within the area are identified, the co-presidents register all inhabitants of their commune in the commune assembly notebook. The Kurds who were identified as *ajanib* and *maktoumin* were also registered and handed IDs made by TEV-DEM. Moreover, one of the daily tasks of the commune is the preparation of the "commune document." The autonomous government made it mandatory for people who want to do any work in the Rojava cantons, who want to travel, send their children to school or open a store or business, to present their commune document. This document, which is a kind of residence certificate, states that the person living in the commune does not support any armed organization opposed to the Autonomy and participates in the organization of the democratic autonomy in their commune. Today, in Rojava, this document is still used, in addition to the ID. This is also the document requested by the society guards, *Asayish,* at the road checkpoints when traveling to any point in autonomous regions. The commune document is not only for individuals. Due to the war, the *Asayish* request documentation in case of any kind of movement of people or things. This document, which includes the signature and stamp of the commune co-presidents, certifies that the commune recognizes these persons or their actions.

The authors of the book *Revolution in Rojava* note that with the creation of communes many more people became active in the cities (Ayboğa, Flach and Knapp, 2018, p. 89). Indeed, when I visited Rojava in early 2018, I was struck by the mobilization capacity of the people. People previously oppressed by the state, who did not have the right to speak or live freely, were now actively participating in the processes of self-management and determination of autonomy, with their voices, their ideas and their decisions.

Generally, the people of Rojava work until 2:30 p.m., return to their homes to eat and rest, and then go out again to attend an assembly meeting. From 5:00 p.m. onwards, there are commune, assembly, cooperative, women's, martyr's families or municipal meetings. It is noticeable that no one stays at home or is unoccupied. For absolutely everyone, there is some public meeting to attend. This helped me understand that all the people in Rojava are part of the debates and the political process of autonomy through some form of popular meeting. In addition to this, there are other political activities in which people participate almost daily, such as border resistance, marches, demonstrations, solidarity campaigns, celebrations or mourning. These political-popular activities are noted and analyzed in the report that the commune coordination body prepares each month as a draft to present to the monthly assembly. The report is finished after discussions with the people of the commune.

As a counterpart to the contradictory practices I mentioned in the previous section, during my second visit, in December 2019 to complete my research work, I observed that the villagers were now participating much more actively in the autonomous processes. The people who two years earlier were much more influenced by the political perspectives of the cadres, had now formed their own perspectives and had their own thoughts; they had stronger opinions and were more open to participating in discussions, expressing their opinions and opposing others. It is very clear that the right to direct participation has allowed the people to express themselves freely in all autonomous spaces, which contributes to developing and strengthening social motivation for the autonomy project day by day. The strengthening of the people through their participation in the communes is helping to overcome the contradictions and risks mentioned when discussing the emergence of a ruling class and a hierarchy. Once people create the collective capacities to manage themselves and learn to use them to decide on all aspects of their daily lives, they no longer need an apparatus above society. The administration of daily life from below is created autonomously. An autonomous government, or as they call it in Rojava, the Autonomous Administration, created from below by the communes that organize themselves in all sectors of life, is able to overcome the top-down, government-governed contradictions.

Assemblies as a movement

In July 2011, at the time of the beginning of the Syrian civil war, but prior to the organization of the communes, the PYD started to form the first popular assemblies in Kurdish neighborhoods. Such assemblies were led by small political groups that had previously been organized clandestinely. People call them "patriotic families," referring to the fact that they are the families that have been supporting the PKK for a long time. When the regime began to withdraw from the region, these clandestine groups began to work openly and turned their meetings into open neighborhood assemblies, in which all Kurds could participate. The PYD already had some popular support within Kurdish society, and went on to ally with other Kurdish political actors and parties to form the TEV-DEM. Therefore, the people's assemblies were not formed under the name of a party, but under the TEV-DEM, because their aim was to organize as a democratic people's movement. In other words, "the assemblies that later would become institutions of self-rule, sought to organize society and achieve democratic autonomy, independent of party structures" (Ayboğa, Flach and Knapp, 2018, p. 87).

> In spring 2011 (after March), the movement created the people's assemblies, independent from party structure. That happened very quickly and much earlier than planned. A system of assemblies began to function in large and small towns in Rojava, as well as in Aleppo, within months. Those who did not support the PYD at first (but did not consider them enemies either) and who thought that self-organization was useless, began to show interest in these new democratic structures. At that point, assemblies were not yet present in all neighborhoods. This was especially the case for those where the majority of the population was Arab, Assyrian (Syriac) or any other non-Kurdish population, and also in those places where the residents were aligned with the ENKS. Also, many rural areas lacked popular assemblies. (Ayboğa, Flach and Knapp, 2018, p. 87)

The movement cautiously avoided conflict with any other political group and with the Syrian regime; instead, it worked on developing a self-management or self-organization mindset by supporting the popular assemblies. During that time, the first Community Houses (Mala Gel) were established, followed by Women's Houses (*Mala Jin*). The Kurds gathered there to start discussing their goals. The Kurdish political actors who united under the umbrella of the TEV-DEM followed the *Apoist* line. Actually, most of the leaders of the people's assemblies came from families that had personally met Abdullah Öcalan. It was clear from the beginning that the situation in Rojava would evolve towards democratic autonomy. Nonetheless, it was necessary to discuss the basis of the concept of democratic autonomy and how to build it. This was precisely the objective of the first popular assemblies. Besides building democratic autonomy, it was necessary to simultaneously build self-defense in the context of war. In July 2012, when the YPG declared it was in control of the main Kurdish cities, popular assemblies were ready to become political spaces to work on the process of self-management and organization of society on the basis of democratic autonomy. This was the most important concrete result of the Kurdish Movement's organizing work in Rojava after the Qamishlo rebellion in 2004.

Telat Yunis, Co-president of the autonomous government of the Cezîre region, explains that during that period, the Syrian regime's oppressive policies rejected the Kurds. Their identity was not recognized and they were denied Syrian citizenship. It also denied other peoples the right to live:

> In Syria, having a different opinion and political opposition were forbidden, not only in the case of the Kurds, but also for everyone else. However, the Kurds, compared with other people, were more organized. The Kurds were interested in politics, especially because of the oppressive policies against their identity and language. Even though it was forbidden, people were secretly involved in politics. Hundreds of politicians who struggled were tortured, detained and some martyred in the clandestine prisons of the regime, just for politically organizing. The Kurdish people were organized to a certain extent. The life of Serok [Abdullah Öcalan] and the Freedom Movement played an important role in Syria in terms of organizing and transmitting political experience. But not only that, they also taught people how to protect their own culture from cultural genocide. How would people protect their own existence by organizing? It had a great impact. This new mindset and way of organizing had its results: people were always willing to rise up, fight and engage in revolution whenever an opportunity came up. I mean, people, as a result of that mindset and way of organizing, were always ready. In any case, they would rise up whenever the opportunity came up, and they would fight and engage in revolution. (Interview with Yunis, 2019)

The opportunity finally came with the Qamishlo rebellion. Unfortunately, at that time, there was no common mindset among the Kurds and the conflict and hostilities with the Arabs were decisive elements in the failure of the revolt. The hundreds of thousands of Kurds who took to the streets missed the opportunity to carry out a revolution. However, once they withdrew from the streets, the resistance and organization of the people continued. The Qamishlo rebellion was the first spark of the Rojava Revolution. Yunis, who also participated in the rebellion, pointed out that the people understood that "they were ready, they had the power to engage in revolution and, if they were well organized, they could change everything in one night." According to Yunis, when the Qamishlo rebellion occurred, the brotherhood between Kurds and Arabs had not matured yet, and the regime, as it had always done, turned the Arabs against the Kurds. By spreading fear of the division of the country, they suppressed the revolt. Nonetheless, the Rojava Revolution became possible when rebelliousness against the regime became common in all villages across Syria. This had not been the case at the time of the Qamishlo rebellion (interview with Yunis, 2019). Precisely because of this, in addition to the military control of the YPG in 2012, the People's Assemblies started to become spaces where autonomy materialized. And not only for Kurds, but for all the Rojava community:

> Since there was no practical and concrete experience from the past (in Northern Kurdistan the organization was not very powerful), in 2011, people's assemblies were still not very competent on how to develop solutions for all social, cultural and economic problems in a neighborhood. However, the neighborhood assemblies began to understand what they could do from month to month and with every discussion they started becoming a real alternative to the state. Also, more and more people attended the assemblies to find solutions on issues of justice, social solidarity and security. (Ayboğa, Flach and Knapp, 2018, p. 88)

As the authors point out in the above quote, the Kurdish Movement had not yet developed a comprehensive experience of self-management for autonomy in Bakur. Even though the Kurdish Movement there was very strong in terms of social organization, it could not make progress due to the violent policies of the Turkish state. And although there were popular assemblies, they only played a role in political processes and activities, and it was mostly only partisans who participated in them. They never reached a stage that would allow them to play a role in the organization of the entire daily lives of regular citizens; thus, popular assemblies in Bakur remained fragmented, scattered and non-inclusive. The Bakur experience was very important, but it was not sufficient for the reality of Rojava. Rojava was creating its own autonomy experience and the Kurdish Movement was nourishing that experience. Unlike in Bakur, the people in Rojava were not used to the state of emergency; they had not developed the habit of sustaining their collective needs. The Syrian state had centralized the supply of basic necessities, such as bread, diesel and sugar. The people were used to working on the land of the soldiers and the state, and the state provided for people's needs at very low prices or in the form of subsidies.

The bread issue was decisive in this regard. The Syrian state bought all the wheat that peasants grew each year; the peasants were obliged to sell all their wheat to the state, which stored it in silos and then delivered bread to centralized bakeries in the villages. The fact that people did not have wheat or flour when the war began made the situation harder in many parts of Syria. The population had become sociologically more dependent on the center of power. Thus, when the Kurdish Movement declared its military and political control of the region through its seizure of silos, the people expected to have their needs met through the intervention of a central power, as it has been before the revolution. But it did not happen that way—the movement had not expected the people to make this request. This illustrates the total lack of social organization. The movement also came to realize that the people's assemblies that had been organized to discuss the new political organization were inadequate. Indeed, it was going to be difficult to organize society without being able to meet its vital needs. In times of war, the more logical option for those who are not able to meet their needs is to cross the borders, to migrate. If the Kurdish Movement had not found a way to sustain society's needs, it would have lost its social support. The spokeswoman of the Women's Economy Committee (*Aboriya Jin*) explains:

> When this war started, the bread issue was much discussed even in the mountains; since all the problems in Rojava reached us in some way. The Rojava comrades had not been able to solve it, so we got involved in trying to solve the problem with bread and bakeries. As the Economy Committee we said, "Let's see, what is to be done?" There were serious life problems in the social sphere. If it were up to us, guerrilla people, we would create a commission and the commission would have to solve the problem, but no, in society it is not like that. In a short period of time, comrades came to Rojava and organized many meetings. Imagine, they wanted to solve the bread problem by holding meetings. [...] Believe me when I say that the bread problem affected the organization until 2017. Anyway, after many meetings, the comrades met at a family's house. The problem was: there is a big bakery confiscated by the community and it must be decided how it is going to work. Six hours of discussion without a concrete conclusion. While this happened, the house owner was listening to the comrades' discussion and he suddenly said: "Excuse

me, my friends, but I'm going to ask you something. Have you ever seen a bakery like this?" They say they haven't. Then the house owner says: "Well, what are you even discussing? Go and see for yourself!" And there they went... (laughs). What I mean by that is that life's problems cannot be solved only with ideology. You first need to socialize, if you want to solve a social problem, even if you are a guerrilla fighter. Otherwise, the people would reject us, if we couldn't even solve a bread problem. (Interview with Delal, spokeswoman of *Aboriya Jin*, 2018)

Thus, the communes were first organized out of necessity. The movement's aim was to organize them quickly, starting from smaller communities to ensure that it was the people taking initiative to organize social life across Rojava. This was not an easy process for the movement's militants (cadres) nor for the members of society, who had forgotten how to self-manage. The people expected and demanded that the movement take the initiative, that is, act as a state. However, the movement expected and demanded that the people develop their own communitarian initiative, create their own autonomy. This tension between statization and autonomization has been the main conflict at the core of what we have called the Rojava Revolution for the last ten years. Communes and people's assemblies were the most important way of communitarian organization for autonomy. People in Rojava and northern Syria became more and more experienced in assembly practice. People's assemblies formed the autonomous government through elections, and now in Rojava it has become natural to form the assembly of each autonomous organization. Common decision-making in assemblies has left behind any notion of making decisions on behalf of the people. Forming the assembly on the basis of a democratic nation is an important practice. Participation is not only about making political decisions, but also about people participating in common living. That is the essence of assembling.

Pervin Yusif was elected in 2018 from the Kongra-Star list to be part of the Qamishlo canton assembly for three years and was later appointed canton co-president by the assembly. She reported that the canton assembly is made up of 82 assembly-people. They appointed two assembly-people for the co-presidency and two for the vice-presidency, then they formed 10 committees, one for each sector of the Autonomy: Women, Youth, Economy, Health, Municipalities, Self-defense, Education, Culture, Justice and Social Affairs, along with a supervision committee. Yusif pointed out that the co-presidents and co-spokespersons of the committees have a coordination meeting twice a month and then once a month there is a cantonal assembly attended by all assembly-people.

There are 10 committees that work with the councils (destaye) and there is another committee to do follow-up, we call it the "supervision committee" (*komiteya şopandin*). The committee's purpose is to follow up on the work of the 10 committees. For example, in summer, municipalities work on road maintenance, and so the Supervision Committee works alongside the Municipalities Committee. But when schools open, the Supervision Committee supports the Education Committee. They go and check: have they accomplished the planned work, or have they solved the people's problems? The Supervision Committee assists other committees and reports to the assembly. The cantonal sector committees establish connections with their sector committees working at the provincial and city levels. All the committees in each sector work together through their own assembly. In the region, each sector has its own council (*destaye*). So, the committees are connected horizontally and vertically. Every committee reports to its assembly, the cantonal assembly and also to the assembly of its autonomous sector. (Interview with Yusif, Co-president of Qamishlo Canton Assembly, 2019)

After the sector committees are formed in the canton assembly, as Yusif mentions, the task of each cantonal committee is to organize its own sector assembly. The co-spokespersons of the economy committee, Jinda *(Kurdish woman)* and Mohammed *(Arab man)*, said that, as they were elected by the cantonal assembly, the first thing they did was come together and discuss how to articulate the way of organizing with the previously existing structures, particularly with the previous economic coordination body. The co-spokespersons said that, firstly, they established contact with those chosen for the economy committees in the province and city people's assemblies so that they could transfer the information on decisions and cantonal policies to the communes. That was a bottom-up process; they have created a network that allows the work of local commissions to be reported to the canton, and from there, to the economy council (*destaye*). Secondly, along with the directorates of the different economic areas (agriculture, industry, trade, cooperatives, bakeries, expertise, or *pispor*), they created a cantonal economic assembly. Previously, these directorates worked with the economic coordination body, without having any relationship with the popular assemblies. This assembly brings together the economic co-directorates, the co-spokespersons of the economic committee and a movement cadre. Jinda and Mohammed said that in that assembly all decisions in the economic sector are articulated with the Qamishlo canton people's assembly (interview with Jinda and Mohammed, co-spokespersons of the Economy Committee of the Qamishlo canton).

Similarly, in the Hesekê canton, an economic assembly and an assembly for each of the other sectors were created. In other words, each of the sectors of the democratic self-government (Women, Youth, Economy, Health, Municipalities, Self-defense, Education, Culture, Justice and Social Affairs) has its own assemblies in each canton. These sectoral assemblies at the cantonal level are linked to the respective councils (*destaye*) at the regional level. The economy assembly of the Qamishlo canton, for instance, submits its monthly activity report to the Economy Council (*Destaye Aborî*); the Qamishlo assembly of municipalities does the same with the Municipalities and Ecology Council (*Destaye Şeredarîyan û Ekolojî*). The Economy Council of the Cezîre region merges the Qamishlo and Hesekê canton reports into one document to be presented at the autonomous government assembly of the Cezîre region, which is composed of two co-president, four vice-presidents, the co-spokesperson of 10 councils (20 people) and 11 legislators. In addition, in this assembly, the regional autonomous government drafts its own laws (interview with Yunis, 2019). Its meetings are held after the lower-level assemblies.[16]

Thus, each committee organizes itself as a sector. The organization by sector operates in all the structures of the democratic Autonomy, while preserving its own autonomy; that is, it organizes itself and creates its assembly and coordination as an autonomous organization. The Economy Committee is in charge of organizing daily life in the communes. It works in coordination with other commune committees, like the Municipalities and Ecology Committee. At the canton level, it works together with other economy committees and coordination teams to join in the assembly of its own sector. Like the people's assemblies, the sector assemblies are formed by province, canton and region.

Reports are used to coordinate and exchange information between structures and sectors of the democratic Autonomy. Mutual reporting ensures a constant flow of information from the smallest organizational level (commune) to the largest organizational level (cantonal assembly). Writing reports ensures that there is no hierarchical relationship between the levels of the Autonomy; everyone is responsible for their own level. When analyzing the contents of reports, the most interesting part is *rexne û rexnedayin* (critics and self-critics). Every report starts with a brief update of the political context and then delves into activities carried out during the month. After evaluating the people's participation or interest in

---

16 The schedule of assembly meetings I attended in December 2019 is as follows:
   December 19 – Economic Assemblies in Provinces (Derik)
   December 20 – People's Assembly in the provinces (Derik)
   December 23-24 – Economy Assembly in the canton (Qamishlo-Hesekê)
   December 26 – People's Assembly in the canton (Qamishlo-Hesekê)
   December 29 – Autonomous Government Assembly in the region (Cezîre)

The organization of the Autonomy

(The people's assembly of Qamishlo, the economic sector and the autonomous government of the Cezire region).

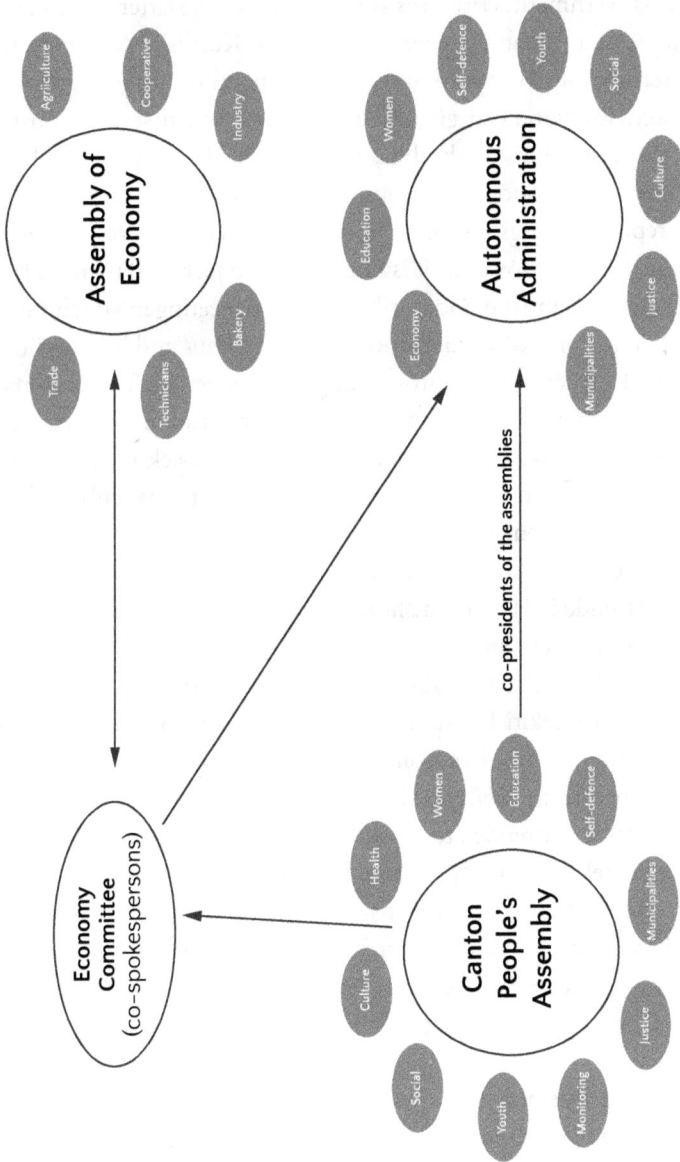

The cantonal people's assembly is organized into more than 10 committees of democratic confederalism dimensions

Dimension of democratic confederalism corresponds to the 10 councils that constitute the Autonomous Administration

the activities, in the last part of the report, every sector or autonomous structure presents a self-criticism, pointing out the obstacles to implementing the activities planned in the previous meeting. If such obstacles are caused by another structure of self-government, criticisms are addressed to the latter structure. The *rexne u rexnedayin* is a valuable mechanism that the Kurdish Movement has used in its organization for many years and that prevents the emergence of the phenomenon power. Everyone can give their criticisms, but first they must also share their self-criticism. This method has socially spread in Rojava and has become a practice that the Autonomy develops in all spaces.

The reports were given orally in the first years of the revolution; now they are given in writing. However, it is not enough to just send them to the meeting. One or two people must mandatorily attend the meeting in which the reports are presented. This form of participation is called *tekmil* and it allows one to learn who or which structures are participating in the meeting. The persons attending the meeting are both the collective voice of their autonomous structure and also those assigned to report the results of the meeting back to their structure. For example, I would like to share my observations from the assembly of the Cooperatives Unit (Yekîtî assembly).

I attended a Yekîtî assembly on March 18, 2018 to observe and listen. Forty-five people attended: 31 were the heads of the 11 Houses of Cooperatives (*Mala Kooperatifan*) of Serîkanîyê, Dirbesiye, Amûdê, Dêrik, Tirbespîye, Hesekê, Şeddade, Girkelege, Tiltemir, Zirgane, Qamishlo, and seven were from the coordination body of Yekîtî (co-spokespersons, organization unit, accounting, law, etc.). In addition, two cadres from the TEV-DEM economy coordination body and two women from *Yekîtîya Kooperatifa Jinan* (Women's Cooperatives Unit) of Kongra-Star also attended to present the monthly report of the women's cooperatives. The Yekîtî assembly meeting lasted more than four hours. Before the meeting, every House of Cooperatives had a similar meeting with their regional cooperatives in order to prepare the monthly report on the development of the cooperatives. For example, before attending the Yekîtî assembly, the Serîkanîyê House of Cooperatives had met with the co-spokespersons of all the cooperatives in its region.

The Yekîtî assembly was held as follows: The cadres of the TEV-DEM first gave updates on the political context and reported on how the TEV-DEM economy coordination body was supporting the resistance of Afrîn's peoples and how the war was affecting the economy. Then, each House of Cooperatives read its previously prepared report. Next, Yekîtî read the draft of their monthly report. For the report to be complete, Yekîtî had to include the discussions that took place in the assembly. Once completed, Yekîtî would present it at the monthly meeting of the Economy Council (*Destaye Aborî*).

Once the mutual reports were read, we moved on to the discussion, opinions and suggestions. This section was significant in terms of me being able to see how autonomy develops: interinstitutional relations within autonomous organizations are democratized through mutual reports and their assemblies. The dialogue allows for an analysis of the organization and the development of each sector and to solve problems on a basis of common learning. This is how common learning and decision-making of autonomy begin. Instead of simply sending reports, people have to go, participate, be present, voice their opinion, think and decide collectively from their own and their collective experience. This confirms that democratic autonomy is not only based on a system of political administration, but also on the people's social organization, which allows them to make decisions about their lives.

In short, for me, autonomy is transforming the capitalist order and reorganizing social relations in everyday life. The research conducted in Rojava shows that communes and assemblies are (non-physical) spaces where people socially interact, transform the capitalist order and produce new (non-state) ways of relating with each other. Each person involved in the organization of the Rojava autonomy participates in at least three monthly assemblies. Moreover, as members of society, they participate in the assembly of the commune where they live and in extraordinary people's meetings. The assembly structure is not fixed; on the contrary, it entails movement with a great capacity to mobilize society. People mobilize every day to make decisions about their own lives, ranging from the need for water to the need for self-defense. The practice of assemblies as a movement generates a mobilizing organizational experience. No one is above society, the people participate directly in everything through one or more assemblies, with their own voice, their own decisions and their own actions. In this sense, the true understanding of autonomy goes beyond the mere administration of society, becoming a creative power that allows the reorganization of social relations in a new way.

CHAPTER 4

The Anti-Capitalist Economy in Rojava

As long as there is bread and water, the struggle continues!
– Hevrin Khalaf[1]

For autonomous anti-capitalist movements that seek social liberation and emancipation, it is imperative to think about and organize alternative economic relations that undermine the dominant capitalist system. It is impossible to profess that a political organization, in which capitalist exploitation and alienation are reproduced, is truly autonomous. As Coraggio opines, "Imagining an alternative economy implies recognizing and criticizing the one we have today. It is very difficult to imagine something different without first analyzing the negative aspects of the current economy, so as to base our analyses on a negation of those very aspects, if we want to overcome them" (Coraggio, 2019, p. 61). For democratic autonomy in Rojava to deepen and strengthen it is necessary that it break with the dominance of capitalism by organizing an anti-capitalist economy.

The Kurdish Movement has had an anti-capitalist vision since the foundation of the PKK. Yet it only began to discuss organizing an alternative economy in earnest in the context of the peace talks and the debates on autonomy held during the Democratic Economy Conference, organized by the DTK (Democratic Society Congress), on November 8 to 9, 2014, in Turkey. I had the opportunity to participate in these initial discussions, joining the Democratic Economy Committee[2] of the DTK. Most of the arguments I discuss in the current section are heavily informed by my two years of active experience on this committee. The

---

1 Hevrin Khalaf was the Co-president of the Economic Council when I met her in 2018. On October 12, 2019, three days after Turkey launched its military offensive in northern Syria, she was brutally assassinated. According to reports from the Syrian Observatory for Human Rights, she was dragged out of her car and shot in cold blood by the side of the road. An autopsy revealed that she was shot, hit with heavy objects and dragged by her hair until the skin was torn from her scalp.
2 The DTK, an autonomous popular congress, is organized in committees in accordance with the ideas of democratic autonomy and leads efforts to construct autonomous systems. The committees are co-spokesperson by two political cadres and can be expanded if needed. The committees determine their own size according to the work they will carry out. They can expand, be organized into subcommittees, and, if necessary, take the form of coordinating bodies. Their precise form is determined by the practical needs that arise. At inception, the economy committee that I participated in was composed of seven people, but it grew to a coordinating committee of more than 30 members. Although the committee was tasked with practical work, we were able to organize a great number of discussions in order to further deepen the economic perspective of democratic autonomy.

debates that took place in the popular meetings in different areas of Bakur (North of Kurdistan) and the contradictions we experienced—between the perspective of the communal-democratic economy and the practices that we tried to carry out in line with this perspective—helped me reflect on the organization of an anti-capitalist economy in Rojava (West of Kurdistan) as I did my field research.

During this Democratic Economy Conference, eight thematic factories were held on agriculture and livestock, energy, water and mining, industry, work, commerce, local governments, cooperatives, and the women's economy. The main objective of these factories was to socialize production and establish a community-based economy that could ensure self-sufficiency (Aslan, 2014). As a result of said conference, the DTK, on behalf of the Kurdish Movement, defined the economy within the democratic autonomy model as communitarian-democratic, ecological and women liberationist:

> We intend to establish our self-sufficient economy within the democratic autonomy model, and we believe that the democratic, communitarian, women liberationist, ecological, egalitarian, and solidary paradigm based on self-sufficiency, promoted by Abdullah Öcalan, the leader of the Kurdish people, will be the solution for a social economy. The goal of this paradigm—which saves the economy from the trap of individualist and statist paradigms, and focuses on human emancipation, nature, and women—is, basically, to socialize the economy. (DTK, 2014)

In a communal-democratic economy, the socialization of the economy will be carried out through assemblies, communes and cooperatives, eliminating any relationship between collective work and salaries. Its goal is to create solidary markets and it plans to organize an anti-capitalist autonomy by improving the self-management of society within the economy. Thus, one of its main battlegrounds is the creation of new communal spaces and not leaving existing ones at the mercy of capitalist logic.

Various terms have been used to define this form of economic organization. Öcalan calls the economic organization of democratic confederalism "economic society"; the PKK calls it the "communal economy." The DTK in Bakur has named it "democratic economy." While Öcalan criticizes capitalist modernity and the socialist economy in order to develop the concept of "economic society," the PKK's "communal economy" emphasizes the vital importance of existing communal relations in Kurdistan's society in order to reorganize the economy. I prefer the term "communal economy," but in this section I will use the concept of "social economy" (*aborîya civakî*), as it is particularly widespread in Rojava.

Although the conceptual definitions change, the thoughts and policies that "social economy" refers to have their roots in the discussions first advanced by Abdullah Öcalan. Therefore, in order to understand the practice of the social economy in Rojava, it is useful to review the sources that have shaped the Kurdish Movement's economic outlook. To this end, I will address some of Öcalan's analyses of capitalism and the economy, as well as the ideas of a communal-democratic economy developed by the PKK at the Abdullah Öcalan Academy of Social Sciences,[3] and the discussions that took place at the economic conferences held in Bakur (November 8 to 9, 2014) and Rojava (October 16 to 17, 2015) in order to understand the theoretical bases of the social economy and how it is organized in Rojava. This will also enable an analysis of the extent to which the problems and contradictions that arise during the process of organization are fueled by conformity to this theoretical perspective. Simply placing the anti-capitalist economy at the horizon easily leads to idealized discussions; anti-capitalist practice seeks to create a lived experience that draws ever-closer to that horizon.

Discussions of alternative economies and perspectives on the social economy

First of all, it is necessary to underline that the proliferation of concepts used to define anti-capitalist economies is not exclusive to the Kurdish struggle. Specialized literature uses a variety of terms, such as: another economy, solidarity economy, social economy, community economy, communal economy, public economy, feminist economy, ecological economy, alternative/anti-capitalist economy, etc. These concepts are used to define concrete phenomena (formal institutions, social practices) and abstract ideas such as projects, values and perceptions that do not correspond to the conventional economy, as well as its practices (Cattani, 2004, p. 25). Although they are similar in many ways, there are differences between the precise definitions of these terms, which can be traced back to their differing political and intellectual roots. Currently, various discussion platforms are guiding the anti-capitalist economy debate of the 21st century: Marxism, libertarian anarchism, the social and solidarity economy, the Network of Alternative and Solidarity Economy Networks (*Red de Redes de Economía Alternativa y Solidaria*, REAS), feminist economics, ecosocialism, ecofeminism, *Sumak Kawsai* (Good Living), and *Vivir Bien* (Living Well). Luis Miguel Uharte emphasizes that these discussion platforms and alternative economic experiences are fueled by and in with emancipatory thoughts—socialisms, feminisms, envi-

---

3 The Abdullah Öcalan Academy of Social Sciences (*Abdullah Öcalan Sosyal Bilimler Akademisi*) is an academy located in the Kurdish mountains where guerrillas receive theoretical and political formation. This academy, through its publication of brochures of collective discussions, plays an important role in developing political perspectives in the various fields of the democratic autonomy model.

ronmentalisms, Indigenous communitarianisms— (Uharte, 2019, p. 12). To this list we can add autonomism.

The concept of social economy, used to express the anti-capitalist, autonomous and democratic organization in Rojava, has emerged as an alternative to economic liberalism and the centralized planned economy (Yusuf, 2015, p. 264). The social economy is defined as a self-sufficient, autonomous economy that is at the service of the people, where social resources are public in nature, and the people decide how best to use them. In other words: social wealth is under the collective management and control of the people. This work is to be carried out through cooperatives organized and planned by communes and popular assemblies. In this way, the people will be able to satisfy their needs, so that, eventually, property and social classes will disappear. The social economy is not against private property or individual investments; however, it limits private companies, granting them only "non-excessive economic profit and non-monopolistic economic activity" (Öcalan, 2009, p. 293). According to Öcalan, while a society built in defiance of "capitalist society" can be given many names, it is crucial to construct "an economy and a social weave that are not dominated by a monopoly" (Öcalan, 2011, p. 261). Öcalan here uses the term "monopoly" instead of "capitalism." In other words, Öcalan accepts as a capitalist only the monopoly segment that has large capital and dominates the economy. In this sense, he does not see capitalism as a set of social relations, but as a relationship of domination that monopolistic capital exercises over society through the economy. This is one of Öcalan's definitions that determines the perspective and practice of the social economy. The Kurdish Movement, which has adopted this definition as its fundamental point of reference, does not consider associating with "small" capitalists to be outside the understanding and practice of the social economy, unless those capitalists possess a dominant share of the capital. Therefore, while the social economy is based on the organization of communal relations and spaces, it does not exclude small-scale private sector production. The assumption is that the communal ethic of society will limit the private sector. In short, we can say that the social economy envisions a mixed economy, in which the communal economy and the subsistence economy of small-scale producers can coexist.

By affirming that the current capitalist system is governed by groups of monopoly capital, the Kurdish Movement emphasizes that in the social economy the subject of decision-making must be society. To this end, all individuals must have a voice and influence over the processes of production, distribution and consumption. In the neighborhood, village, municipal, provincial, cantonal and regional assemblies—or those organized specifically by women and youth—each person, as a member of society, is part of the decision-making processes in which production is democratically planned. How production is carried out or shared is decided communally. In this way, social wealth is managed in accordance with the will and common needs of society. Thus, "it is the community who decides what society needs to survive, as well as how much should be produced to satisfy this need; how, where and with whom to cooperate, and how, by whom and with whom the fruits of production will be shared" (Abdullah Öcalan Sosyal Bilimler Akademisi, 2012, p. 19). Only in this way can society manage the economy for its own benefit. Capitalism's greatest feat has been to rob society of its economic decision-making power—starting with the working class, and slowly enveloping the entire society. Following from this premise, I believe that capitalism can be overcome by the self-management of society, and not only of the working class.

The self-management of society is necessary for a democratic economy

I think it is useful, at this point, to digress in order to emphasize the originality of the Kurdish Movement's self-management principles and its practice of an anti-capitalist economy. As we saw in the previous chapter, the Kurdish Movement has used the concept of self-management to define the various processes of autonomy. In its analyses of the economy, self-management refers to the organization of a communitarian-democratic, ecological and women's liberation economy.[4] Any type of economic organization or economic relationship that does not follow these core principles is deemed a continuation of the capitalist system.

The concept of self-management originates from the anarchist and libertarian socialist tradition. Examples of its practical implementation include the Paris Commune (Ross, 2015); the soviets (Anweiler, 1975); the 1920s' factory councils in Italy; the 1936 libertarian collectivizations in Catalonia, Aragon and Andalusia (Ruggeri, 2018); the recovered factories in Argentina, following the 2001 economic crisis (Ruggeri, 2012); the poder popular (people power) in Chile (Trasol, 2017); the collective work of the Zapatistas (Santiago, 2017); the settlements of MST (*Movimiento Sin Tierra*, Landless Movement); the Venezuelan communes; the Ekojin cooperatives in Turkish Kurdistan (Aslan, 2016); and innumerable other experiences, to which we can add the confederated cooperatives of Rojava and northern Syria.

In the ongoing debates surrounding cooperativism, the emphasis tends to be placed on the self-management of workers/laborers, because, as indicated in the first *Cuadernos para la autogestión* (Notebooks for Self-management), "the most common form of a self-managed company is the cooperative" (Ruggeri,

---

4 This principle, defined as "gender liberation" in the early texts, later began to be referred to as "women's liberation" for unknown and unexplained reasons.

Wertheimer, Galeazzi and Garcia, 2012, p. 7). In addition, "democratic management is one of the most important principles of cooperativism" (Garcia Jané,
2012, p. 10). Thus, cooperatives tend to be equated with a form of economic
organization in which self-management is implemented. In my opinion, cooperatives cannot be discussed as divorced from self-management, as any cooperative
devoid of self-management cannot be said to be organizing anti-capitalist social
relations or an alternative economy. Cooperatives without democratic self-management do not possess any anti-capitalist potential. It is worth noting that "not
all cooperatives are organized according to the principles of self-management"
(Ruggeri, Wertheimer, Galeazzi and García, 2012, p. 7). Many structures that
self-define as cooperatives are without any higher-level management, yet continue
to be organized hierarchically and vertically. Therefore, even if they are referred to
as cooperatives, they operate similarly to any capitalist company, becoming subject
to market forces, even making profit off of the exploitation of wage labor. Thus,
we consider that democratic self-management is the basic principle of cooperatives. Though, as García Jané says, often "it is easy to agree on what a cooperative
is, but harder to say what self-management is" (Garcia Jané, 2012, pp. 9-10).

Today, when workers in the recovered factories and cooperatives of Latin
America, especially those in Argentina, speak of "self-management," the reference
point is often the classical definition of the term, harking back to the 19th and 20th
centuries. That is, self-management as the collective control and management of
economic units by their workers (Ruggeri, 2018, p. 23). Here, "self-management"
is associated with workers' control over factories and the means of production.

According to the Kurdish Movement, self-management should belong
to society and not to a particular class. The "Contract on Cooperatives of the
Democratic Federation of Northern Syria," written as a concluding document
for the Assembly of Economic Organizations on Cooperativism, defines democratic self-management as a precondition: "There is a complementary and holistic
relationship between cooperatives and other institutions and units of democratic society. The presence of cooperatives, as well as communes, assemblies, city
councils and congresses, requires the existence and functionality of democratic
self-management mechanisms" (Assembly of Economy of the Democratic Federation of Northern Syria, 2017).

The social economy is regarded as an economy organized on a democratic
basis (Commission for the Preparation of the Democratic Economy Conference,
2014). Today, all local people's assemblies of Rojava have economic commissions
in charge of effecting economic activities through communes and cooperatives.
The goal is to establish a network of economic committees and cooperatives.

To summarize, within the Kurdish struggle, self-management is society's method of democratic decision-making. Its scope is not limited to the economy, but encompasses all areas related to building autonomy. Thus, the principle of self-management also applies to areas such as education and health. In the economic realm, self-management is implemented through cooperatives, economic committees and assemblies.

Later, after outlining the organization of cooperatives, I will discuss the term in more detail. For now, suffice it to say that for the Kurdish Movement, the self-management of society is crucial in establishing the link between cooperatives and communities. Furthermore, it must be specified that decisions concerning cooperatives are not taken solely by its members, but also by the assemblies of the communities where the cooperatives are located. This collective process allows the larger community, and not just the workers, to create a culture of production that meets their needs. The underlying assumption is that the formation of cooperatives must develop independently of market conditions in order to enable the creation of autonomous power. Argentina's recovered factories, which remained rooted in the logic of the market, were unable to develop autonomous power for this reason.

The fact that it is not just members and workers who have a voice in cooperative decision-making is what differentiates the self-management practice of the Kurdish Movement decisively from other, more classical approaches. It means sharing the ability to self-manage beyond a single class, making self-managed labor serve the needs of the wider community. The "commitment to the environment" (*compromiso con el entorno*), one of the basic principles of solidarity economies (REAS, 2020),[5] has already been implemented by Rojava cooperatives. This commitment allows "the proper/good [buena] reinvestment and redistribution of generated wealth" (REAS, 2020). Of course, the commitment is not based purely on political solidarity, but is rather considered a condition for life and the anti-capitalist struggle. Thus, the work carried out in the context of cooperatives becomes a holistic project that effects real social change.

A non-capitalist economy is an anti-patriarchal economy

Another defining principle of the social economy is the liberation of women—which also implies gender equality—for, without it, democratic relations cannot exist in society (Commission for the Preparation of the Democratic Economy Conference, 2014, p. 72). The Kurdish Movement, building on the feminist

5 The six principles of the solidarity economy outlined by the REAS (*Red de Redes de Economía Alternativa y Solidaria*, Network of Alternative and Solidarity Economy Networks) are equity, work, environmental sustainability, cooperation, lack of profit motive, and commitment to the environment.

tradition, posits that, in the capitalist economy, women become invisible, as their work is unremunerated or is made invisible. The main reason is that, in the capitalist economy, women are excluded from decision-making processes, even when their work is salaried like men's (Aslan, 2016). The fight for the remuneration of women's work, therefore, is a deflection of socialist thought into feminist thought. The creation of the female working class is nothing but the commodification of women's labor. That is why the social economy advocates for the socialization of women's work through collective and communal economies (Jineoloji Academy, 2016, p. 218). According to Öcalan, "the most brutal period for women occurred when they were excluded from the economy during capitalist civilization." He calls this "the destitution of women in the economy" (Öcalan, 2013, p. 47). The "Women's Work" workshop, held in February 2016 as part of the Women's Economy Conference (Bakur), stated that from the time of hunter-gatherer societies, women have played an essential role in sustaining life. However, the subsistence economy, organized by women through use value, was subsumed and its activities aimed at satisfying society's basic needs became hidden labor or, rather, a gendered responsibility. In the following period, the driving force of the economy became the exchange and surplus value. However, exchange value, surplus value, and then the market, were regulated by patriarchal power, which men had acquired by seizing control of the economy from women.

The social economy requires a social reality in which women return to the economy; an economy organized by women's hands and minds (KJA-Democratic Women's Movement, 2016). The social economy prioritizes the creation of spaces and relationships that allow women to return to the economy as "decision-making subject" (*sujetos de decisión*), instead of advocating for their participation in the capitalist market. A fundamental condition of democratic autonomy is that women create their own economies and become the subjects of the social economy. Thus, women could rejoin the economy with their own conscience, organization and willpower, creating areas of co-representation and self-organization[6] in the social economy, as in all areas of democratic autonomy (Abdullah Öcalan Sosyal Bilimler Akademisi, 2012, p. 85). Women's communes and cooperatives are thus to be organized as areas for women's emancipation. Although the women's economy (*aborîyaJIN*) is part of Rojava's social economy, it has always been organized separately and autonomous.

---

6 "Co-representation" means that women participate and are represented in half of all areas of mixed-gender organization. "Self-organization" is defined as an organization in which only women can participate, make decisions and implement them.

An economy in which women are the decision-making subject is an ecological economy

Another characteristic that defines the social economy is ecology. This ecological principle is directly related to women becoming decision-making subjects in the social economy. The Kurdish Movement insists that a women-led economy—based on satisfying society's basic needs and on use values—would be one based on subsistence and not on exchange value, as is the case under capitalism. That is, it would be an ecological economy (Aslan, 2014). The exclusion of women, whose relationship to nature is based on sustaining life, has made exchange value dominant in shaping society's relationship to nature. Natural resources, society's common goods (or commons), have become the inputs of industrial capital through industrialism, the cost of the production process, and a market component mediated through money, that is, a commodity.

Öcalan's analysis of ecology has two reference points: women as defenders of nature, and industrialism as its enemy. According to him, industrialism became an ideology based on the exclusion of women from the economy and the formation of the nation-state. In the era of industrialism, the formation of the nation-state was idealized and carried out with the aim of obtaining monopolistic profits (Öcalan, 2012, p. 356). According to Öcalan, "The greatest destruction brought about by industrialism took place in the field of agriculture and in small communities, which are a precondition for the existence of the social." Following from this idea, the establishment of eco-communities, that is, of communes, is one of the core economic principles of democratic autonomy (Öcalan, 2009, p. 251). Building on the ideas of Murray Bookchin (2014), Öcalan states that eco-communities should also be established in cities, since "they have the optimal size to function as [self-contained] units, where non-profit economic activities are able to fit each city's unique features, and where the goal is to eliminate unemployment and poverty for the people who live there. People can divide themselves freely across these units according to their structure and capability" (Öcalan, 2009, p. 251). In other words, the social economy does not reject industrial production as such, it rejects "the ideology of capitalist nation-state industrialism." Industrial production should be limited by ecologism and serve to cover basic needs. There should be no industrial production that exceeds these two limitations. An industry resulting from such restraints would be an eco-industry. (Öcalan, 2014, p. 11).

Öcalan furthermore asserts that, in an economy built within the limits of ecology and serving only to cover fundamental needs, unemployment, overproduction and underproduction in underdeveloped countries and regions will disappear—as will the contrast between villages and cities, class differences, economic crises and wars. In essence, the breeding ground for a dominant society will cease to exist (Öcalan, 2009, p. 248). Essentially, democratic autonomy is based on an ecological economy and society. As with all other segments of the communal economy, industry, too, should be ecological. Industrial production should be subordinated to the collective needs of society and organized by its communal decisions (Abdullah Öcalan Sosyal Bilimler Akademisi, 2012, p. 85). The most important function of the commune is to create a social organization that can turn these communal needs and decisions into actions.

Ecology is one of the most contradictory areas of the social economy. As we will see later, when I analyze the organization of the social economy in the industrial sector, it is not easy to determine where to draw the line for industrial production, or to determine the nature and ecological conditions of production in other fields, such as agriculture. Compounding this is the fact that capitalism's global impact on the environment often tends to frustrate the efforts of local ecological economies. Nevertheless, the fact that the social economy is based on collective needs and defined by women implies a truly anti-capitalist vision, as it takes the debates on ecology far beyond mere concepts like respect for nature or organic production,and centers the economy around a moral-political approach.

The social economy reinforces pre-existing features of society, but organizes them in an anti-capitalist way

The Kurdish Movement states that the origins of the social economy—defined as collective, communal, egalitarian and solidary—are based on natural society (Abdullah Öcalan Sosyal Bilimler Akademisi, 2012, p. 78) and that multiple traces of these roots are still visible in Kurdistan's society. However, these are useless and valueless in the capitalist system. Since the new economy must be built on these roots, it implies that the movement will need to counter capitalism by creating a more integrated organization that can transcend the status quo. Jorge Santiago, who under the umbrella of DESMI has provided important support to a number of projects of the Zapatista's economic organization through training and assistance, emphasizes the aforementioned point when he describes the "solidarity economy" as a model of organic relationships, and a consciously-transcendent model:

> When the latter comes into being, a so-called solidarity economy begins to sprout. The term "solidarity economy" denotes an outgrowing of previous models, which were merely social constructions of cooperation. These are models of mutuality that continue to exist and that still serve as

the base for many activities, but that lack the awareness to grow into an alternative model. Their consciousness remained anchored solely in the participation in the existing model (Santiago, 2017, p. 32).

The working assumption here is that communal models have survived even under the dominance of capitalism, but are unable themselves to overcome it. In fact, on this point, Santiago concurs with the Kurdish Movement.

In the field of economics, society does not have to organize itself from scratch. Important experiences, leaders and organized struggles have emerged from within this field of moral-political society, along with its culture and values. Numerous social struggles—from the nameless mythic woman-mother who planted the first wheat seedling to today's democratic cooperatives—all are the economy of democratic modernity itself. Even today, a large part of community life and the economy is made up of communal economies, communitarian economies, associations, foundations, unions, cooperatives, domestic economies constituted of organizations, such as small- and mid-scale producers, and small-time commerce. These non-monopolistic structures are within the scope of the moral-political society's economy. What is necessary—based on an understanding of the democratic-autonomous nature of these economic structures—is to ensure their reorganization and transformation in a democratic-autonomous-communitarian and confederal manner" (Commission for the Preparation of the Democratic Economy Conference, 2014, pp. 76-77).

This posits that the power of autonomy is a potential force for the creation of modes of reorganization that can strengthen and reproduce communal models.

The economy of democratic autonomy is thus to be understood not as a centralized institution, but rather as a general understanding that is expected to take hold in society. An anti-capitalist economy cannot be organized by the creation of a hierarchical, centralized power. Instead, it must be organized by implementing forms of mutual aid, solidarity, community and resistance, along the lines of those societies that have preserved these values for centuries. The essence of moral-political society lives on in these societies, which can be interpreted as a resistance against capitalism. The revitalization and strengthening of these societies form the basis of the social economy.

The creation of anti-capitalist economies: the organization of a social economy in Rojava

For over ten years, the de facto autonomy of Rojava has brought about autonomous practices and experiences in a variety of areas. Since the announcement of the first Social Contract of Rojava (2014), the nature of autonomy has changed and has been in constant flux as political and social needs, too, have morphed. I have previously stressed that I am not analyzing a completed model, but rather an ongoing experience. One of the areas in which this ongoing revolution is still most noticeable is that of economy. As was highlighted in Chapter 3, the autonomous model has made considerable advances in the organization of decision-making processes in the field of politics, as well as in women's participation. Although a lot of experience in the field of economics has been gained already, the Rojava Revolution as a whole has yet to challenge the forces of war and capitalism. In order for the autonomy model to have a future, it is imperative to organize self-sufficient people's social economies and to overcome the dominant capitalist system. The Kurdish Movement, well aware of this need, has put people's economic self-sufficiency at the front and center of its autonomy-focused politics since the beginning of the Rojava Revolution.

The revolution, which began in 2012 with the seizure of wheat silos controlled by the Ba'ath regime, focused on meeting the collective needs of the people through the early formation of the very first neighborhood assemblies. During this period, assemblies and communes played an active role in covering citizens' basic needs. The Economic Development Center of Rojava (*Navenda Geşkirina Aborîya Rojavayê Kurdistanê*, NGARK o NAR, July 13, 2014) was established in concert with the construction of a social economy based on the vision of a communal-democratic, ecological and women's liberation economy, as previously mentioned. With the declaration of the cantons and the system of democratic autonomy in 2014, the autonomous administrations and the Economic and Trade Council affiliated with these administrations came into being. Agriculture, which today is included as part of the Economic Council, was given its own council at the time (Rojava Social Contract, 2014).

Following this period, Rojava held its first economic conference. Reclaiming the slogan of the 2014 Democratic Economy Conference in Bakur[7]—"We communalize our land, water, and energy; let's build a free and democratic life"— the Rojava conference was held in the city of Rimelan from October 16 to 17, 2015.

---

7 To recap: the Kurdish Movement established an organizational system on the basis of the KCK system as confederated peoples' congresses in each part of Kurdistan. Based on this system, perspectives and experiences are shared between economic committees.

As the Kurdish Movement discussed the economic perspectives first arrived at in Bakur, and initial agreements between different sectors of society were established, the first experiences of the communalization and cooperatives were also underway. In fact, at the Rojava Economic Conference, the discussions that took place on the organization and practice of the social economy dealt with their real-world application, and were not simply discussed on the basis of a purely theoretical understanding of the economy. When the concluding documents of the Democratic Economy Conference and the First Social Economy Conference of Rojava are set side by side, it is apparent that both stem from the same perspective and are thus related. However, there is a difference: in Bakur, the discussions on a future economy were based on a peace settlement yet to come. In Rojava, the Economic Committee approached the topic as part of the region's self-defense, taking into account the conditions of war.[8] At this time, the organization of autonomy in Rojava was becoming increasingly complex, even as it made great strides. While, on the one hand, all civil and social spaces were constructed by both the Kurdish Movement and the women's movement in accordance with the tenets of democratic confederalism, on the other hand, an autonomous administration was being established and forming councils following these same tenets. In 2015, a Social Economy Committee consisting of political cadres of the KCK, political leaders of the Movement for a Democratic Society (TEV-DEM), and the Social Economy Council of the Autonomous Administration, made up of local Rojavans, formed a parallel body. In addition, the Rojava Women's Economic Committee, affiliated with the Women's Congress (Kongra-Star), was also founded. This situation caused confusion as to the division of roles and responsibilities in the decision-making processes:

> Before the founding of the Autonomous Administration, the TEV-DEM institutions ran centers for the development of the economy, and continue to do so today. When the General Council of the Autonomous Administration was established, it created governing institutions as well; the TEV-DEM institutions were closed. Thus, only a single economic institution carried on doing this work. For instance, an Agriculture Council existed here two years before I began my work, but it had nothing to do with agriculture. [It was tied to the] Economic Development Center, which was also conducting research into agriculture. We had great fights over this for the first six months. For example, we set agricultural policy:

---

8 The Democratic Economy Conference in Bakur was held in the shadow of a dialogue process between the PKK and the Turkish state. This came to an abrupt end due to the Kurdish Movement's advances in autonomous organization in the aftermath of the victory at Kobane. In 2015, the war between the PKK and the Turkish state was reignited.

what to plant, what not to plant, where to buy seeds, etc. We decided on all of this, but it was not clear who was going to execute it. The Economic Development Center of Rojava (NGARK) on one side, the responsible people of TEV-DEM agriculture on another, and us, on a third side, all worked independently of each other. Working in two different ways does not work, and it will create two parallel responsible bodies. For example, we rejected launching a product, but a co-responsible at the NGARK then told us that he had approved the same product. We told them: "Let's get together and eliminate this dual system," but it took us six months to convince everyone. It took even longer to merge and learn to work together. So, our objective is to take common decisions and let everyone apply them in their field. A plurality of voices in the institutions, but unity in decision-making is key. In other words, let there be no opposition between us. Once we all agreed on these principles, we created an economic coordination body, together with an Economic Council (Destaye Aborî) and a NGARK committee—that is, committees for the general economy (TEV-DEM) and women's economy (*AboriyaJIN* – Kongra Star). In other words, they no longer make decisions without the council, and we no longer make decisions without them. Instead, we make decisions in the coordination. (Interview with Khalaf, 2018)

The reigning confusion between the competing roles of the Kurdish Movement and the Autonomous Administration in 2016 had a negative impact on the practice of autonomous organization. Due to the previous of experience of the Kurdish freedom movement, the "failure of the local development initiative" was laid bare, which made clear the need for wide-ranging restructuring. As a result, a 21-person Social Economy Coordination body was soon established:

Many economic committees, organizations and institutions have been established. However, they are independent of each other, and are scattered and fragmented. Therefore, a complete economic system does not yet to emerge. A coordination body must be established in order to overcome this deficiency. On this basis, coordination is established between the mixed (general) economic committee, the autonomous women's economic committee, the agriculture committee, the economic council (*Destaye aborî*), the agriculture council, the ecology and municipalities committee, the municipalities council (*Destaye şeradariyen*), the *Temwin* (oversight) commission—which oversees basic necessities— and the all coordination body of the co-construction of autonomy.

All organizations and tasks related to the social economy are thus connected through this body. The overall approach, measures and programs have to be settled at this level. However, the coordination body cannot make decisions in all economic matters but it does set its own agenda. General decisions are settled in cantonal assemblies, in the assembly and economy departments, and at conferences. The coordination body performs, controls and coordinates the decisions taken by the assembly. It works at a cantonal as well as at an inter-cantonal level. (ANF-Firat News Agency, 2015)

At the Economic Conference, a number of decisions were taken to streamline the economic sector so that its activities could be carried out in a more coordinated and organized manner. Many of the practices already successfully implemented were settled here and later applied as an autonomous policy endorsed by the autonomous assemblies of Rojava. The conference emphasized that an economic model has yet to be implemented in Rojava, and identified women, peasants, herders and small-scale merchants as the economy's main actors. Another noteworthy decision taken at the conference was the acknowledgement that the women's and general economies must be organized in harmony. At times, the women's economy that I was witness to in Bakur and Rojava and the general economy were at loggerheads. The women's economy, in particular, has not been able to benefit equally from the use of common resources. This is due to the fact that the women's movement defines the communal economy as a "moneyless" economy and does not allocate special resources for the organization of the Women's Economy Committee (*aborîya jin*). The *aborîya jin* (affiliated with Kongra-Star in Rojava) receives no budget and no support, except for land and basic needs like gasoline, electricity and water. On the other hand, the Autonomous Administration allocates a budget to the general economy, which is used for the organization of the social economy.

To compensate, the Social Economy Coordination body—which I interviewed in early 2018—as an assembly of the general economy, the women's economy and the Economic Council, decided on and harmonized their policies. While the Economic Council took over the management of the economy at the Autonomous Administration and regional levels, the General Economy Committee and Women's Economy Committee organized the social economy in coordination with communes and assemblies, so as to use existing social resources to serve peoples' collective needs.

The economy is composed of three sectors: agriculture and livestock (*çandinî û sewaldarî*), market and trade (*bazar û tîcaret*) and industry (*pîşesazî*). The social economy approach aims to create cooperatives (*kooperatîf*) in all three sectors, since cooperatives are considered the basic organizational mechanism. Cooperatives and economy academies, which provide training on cooperatives and economics, stand out as two important tools for the socialization of the economy.

Agriculture and land

The most distinctive feature of Rojava's geography, unique to this part of Kurdistan, is its vast open fields. For Kurds growing up hearing stories centered around the mountains it is surprising to see Rojava's seemingly-endless steppes. The only mountainous area in Rojava is the Afrin region. Cezîre and Kobanê, on the other hand, are home to some of the most fertile lands in the Mesopotamia region, flanked by the Euphrates and Xabour rivers. The main economic activity in the region is agriculture. In Rojava and northern Syria, where industrial production was never developed, trade was carried out as "border trade" until the civil war. According to my interviewees, the Syrian state forbade all private industrial activities in these regions. The few existing factories were state-owned and engaged in agricultural processing, including the Hesekê weaving factory, which employed 1,500 workers. The Syrian state concentrated its industrial production mainly in Deir-Ezzor and Damascus. Rojava's Kurds interpret this to mean that "the state had sentenced the Kurds to a life of perpetual peasantry." Although there are no factories in the region, wheat production is fully industrialized. One of the most important factors that contributed to this state of affairs was the Ba'ath regime's land and agriculture policy.

> Following the Ba'ath regime's seizure of power in 1963, the new administration distributed a lot of land to groups of recently-settled semi-nomadic farmers, who began to grow grain and cotton. As part of the Xabour project, dams and canals were built to irrigate 16,000 square kilometers of crops, which would end up forming "Syria's breadbasket." Adding to the continuous expansion of cultivated land across the steppe, the area's population grew as well, both of which increased water scarcity in the area. (Ayboğa, Flach and Knapp, 2018, p. 24)

Therefore, during the Ba'ath regime's process of nation-state formation, Syria was integrated into the capitalist system. Nonetheless, a large sector of the economy, outside of trade, remained beyond the reach of private capital and firmly in the hands of the Syrian state. The state organized the agriculture and industry sector, as it was the country's largest capitalist and landowner, and dominated Syria's economy.

During the regime's rule, no one could carry out agricultural activities for their own benefit; all agriculture was carried out for the benefit of the state. For example, if someone owned 100 hectares of land, the state told them that 50% of it was reserved for wheat production, 25% for cotton, and that the remaining land would be horticulture. The State would tell you that you could not sell to anyone else. "You will plant all of it for me, and I will take it all." Some years, 100 tons of wheat would be needed, so the state forced people to grow wheat in order to extract those 100 tons from the Cezîre region. We were not allowed to plant anything but wheat, cotton and barley. Landowner or not, all worked for the benefit of the state. Moreover, the state was buying up everything that was produced, but it also determined the price. For example, the last price of wheat before the revolution was 11 *varaka* (Syrian pounds), as far as I remember, and now the Autonomous Administration pays 137 pounds. The price has increased due to the war, but the Autonomous Administration pays a fair price. The state gave us barely enough to feed ourselves. (Interview with Ciwan, Co-spokesperson of the Dirbesiye Agriculture Administration, 2018)

Fehim Taştekin—following in the footsteps of Brazilian academic Paulo Gabriel Hilu Pinto, who previously conducted fieldwork in Syria—argues that the decrease in income from agricultural production, due to an increase in severe drought, and the subsequent increase in unemployment, were the main catalysts for the outbreak of the Syrian civil war. Additionally, Taştekin points out that the spending habits of the elite and the levels of luxury created by the state's neoliberal policies caused the greater exploitation of rural areas, in particular when Bashar Assad took power (Taştekin, 2015, p. 57).

The civil war was not as widespread in Damascus, where the political elites and wealthy families lived, as it was in rural areas. The transfer of social wealth from rural areas to these regions during the Ba'ath regime was what kept Bashar Assad in power.

According to Ciwan, Co-spokesperson of the Directorate of Agriculture in Dirbesiye province, the Ba'ath regime provided seeds, fertilizer and diesel to ensure production; it drilled water wells and sent agricultural engineers to fight diseases (interview with Ciwan, 2018). The lands were exploited through various contractual relationships; peasants became the tillers of state land. Producers had no say in either the production process or the allocation of the product. The state was the seed distributor and, also, the sole buyer. The purchase price was determined before harvest time; the wheat was transported to silos throughout Syria. After oil, wheat production in the Cezîre region and cotton production in the Raqqa and Tabqa areas were the Syrian state's most profitable economic activities. This dynamic was made possible by the Ba'ath regime's land tenure system.

The political regime of land tenure in Syria

In Syria, land tenure essentially takes two forms: private property and state property. It is estimated that privately-held land accounts for roughly 20% of all existing land and is concentrated in the regions of Damascus, Aleppo, Hama and Deir ez-Zor (Batatu, 1999, pp. 29-37). The existing state-owned land dates back to the 1970 coup d'etat by the elder Assad. The regime then passed an expropriation law under the guise of land redistribution (Decree Law No. 88), expropriating 1.4 million hectares of land until 1975. However, only a fraction of it was ever redistributed (http://www.country-data.com/cgi-bin/query/r-13526.html). Thus, Gamal Abdul Nasser's land reforms implemented during the short-lived United Arab Republic (UAR, 1958-1961) notwithstanding, the lands nominally earmarked for landless peasants in fact remained in the hands of the state, which became the country's largest landowner. This was the outcome of the so-called "statist socialist approach," which the Ba'ath regime proclaimed during that period. The state expanded its application of intifa (usufruct), giving peasants the right to use state land only by renting it, thereby assuring that they would never be able to accrue enough savings to break free of this system. The sale of all agricultural production to the state, at a price determined by the state itself, became mandatory. Ahmed, who worked in the Agriculture Directorate before the revolution and was the Co-spokesperson of AANES' Agriculture Directorate at the time of our interview, believes it is necessary to carry out agrarian reform in northern Syria. This has yet to be achieved and, thus, the old system persists:

> There are the following types of land tenure here: there are the *milla*, that is, privately-held lands. There are [also] types of lands that we call *intifa*. These are state lands, but the right-to-use has been handed to the public for a determined period of time. Purchases and sales of this type of land are prohibited. There are also *curmuse*, which are state lands where the right-to-use has been granted indefinitely. Finally, there are the *makmurî*. These lands are those formerly owned by Kurds, which were settled by Arabs sent up from Raqqa for political reasons, in order to erect the "Arab Belt." We did not carry out any changes, we continued with the same system. This is why many lands in the Cezîre region remain under state control. (Interview with Ahmed, Co-spokesperson of the AANES' Agricultural Directorate, 2018)

According to Ahmed, the lands "gifted" to high-ranking army personnel in exchange for their service are particularly significant in Rojava (interview with Ahmed, 2018). The soldiers who were not able to farm them rented them out to locals. This prevented the development of regional land tenure and any mean-ingful link between the tillers and the lands they worked on. When the Ba'ath regime's power waned with the onset of war, the land that was abandoned by soldiers and the state began to be sold through verbal agreements (*axta berranî*). The only decision taken by the Autonomous Administration regarding these lands in the areas under its influence was to ban their sale. In cases where illegal sales of land without the knowledge of the Autonomous Administration had occurred, the buyers were granted usage rights for a number of years in order to prevent their further victimization (interview with Mizgin, a member of the Land Committee [*Axarî*], 2018).

In agricultural societies, land tenure is one of the areas where social and class conflict is most visible. This makes it a sphere of life in which a revolution claiming to be harbinger of social transformation must intervene most urgently. It is imperative that there be the promise of a land tenure reform that intervenes in what appears to be an ethnic conflict between the peoples of Rojava reorganized by the democratic nation system, but in reality exists as a class contradiction in the social economy.In fact, as part of Rojava's revolutionary process, a series of discus-sions raised the issue of land ownership, with an eye to transforming the capitalist class and existing social relations. One of the main objectives of the Autonomous Administration is to re-evaluate the issue of property, especially that of land. A possible way out would be the communalization of agricultural lands in Rojava.

It is important to take a moment to discuss the idea of private land commu-nalization within the Kurdish Movement. As previously mentioned, Öcalan sees the tension between society and the state as the main social contradiction, while class struggle is only a secondary battleground (Öcalan, 2012, p. 59). Even though the Kurdish Movement does not see society as homogeneous, it nevertheless considers that social differences only lead to artificial conflicts. Öcalan thinks that these conflicts are a product of the state or other monopolistic forces (Öcalan, 2011, p. 250). According to the Kurdish Movement, if a society is plagued by internal strife, it ought to resolve it on the basis of solidarity and not through open conflict. Existing conflicts are artificial; should the powers that created them disappear, solidarity and cooperation will once again prevail. In summary, capital domination created class conflict and, when individuals come to realize this, they will abandon capital.

The Autonomous Administration has no plans to change existing inequali-ties in land tenure through any apparatus based on power because it did not adopt or establish rule through power. On the contrary, the negation of power in polit-ical and social terms allows the AANES to move towards an organization based on the communalization of the land, which will be able to sustain society as it faces capitalist forces. Such a configuration is entirely without transformative or abusive power. Rather, society will possess a moral-political structure, since it will organize itself. Those who own property will renounce it. Property will lose all meaning, because, as state and monopolistic forces disappear, society will return to a communalist way of life. According to Öcalan, communalism is the basis of socialist life (Öcalan, 2012, pp. 56-58). The main role of the Kurdish Movement in this process is to negotiate, on a revolutionary basis, with the capital that possesses the means of production, in order to direct the reorganization of society.

In this idealization, the phenomenon referred to as "society" is highly romanticized. Since the Kurdish Movement appears to have the support of all sectors of society today, it imagines that this support will be unwavering, even under changing material conditions. In this regard, it should be noted that Kurdish capitalists of Bakur actively participated in the Democratic Economy Conference in Wan (Bakur) and pledged to provide unlimited support to the Kurdish Movement for the organization of the democratic economy. In fact, in the process of implementing the decisions of the conference as it drew to a close, negotiations began with the owners of capital and land, who were referred to as "patriots".

I remember a meeting on regarding the establishment of an agricultural commune and a cooperative with the owner of a vast estate, who employed thousands of workers, in a district of Amed (Diyarbakir), Bakur. The Economy Committee requested part of his land so that 17 families could cultivate it and ensure their own livelihoods. The owner requested 40% of the cooperative's future income in exchange. The Committee then explained to him how the cooperative would work and the community organization they intended to develop. When the landowner realized that he would not be making a profit, the "revolutionary negotiations" hardened. At the end of this conversation, which was characterized by patriotic agitation, the landowner willingly handed over part of his land to the commune in exchange for just 10% of its income.

Many similar meetings were held at this time with factory owners, merchants and the construction industry. Many of these negotiations were fruitful in further developing the cooperative system. Some meetings lasted hours, others were conducted over the phone in mere minutes. Some negotiations also failed; the only consequence for these owners, however, was that their patriotism (welatparezî) came into question. The Kurdish Movement, with a long history of organizing people, actually negotiated with each of these individuals, one by one. This approach sets its revolutionary practice apart from that of other movements: even though it is an organized movement, backed by armed, political and social power, it did not use violence or any other type of coercion in the negotiation process. Instead, organizational power was employed in order to persuade and to create a revolutionary will.

This same process has taken a different shape in Rojava. First and foremost, it is no longer a pilot project, as was the case in Bakur. In a society-wide transformation like the one occurring in Rojava, communalization cannot keep up with the pace of transformation. On the other hand, there is no such thing as an industrial-capitalist class in the region, and large landowners tend to be Arab families. Although these Arab families are actors in the struggle for autonomy by their participations in the self-goverment, assemblies and communes, they are far removed from the idea of communalization as a political project, because, as I have previously stated, the Kurdish Movement associates the communalization of land and wealth with "patriotic" sentiments. That makes it appear as if only Kurds are convinced by the drive towards communalization. And, in fact, political cadres conduct negotiations exclusively with Kurdish "patriots." One can argue that the process the Kurdish Movement is carrying out under the name of "revolutionary negotiations" really only exists for Kurds.

In this sense, unless property interferes with policies such as agrarian reforms, in what Öcalan refers to as the "transitional" phase, different forms of property can coexist and become permanent if this offers the greatest benefit for society. After coming to this realization, following years of accumulated experience, the Agricultural Committee is trying to ensure the unity of peasants and tillers of the land, combining the social power of the smallholders and the landless in order to oppose large landowners. It is naive to believe that someone who owns thousands of hectares of land and has the potential to accumulate a certain amount of wealth every year will have the same willingness to communalize as a subsistence farmer working on that same landowner's land. Acting on such an assumption would be based entirely on ideology and dogmatism.

In short, the issue of agriculture and land, the main arena of economic life, shows the centrality of class struggle, which the movement sees as a lesser issue in the debates surrounding the construction of democratic confederalism in Rojava.

The implementation of agrarian reforms, for example, show that autonomy is no only a political decision, but also carries with it a social transformation. This transformation is directly proportional to the political potential of autonomy and can further strengthen it. The power of autonomy created by collective decision by popular self-determinations assemblies becomes a force that can create alternative relationships in the field of economics, where one finds the most fundamental relationships of life. Both Ahmed and Mizgin point out that the Autonomous

Administration meant to carry out land reform, as it wanted to solve the issue of the makmurî, but that it was considered socially dangerous to do so:

> We are doing what we can with our current knowledge; we try not to be too conservative or too radical. As I said, it is not possible to carry out something radical without first gaining political status. We are still politically weak, we still have very serious social weaknesses. If we rise up today and carry out a very radical decision, it will create a very serious problem for us. People are turning their backs on us. Therefore, we cannot take a radical step. We say that we have time, that there will be a more suitable moment. For instance, we wanted to tally all agricultural land, but there was an immediate reaction from people: "What are you doing? Why?" The fear spread immediately, so we had to stop. We saw the risk of a renewed revolt. (Interview with Mizgin, 2018)

Makmurî, as explained before, is a term used to identify those Arabs who were brought up from Raqqa and settled on land confiscated from Kurds in order to create an "Arab Belt," and dispossess the local Kurdish population. These lands, confiscated by the state, were not given to the Arabs who settled them. Rather, the *makmurî* became laborers who farmed the state's land for the state.

Many Kurds hoped that, in a reversal of such practices, the revolution would give them back their land and the *makmurî* would be returned to Raqqa. The Autonomous Administration considers such an action unfeasible and that expropriation and redistribution of these lands are not in line with its own autonomous perspectives. Although the Autonomous Administration considers the *makmurî* a "problem" in need of solving, it does not consider expelling them from the lands they have inhabited for nearly 50 years to be a solution. Mizgin affirms that this would mean repeating the state's policies, acting in the same way as the state:

> When the revolution happened, the complex history of these lands turned out to be a very serious problem for us. How did it turn out to be a problem? For example, many former landowners, that is, people whose lands were seized by the state, came to say "we want our lands back." But others came and said "this land has been ours for 40-50 years. How can they kick us off our land?" The main discussion surrounds the fate of the *makmurî*. A political decision on the *makmurî* is required. For example, when the revolution started, many Kurdish reformist parties came to us and said: "Why don't you tell the *makmurî* to leave these lands anymore?" They said that they should leave Rojava. We said that

this would not be a solution, I mean, how can this be the solution? These people have been living here for 40 years, how can we tell them to leave this place? There must be another solution. For example, once the Arab lands of Raqqa, of Deir ez-Zor, are liberated, they can leave voluntarily. But if they don't want to, they should stay. This can be the only proposal for a solution. We cannot confiscate people's lands in the same way that the state did at that time. We say that we can solve this politically and look for alternative solutions, but we cannot do the same thing the state did. We do not think this is good. (Interview with Mizgin, 2018)

A different solution could be that the makmurî, through cooperatives, could make use of the lands previously held by the state, and now in the hands of the Autonomous Administration.

Communal lands

One of the greatest concrete achievements of the transformation towards autonomy that spread from Rojava to all of northern Syria in 2012 was the loss of control by the Syrian Ba'ath regime over lands they held in the region, and the fact that these lands remained in effect "ownerless." There is an estimated 500,000 hectares of arable land in Rojava and 1 million hectares in northern Syria (interview with Şiyar, 2019). All of it is agricultural land. However, it should be noted that not all of these lands were previously owned by the state. During the war, large landowners and families who had joined ISIS's armed wing lost their property rights in the eyes of the autonomous movement. Although the Autonomous Administration does not refer to it in these terms, the lands of individuals and families who joined ISIS were confiscated because these people had committed crimes against society:

> When the revolution began, many people fled to Turkey with their families; some of them were jihadist terrorists. Some returned. We established the land registration committee in order to clarify the situation of those who were deemed terrorists. Our goal is not to confiscate anyone's land. If they did not join any terrorist group, for example al-Nusra or groups like ISIS, and if there is proof of that, we hand them back their land. We have a committee called the Axarî Committee in Qamishlo, including representatives of the Asayish, YPG, the municipalities and individuals from the field of agriculture. They investigate whether these people joined terrorist outfits or whether they committed any other crime. If the representatives of all the sectors give a positive review about

a person, the Axarî Committee will decide to return the land to them. At this point, we are preparing a new registry of lands confiscated by the state in order to return land to them. (Interview with Ciwan, 2018)

The classical conception of revolution under the Leninist canon holds that private ownership of the means of production, especially land, will disappear and the tools of production will be handed to the proletariat, thereby socializing private property. However, "in the practical experience of the Soviet Union and other 'communist' countries, this had little effect in transforming the doing itself or in holding the doers themselves accountable for it" (Holloway, 2011, p. 280). In practice, it became socialist state property; later on, Tony Cliff would term this "state capitalism" (Cliff, 1990). Since "the Soviet Union adopted the 'capitalist heavy industry definition of economic modernization,' socialism was trapped in a very specific model of capitalist economic development" (Dean, 2014, p. 21).

Many Marxists believe that, in practice, the existence of state property is a necessary stage towards the establishment of social property. For example, one of Turkey's Marxists-Trotskyists, Sungur Savran (2011), defines state socialist ownership as the most primitive form of social ownership and deems its existence necessary. In other words, the means of production seized by the revolutionary power are expected to be handed over to the socialist power. Private property becomes public property rather than social property. However, the most crucial cause of the collapse of real existing socialism was that property changed hands in favor of the state and then in favor of the capitalist classes, but never in favor of society. I believe that a new revolutionary process should take possession of property applying a novel and different perspective. Taking over the state is no longer seen as an option on the path to revolution and social transformation. Nor does the new revolutionary organization based on autonomy and self-determination see it that way.

Haydar, one of TEV-DEM's co-spokesperson and the person responsible for the economy at the time of the interview, mentioned that many socialists do not see the transformations that took place in Rojava as a socialist revolution, since neither power nor property had meaningfully changed:

Look, Azê: in all the revolutions in history two things have always changed: those who hold power and those who own property. None of that happened in Rojava. So, are we the power or the state? Neither! Did we take anyone's property? Nope! So, are we revolutionaries? Of course we are revolutionaries! Is the system we organize a socialist system? Of course it is socialist! (Interview with Haydar, Co-spokesperson of the Economy Committee for TEV-DEM, 2018)

In the words of Jodi Dean, a "communism of the present" was created in Rojava (Dean, 2014). In Rojava, as for all means of production, the answer to the question "Whose land is it?" determines the scope and limitations of the social transformation that the "communism of the present" can effect. In the Rojava Revolution, the answer to this question is ideologically unambiguous: the land belongs to the people. However, in the Kurdish struggle, this maxim does not translate into the transfer/distribution of land to the people themselves, because, according to the Kurdish Movement, giving land to landless peasants reproduces patterns of land ownership. Instead, the goal of the movement is to render property meaningless and useless by collectivizing and communalizing land.

Considering that even "common/collective property," a concept frequently used by left-wing activists and academic circles, refers to a form of ownership, the transformation of social relations, established around community-based means of production, becomes central to the autonomy of Rojava. One can thus say that the means of production have become a commons on the basis of communal relations—that is, they belong to everyone and no one simultaneously—emphasizing the fact that everyone has the right to use them, but no one has the right to own them. Here, a reference is made to the position of social wealth in natural society. However, it is not an implicit natural society, but one that constructs its own social ecology. According to Öcalan, natural society is a spontaneous form of ecological society. In this sense, I believe that the end of capitalism will not come about spontaneously; an ecological society can only be built through conscious activism. It is the coming together and the functioning of society on the basis of community relations that will render property meaningless. In the Kurdish Movement's understanding of struggle and the revolution, it is futile to confiscate private property in favor of the state or other individuals:

> The democratic-communitarian economy rejects both extremely individualistic, antisocial and anti-nature property, as well as state property under the name of collective or public property. Because in both forms, social values are confiscated under the name of property, and the control of society over the confiscated values and means of production is eliminated. For these reasons, it is not property but the right to social use that should be its base. (Abdullah Öcalan Sosyal Bilimler Akademisi, 2012, p. 89)

Ownership of property and the means of production, it is claimed, will lose its meaning in the eyes of society, which will instead base itself on the rights to use, produce and share communally. This is not a process that will come about overnight. To persuade the owners of capital, so that society may abandon its sense of property, is one of the objectives of the revolutionary process.

As Caffentzis and Federici write, history shows that the main principle under which humanity has organized itself for thousands of years is that of "commoning" (Caffentzis and Federici, 2014, p. i93). Therefore, it is far from impossible to think that non-capitalist social relations will become the basis of society. However, radical revolutionary practices are necessary to activate this process. Öcalan does not see this as a homogeneous process either; different forms of ownership can coexist during long periods of time:

> In the economic units of democratic modernity, property loses its impor-tance and remains only a secondary concern. Property, of course, will still belong to the organized communities. Neither family-held nor state property can provide an answer to the modern economy. State and family ownership of the hierarchical era cannot survive capitalist modernity. Even companies are increasingly entering joint-ownership agreements with employees due to economic factors. Nonetheless, we should not draw hard lines separating these rights to property. Just as both systems of civilization live together, these property systems will maintain an interconnected coex-istence for some time to come. Just as family property will continue to exist within community property, the existence of the state and its property will continue to influence it. The important thing is to be open to flexible property rules that could be the solution to problems of the environment, productivity and unemployment. (Öcalan, 2009, p. 252)

Beyond the idea of ancient communion, it is the communes, popular assemblies, cooperatives and academies built as a social organizational structure of demo-cratic autonomy and confederalism that will create a communal society, not the ideology of the nation-state. In Chapter 3, we saw that this is not just a prediction; these structures are already reconstructing the social fabric in Rojava.

An autonomous policy and practice in Rojava are the organization of cooper-atives based on communal lands as the fundamental form of organization, through which communalization can then be carried out. Cooperation and communal production on peasants' lands is the core of the proposed social economy, but no progress has been made in this regard. According to Melsa, Co-spokesperson of Rojava Cooperatives, people either do not know or have a negative view of cooperatives. This is a direct consequence of their experience with the coopera-tives established during the Ba'ath regime. "We started building cooperatives with the lands the regime left behind in order to break this perception and introduce the people to cooperatives." (Interview with Melsa, Co-spokesperson of Rojava Cooperatives Committee, 2018)

To this end, the Agriculture Committee asked the people to cultivate their land in accordance with their possibilities, in order to establish economies based on collective agriculture. They announced to the public their intention of organizing cooperative structures in the territories controlled by the Autonomous Administration:

Dear peoples!

We are organizing cooperatives on the communal lands of the Autonomous Administration.

Our country is still in the midst of a long war and the embargo continues. Our economy was marked by looting and colonial practices. Poverty is widespread in our country. Our struggle against poverty and hunger, as the Economy and Agriculture Committee, is constant and organized. In our opinion, the solution is to erect a social economy system and become self-sufficient. This struggle requires immense work, agreement and coordination. We are working on it. However, due to the grave problems we face, we urgently need to find solutions and mobilize all of our options. On this basis, we will organize agricultural and livestock cooperatives on the lands we control. Of course, these lands are only a small part of the agricultural lands in Rojava and northern Syria, so there will not be enough to cover all of the poor. Even so, we want to distribute these lands to the communes and agricultural cooperatives in the fairest and most precise way possible.

At this point, we need to focus on those people who are very poor and in need of support. Although we cannot include all the poor at once, our overall objective is to include all these people step by step within the agricultural cooperatives. We will not include in the cooperatives those who can earn a living by their own means. For this reason, many people may be left out; we want our peoples to understand this reality. We hope everyone will participate in everything approved and promised in the Contract on Cooperatives. All the work of the cooperative will be carried out by the members of the cooperative. Everyone who forms part of a cooperative must participate in its work under the cooperative's program.

This is basically our announcement: let's grow our crops together, let's communalize and turn our land and crops into cooperatives; let's build our economy and our country, and live off of our work. (Agriculture Committee–*Komîta Çandinî-Sewaldarî*, 2017)

At the Rojava Cooperative Conference, in the fall of 2017, discussions were held on the Qesrik project, which includes 57 agricultural cooperatives on 370,856 hectares of land located in the Cezîre region, as well as different cooperatives in Dirbesiye province. At the same time, the Autonomous Administration assigned land to seed and fertilizer development centers within the Agricultural Directorate to be worked on.

Later we will see how cooperatives work and if they really have an effect on the communalization and the dysfunctionalition of property. The aim of the Agriculture Committee is to bring about a profound agricultural transformation in Rojava. To this end, unlike the way industrialized agricultural production operates, it is trying to increase the variety of products. Thus, production has started on chickpeas, lentils, and beans—none of which was previously cultivated—occupying 25% of the cooperatives' agricultural land; with cotton production on another 10% and vegetables on 5% (Internationalist Commune of Rojava, 2018, p. 72). The recommendation to communes also includes creating gardens and planting edible herbs. To diversify crops, seminars are held for farmers. In addition, the agriculture committee provides farmers with basic materials, such as diesel fuel, fertilizers and irrigation. This drive towards diversification was further aided by the planting of several hundreds of thousands of fruit-bearing trees.

Tree planting has two objectives. First of all, we want to diversify our produce; secondly, it helps the ecology and soil regeneration. A proverb says that "if you want a product for a year, grow wheat, if you want a product for 10 years, plant a tree. But if you want a product for 100 years, cultivate a person." The Ba'ath regime only allowed cultivation for one year. People grew wheat. The following year, so families would not starve, many young people were forced to work in factories. If there were a variety of products here, if there were trees, those young people would have been able to stay here, work on their own land and benefit their own communities. Having gotten rid of Ba'ath politics, we can revive the love and loyalty between a people and their land. (Interview with Khalaf, 2018)

Tree planting in Rojava is a collective effort that usually incites great participation and enthusiasm. Under Ba'ath rule, planting trees, even in private gardens,
was forbidden. Now, with each new tree planted in northern Syria, the people
develop a stronger bond with the land and nature.[9] (Interview with Hevre,
Cerûdiye commune, 2019)

Strengthening this link is essential to further developing ecological farming.
The example of Rojava shows how ecological problems are intertwined with
centralization, the capitalist economy, and the exploitation of both nature and
people (Internationalist Commune of Rojava, 2018, p. 90). In addition to the
ecological destruction caused by war, the unchecked digging of irrigation wells
and the construction of houses on agricultural land—both a result of the power
vacuum created during the revolution—are among the main problems facing
the Agriculture Committee. This causes serious ecological devastation, which is
why the Agriculture Committee established a Committee for Land Protection
(*Comite Axarî*) as part of its efforts to protect the local ecology. Furthermore, in
order to ensure agricultural and water resources for future generations, digging
wells and building new homes on agricultural land has been prohibited.

In the first years of the revolution, there were no seeds to start agricultural
activities. As Hevrîn points out:

> When the state disappeared, there was no one to hand out seeds. We went
> around, village by village, looking for seeds. We established a seed devel-
> opment center, asking for the seeds people were keeping secretly, because
> we are trying to collect local natural seeds in order to try and break the
> dependency on outside suppliers, which is the main objective of our
> investigates about the local economy. (Interview with Khalaf, 2018)

Despite these efforts, it is very difficult to break established agricultural habits in
Rojava. Many people do not want to diversify their crops because it is labor-inten-
sive. In particular in the Cezîre region, local Kurds are reluctant to stop cultivating
wheat, which does not require much work, and experiment with new plants. The
commitment to industrialized agriculture is not only established on a material
level, but also on a mental and emotional level. According to Hevrîn, "in order
for this barrier to be demolished, people must eat the cucumbers they themselves
produce. Then they will realize that nothing tastes sweeter than that which their
own hands have made" (interview with Khalaf, 2018).

---

9 Hevre, from the Cerûdiye commune—one of a handful of fully-communalized villages, which I visited in the winter of
   2019—stated that "as the people of Rojava lose their children, they plant trees; thus, these lands become more their own."

Industrial organization and factories without bosses

Are ecological industries possible in the Middle East?

It is key to keep in mind that the Kurdish struggle does not identify industry for industrialism. In my analysis of the ideas behind the communal-democratic economy, I mentioned its rejection of industrialism, seen as an ideology of the nation-state, yet its acceptance of industrial production on the condition that it satisfies social needs.

From this perspective, the Industry Committee, founded under the Economy Committee in order to organize local industry, is one of the committees with the most complex agenda. An issue frequently raised during my formal and informal meetings with this committee was the fact that the regime did not develop Rojava's industry, and instead kept the area undeveloped and agrarian. While the Agriculture Committee viewed this positively, the Industry Committee emphasized that the development of agricultural industry was vital for Rojava.

> We were all convinced during our economy workshop: It was not a bad policy that the regime had protected the territory, the agricultural land. What was detrimental was the theft of the goods that had been produced on this land. In other words, they took the products to other, Arab cities, within Syria, to process them, and then put them back on the market in Rojava at 10 times the cost. Our industrial policy needs to start there. Even as seen through the lens of the war economy, it is absolutely wrong-headed not to tackle this problem. The people are bound to the centralized food policy. We need to prevent the overpriced sale of products on the market, and to prevent living a dignified life from becoming too costly. We need to do the following: store wheat and barley. The regime stored enough wheat and barley to face a decade of war. We have to do the same. However, when considering this prospect within the framework of the war economy, some items are needed to process these products before they can reach someone's dinner table. [...]

> Our aim is to improve agriculture-based industry and thus reduce dependence on state centralism. For example, we must be able to turn wheat into savar (crushed wheat grain; a staple in Rojava, like corn or rice) and lentil seeds into lentils fit for consumption. We also need to be able to produce sugar. For example, the fact we were not able to produce sugar, whose price skyrocketed on the black market when an embargo was imposed on our region, caused a crisis that showed us the true face of

war, because sugar is one of the basic staples of the people. (Interview
with Asmîn, member of the Industry Committee, 2018)

Asmîn explains that several attempts were made to build an indigenous agricultural industry, but they were unable to successfully encourage the public to
develop this economic area given the uncertain political situation at that time.
Only the public had the necessary capital to develop and maintain this initiative,
as mentioned by Asmîn:

> Now we are in the midst of war. There are not many people who want
> to invest and bring their capital here during war. Although some such
> interest exists, they will likely wait until our political status is settled.
> There are some who want to come to Rojava and invest, but they say: we
> want security guarantees, if industry and businesses put up their capital,
> tomorrow or the day after they will want security; the capital must also
> be guaranteed. What if they bomb the factory? We must be able to assure
> people that this is not going to happen. (Interview with Asmîn, 2018)

As has become apparent, private capital is seen as a viable avenue for the development of industry in Rojava. For her part, Hevrîn stated that the objective of the
Economic Council was not to end the private economy, but rather to reduce its
influence (interview with Khalaf, 2018). According to Asmîn, private capital was
crucial during the transition process, as there was no other way to improve the
industrial sector under the existing conditions.

> This is a principle-based approach, as I said before, but it can be expanded
> according to the situation and conditions, the needs and the transition
> process. We can define the current situation as a transition process,
> because setting up a large or small factory requires capital. A cooperative
> that develops in the agricultural sector does not require much start-up
> capital, but a cooperative in the industrial sector does. [...] Some of us
> have been discussing such issues again and again in meetings on the
> industrial sector. There are those who previously dealt with trade but
> now want to get involved in the industrial sector. When we talk about
> cooperatives, they say: "Surely we can be affiliated with the organization
> (the Party)." To them, this is synonymous with a guarantee. That is, that
> with the movement their capital will be in safe hands and will not be
> affected. But when we tell them "Let's involve other people in these coop-
> eratives," they tell us: "I'm already earning enough as it is; I don't want
> to take risks." Whoever says something like that must be rich. In other

words, they do not lack money, what they want is to increase their capital. However, we want to develop our industry in accordance with the needs of society. The poor lack capital; the Autonomous Administration does not have a very developed industry. Only the rich have the ability to change that.

Our goal is not to make the rich richer, but to improve the economic situation of the poor. The profit belongs to them and to their work, and should not be exposed to a merchant's exploitation. As we try to resolve the poor's lack of capital, our ideological approach—that is, our understanding of not making the rich richer—brings with it certain tensions. We want to respond to the needs of society, but we are without solutions because of this ideological understandin. I will be clear: if we hadn't approached it ideologically, we would go and call up the rich, "Come here, we need this; come do this." There are many rich Kurds who would be eager to help. Sometimes, we had to do this to strengthen the basis of the war economy. But this also leads to an impasse in developing a seamless industry that includes everyone. There is an ideological perspective, of course, but the current situation does not match our perspective, nor does it come close. We live in a state of ambivalence Sometimes, out of necessity, we act as if we don't have this perspective that we defend, we try to find daily solutions, we take decisions that are not in accord with our political ideology. Otherwise, we experience a situation of insolvency and stuckness. This is the situation we find ourselves in, we are aware of this. (Interview with Asmîn, 2018)

In the real world, one would never act according to the ideological perspective mentioned by Asmîn. The fact that the decisions made based on daily needs contradict this overall perspective is one of the most contested aspects of the revolutionary process. For me, being aware of this and maintaining the will to develop people's autonomous power is the mark of a truly revolutionary process.

The development of an ecological industry or an anti-capitalist economy for a social revolution is not only about what Asmîn calls the "'deadlock'" caused by the society's lack of resources (capital). Many other factors reinforce this situation in Rojava. One of them is that the Cezîre region sits on vast oil reserves, and that today oil is the only source of financing for the revolutionary process. The head of the Trade Committee has tried to take into account the principles of an ecological economy, even considering that oil is not only an economic tool, but also a political tool, and understanding that it has opened many a door for them. But, as Zafer explain, sometimes, they cannot do nothing to counteract the existing conditions:

> We are a society that is living through war; we have no other income but that from oil. Without oil, we can't pay wages, we can't keep up the costs of the YPG, we can't buy weapons. We cannot give it up simply because it is not ecological; the main issue here is that of life. However, the proliferation of oil technology and its damage to the soil is a situation that the comrades of the Industry Committee analyze and try to prevent. That is why, for example, they reject those who want to establish petroleum-based industries. Like the tire industry, for example. We try to organize oil in accordance only with satisfying our vital needs and our defense needs. Is this a 100% ecological measure or not? Of course, that is a separate discussion. To be honest, it is a luxury to discuss such things under these circumstances. (Interview with Zafer, responsible for the Trade Committee, 2018)

Zafer was responsible for trade and the sale of oil fell under his purview at the time we met. He pointed out that, numerous times before, the embargo on Rojava had been dismantled and the other side forced to open their customs offices by wielding the weapon of oil (interview with Zafer, 2018). For her part, Asmîn says that, in this manner, as the Industry Committee, they were able to obtain the machines that allowed many factories to open. It should be noted that the oil extracted in Rojava represents a very small proportion of the existing reserves. This is the main reason why international actors (mainly the United States and Russia) perpetuate war in the region, seeking to ensure that these reserves are fully integrated into capitalist accumulation.

Another aspect that impedes general economic advancement in Rojava, especially in the industrial sector, is the lack of skilled, knowledgeable and experienced labor. Once agricultural production was industrialized and divorced from the peasant production process, the people were subjugated to the positions of client and consumer, both in rural areas and in the city. Capitalism and the state suppressed the autonomy and right to self-determination of the people. A major consequence of agricultural industrialization has been the newer generation's ignorance of the knowledge and expertise necessary for ecological agricultural production. Its effects are even more acute in the industrial sector. According to Asmîn, finding someone able to operate a textile factory abandoned by the regime proved near impossible. Previously, they were able to find former staff, though most have left the region because of the war. The factory thus remains inoperative (interview with Asmîn, 2018). This is one of the most devastating effects of war: those qualified and educated leave. Although there was no mass migration out of the region the first years of the revolution in Rojava, tens of thousands of young people were killed during the war.

Despite these negative aspects, one of Rojava's most notable experiences in industrial reorganization, though it would later lose its transformative potential, was what I call "factories without bosses" and the Economic Coordination body calls "company."

Rojava's factories without bosses

The factories without bosses, which are basically small manufacturing factories, were affiliated with the Industry Committee of the Economic Coordination body in 2018. The organization of the social economy had established these factories in order to solve the contradictions outlined by the Industry Committee and to meet social needs. For undisclosed reasons, in 2019, the factories were transferred to the Finance Council of the Autonomous Administration as part of a tendency towards centralization of the Federation's resources. This change, although it does not seem important, but it illustrates the tendencies of autonomy. According to the information I received in 2019, the factories continued to function as they did in 2018, since only their organizing committee had changed (unrecorded meeting with the Finance Council, 2019). Before addressing the consequences and greater tendencies resulting from this change, it is important to understand how and why these factories were established in 2018.

According to the spokesperson for the Tev-dem Economy Committee, the factories emerged in 2018 due to necessity (interview with Haydar, Co-spokesperson of Tev-dem's Economy Commitee, 2018). These productive factories (lentil processing and packaging plant, fertilizer production plant, potato chip factory, chickpea roasting and packaging factory, chicken factories, carpentry, electricity production plants, etc.) were established by the Economic Development Center of Rojava (NGARK)—*Navenda Geşkirina Aborîya Rojava*) during the initial years of the revolution. Their names are generally the same; some factories bear the name "Roj" and others "Miray." In 2018, when I interviewed the Industry Committee on behalf of the Economic Coordination body, the Committee outlined the following objectives for these factories:

One of our main goals for our companies (şirket) is not profit, but to get affordable goods to the market for people to buy. To provide the goods below market price in order to pull the market price down and make covering people's basic needs more affordable. In other words, our goal was to develop industry in accordance with society's needs. (Interview with Asmîn, member of the Industry Committee, 2018)

The main objective of these factories, which were established by decree of the Kurdish Movement, was to cover people's basic needs and to support their economies. They thus had a double function. As previously mentioned, the Syrian state used to buy up all of peasants' agricultural production and resell it to the local markets once processed. However, when the Syrian government withdrew from Rojava in the course of the war, farmers' agricultural produce found no buyers and remained in their hands, resulting in shortages of many manufactured goods in Rojava markets, as well as inflation due to rising prices. At this point, the NGARK, in the name of the newly-founded Autonomous Administration, established companies to process local agricultural products and turn them into finished products. The NGARK made urgent investments in some sectors in order to assume the role formerly played by the regime, while they considerably lowered prices for finished products on the local market. Moreover, the Kurdish Movement made use of products manufactured in these companies in order to meet the needs of the armed forces and those displaced by war.

Some factories were built from scratch, while others were refurbished former state-owned or private sectors abandoned during the war, or "recuperated factories." The term "recuperated factories" is used in Argentina to refer to factories occupied by their workers in the aftermath of the 2001 crisis, which then became cooperatives with varying degrees of self-management. The factories that were "recuperated" in Rojava already belonged to the workers; the origin of recuperated factories in Argentina is a different one. However, both agree on the principle that people should take what is theirs. In the case of Rojava, there was no need to occupy the factories. Nevertheless, the Kurdish Movement suggested that the workers self-manage these factories.

There are two reasons why I consider these Rojava companies/factories to be "factories without bosses," adopting the term "without boss" (sin patron) from the Argentine and Chilean experiences. One has to do with the nature of property: the property does not belong to anyone; it is not private property or public property, nor is it collective property. Although they are managed by the Economic Coordination body, there is no legal entity or institution that one could call their owner. Moreover, the property—both the means of production and place of production— does not belong to the workers. There is no one to call "boss" or "manager" to direct the workers. The management of the factory is carried out by the factory's workers' council—an expression of workers' self-management.

The second reason why I refer to such workspaces as "factories without bosses" is the practice of self-management, in a classical sense. In factories where everything is determined before work begins, that is, in factories formed on the basis of the division of labor, the workers' council is an afterthought. It is thus similar to socialist workers' councils (Anweiler, 1975): people first start to work, to become workers, then the workers' council can be formed. But in Rojava, the idea of forming a workers' council did not spring from the workers themselves. The council did not develop as a result of the class consciousness of the proletariat, but was formed by the cadres of the Kurdish Movement within the Economic Coordination body.

This practice was set in place in order to provide a "democratic" starting principle. Once such a factory's council has been formed with the participation of all workers, its task is to approve the factory's administration, which is comprised of two co-spokespersons, accountants and marketing. The council can reshuffle the administration at any point, be it through layoffs or by rotating workers' positions. However, it is important to underline that, the rotation that usually serves for role changes in a factory does not apply in these Rojava factories. The division of labor is permanent: the factory is arranged on the basis of the division between administration and workers. Nonetheless, the administration does not become the sole decision-making body, since the workers' council continues to be able to regulate it. The administration's task is to manage the operation, coordination and facilitation of different work in coordination with the Industry Committee (interview with Asmîn, 2018). The administration's responsibility for the internal operations of the factory, of sales, distribution, the purchase of raw materials, and more, are carried out in line with the plans of the Economic Coordination body.

The movement's political cadres I interviewed self-critically shared their concerns about how these factories had developed, as they were not in accordance with the ideas of the communal economy, since everyone saw them as the movement's companies. They were particularly concerned that the people would begin perceiving the movement as the state. In 2018, the Industry Committee (self-)criticized the haphazard way in which this model had been implemented, pointing out that these factories ran the risk of reproducing the *state capitalism*. Therefore, their new objective is to convert such factories into cooperatives and hand them over to the people as soon as possible.

> These companies, established at the beginning of the revolution, were formed around common needs. The people, without giving much thought to which institution or organization would be responsible, took

the initiative. For instance, there was no electricity, so people with good economic prospects bought generators, brought them here, and installed them. Later on, electricity communes were organized and their administrations established. They have often been described as cooperatives, but I do not think that we can say that they were created as cooperatives. In other words, the generators were taken to the towns and then turned into companies that produce and distribute electricity. They have changed their form numerous times. In the beginning, neighborhood assemblies were responsible for these companies; later they began disengaging them from civil society; and now they have been transferred entirely to the Industry Committee. Today, they act as companies under our supervision. One is in Amûdê and the other is here [in Qamishlo]. They are companies, yet they do not turn a profit in the capitalist sense. They are organized to serve society, producing according to collective needs. Each of the generators is located in a neighborhood. They provide amps of electricity to the people in these neighborhoods. People pay for the amps and the company obtains diesel with that money. Our goal is to reorganize them as cooperatives and hand them to the people. (Interview with Asmîn, 2018)

Asmîn, who frequently emphasized that the purpose of these factories is not profit but to meet people's needs, stated that attempts were made to turn these electricity plants into working cooperatives. However, since these factories operate not only without turning a profit, but at a loss, it has been impossible to make this change.

They have remained in our hands; in the state that they are in we cannot hand them over to the people, but also cannot halt production, as the people would suffer. The Autonomous Administration has to cover all expenses. We have diesel through our oil reserves, but we still need to exchange the broken generators and we don't know who will be able to exchange them and how they can continue working. (Interview with Asmîn, 2018)

As Asmîn mentioned, although the electricity plants produce social benefits, they do not produce any economic benefits. However, not all factories generate losses. In particular, the Miray wheat and barley factory, the Roj lentil factory and the Roj potato chip factory manage to generate substantial surpluses. Nevertheless, Şerhat indicated that, though they did not record any losses, they did not earn money either, as they support "the revolutionary war." In other words, they were producing surpluses in order to sustain the revolutionary struggle:

There are newly liberated areas, but there are also areas where war rages on. We send the wheat we buy in the Cezîre region to Raqqa and Manbij. There has been no production there for years. Again, we send a lot of food to our YPG/YPJ and the armed forces. That is how we support the revolutionary war. (Interview with Şerhat, member of the Economic Coordination body in Derik, 2018)

The purchase and sale price between autonomous organizations is based on the cost of production. In the factories I visited, the workers I met said that they were satisfied with their work and that no one ordered them around. The factory's administration set the quantity and type of products to be manufactured according to demands made by the communes and the workers' council decides how they are going to produce them, that is, their working conditions. A young woman I met at the Roj factory specified that she was happy because she had a paying job. When I indicated that she would stop receiving a salary if her factory were to organize itself as a cooperative and that they would instead share their earnings, she expressed her satisfaction with the fund system, since she did not know what a cooperative was. As I explained before, the Kurds, especially in Rojava, consider the fund system to be an important achievement of autonomy, since it provides a regular income—a novelty in this part of Syria. In fact, during meetings organized to promote the formation of cooperatives, many people said: "build a factory, not a cooperative—we want to have a fixed salary." Many consider the meaning of emancipation to be a fixed salary for fixed hours of work. However, the Kurdish Movement's economic perspective rejects capitalist work and remunerative labor, instead stating that the emancipation of society must be achieved without turning people into workers:

> Since the democratic-communitarian economy is based on work that is conscious, productive, creative and social, there is no place for labor and the laborer. An effective struggle is being waged against the capitalization and disposition invoked by the forces of power of capital. Since society, and the individuals who compose it, work and produce for their own benefit, in order to meet their own needs, only real work is essential, not compulsory work. (Abdullah Öcalan Sosyal Bilimler Akademisi, 2012, p. 88)

In the terminology of the Kurdish struggle, work as a societal activity is accepted, while abstract work, defined by exploitation and alienation, is rejected. The following quote highlights the difference between workers and laborers. The Kurdish Movement does not reject working. On the contrary, it states that:

In the communal economy, compulsory work will be eliminated. Work will become a celebration of life. The walls of alienation erected between life and work will be torn down. Instead of a system in all aspects of society are commodified, turning them into products, an unavoidable turn towards an economic system based on use-values will be fundamental (Cooperatives Committee of Rojava and North Syria – *Komîteya Kooparatîfên Bakûrê Sûrî*, 2017).

In other words, instead of a salaried workers in exchange for the exploitation, the Kurdish Movement proposes voluntary work, which generates a community benefit. However, during my field research in 2019, I found that companies/factories had not been turned into cooperatives and were instead transferred to the autonomous governments of their region. Had they been transformed into cooperatives; they could have been used as transitional models in order to develop collective industries based on use-value and create industrial cooperatives. They could have become a common good that the Autonomous Administration could have invested in to the benefit of the people. They could have been built as common production units, owned by no one and managed by workers' councils based on the principle of self-management. They could have been cooperatives turned into the autonomous production power of the people.

However, as a result of elections of the Federation and its new structure, and many another reason of this process gives rise to the need to centralize resources. To this end, the factories without bosses became a source of funding system, continuing the tendency whereby autonomy was distancing itself from its radical roots and toward more liberal autonomy. Another reason is that the changes for the emancipation of society do not occur at the speed required by the revolutionary process. Although it is claimed that these factories continue to operate in the same way as before and continue to serve the needs of society, for me, the emancipatory potential they were imbued with in 2018 has evaporated. This is because, cooperatives or not, the economic and social resources conducted by the revolutionary political will for the social economy are the tools that fed the potential anti-capitalist spaces.

In 2018, the Economic Coordination body supported the development of cooperativism through the income obtained from these factories. It created a direct, non-bureaucratic resource that aided in the construction of the social economy:

We call these structures "companies." However, to be clear, our businesses are entering into the realm of monopolism. Depending on which angle you choose to look at it from, they can appear as monopolies. We call it business by obligation. Wheat, barley, cotton [...] We, as the Cooperatives Committee, also benefit from them. They often lend us money or give us products/seeds free of charge. It provides many benefits to the cooperatives. [...] Not only do we finance the cooperatives, but all our agricultural work benefits. The companies process or sell the agricultural products that are produced in the area. (Interview with Melsa, Co-spokesperson of the Cooperatives Committee, 2018)

In 2018, these companies/factories allowed the Economic Coordination body to balance different economic sectors. In Hesekê, for example, a 10% quota on cotton production was imposed through the Agriculture Committee in order to bring the abandoned state-owned spinning mill back into operation. Once again, although these factories were not cooperatives, they practiced self-management. Self-management—that is, the democratization of a factory's organization—is one of the most important preconditions for the establishment of real cooperatives.

However, when these factories came under the purview of the Finance Committee, this link was severed. Their potential to support anti-capitalist economic organization was dismantled. As for the emancipation of work, the factory's revolutionary potential was limited by its use as a bureaucratic redistributive mechanism—that is, it was reduced to the Autonomous Administration's tool to employ or distribute the social wealth created and thereby strengthen the community economy. In fact, at one of the Economy Committee's meetings in the canton of Hesekê, when a cooperative project was due to be established, the necessary resources were requested from the Economic Council. I was told that the required resources could only be supplied if the Autonomous Administration provided the Council with a budget. Since that process would take a long time, much of the work needed to organize the cooperatives could not be carried out (interview with the Hesekê Canton Economic Committee, 2019). One can say that the time of autonomy was locked up in administrative time.

The direct redistribution of resources on the basis of the wealth produced by these factories and cooperatives went up in smoke in 2019. It was replaced by bureaucracy and planning. The prevalent idea at that time—that the resources should be used for cooperatives or for the development of the communal economy—disappeared. That principle was replaced by the policy of creating the necessary resource for the Autonomous Administration's public services. Of course, this works to the benefit of society, but it undermines the idea that society is able to produce in order to cover its own needs in the form of a self-sufficient economy. It also leads to the growth of the administrative apparatus and the weakening of autonomous social power. This dynamic, laid bare by the factories without bosses, has increasingly become the dominant tendency as attempts are being made to direct Rojava's autonomy towards a form of liberal autonomy.

In my opinion, the reasons for this are twofold: as the Economic Coordination body has not given any space to collective forms of work outside of cooperatives, it has not been able to evaluate its full potential in practice. This is a common attitude within the Kurdish Movement, as it is a movement based on a single political party and its cadres, who insist on a model that they believe to be true. Since the social economy is centered on cooperativism, which asserts that all economic units must be cooperatives and, if they are not, should not exist, the possible experimentation of own modes is ignored. The second reason is related to the policies of external actors—states and imperialist companies— to convert the existing autonomy into a liberal and classical sovereign autonomy. With this purpose in mind, they are attempting to erode the radical aspects of the local autonomy; to guide it towards a statist, capitalist and patriarchal autonomy, subject to the nation-state system in the classical sense. The most important element that feeds this tendency is the centralization of resources and the development of bureaucratic, liberal, and local capitalism, instead of the promotion of anti-capitalist practices of autonomy.

The development of an ecological industry in Rojava requires a holistic struggle against the issues plaguing the industrial and economic sectors. For this reason, it should be noted that the construction of an ecological industry in Rojava has to face a much more complex, contradictory and opposite process, contrary to what we imagine about the revolution and revolutionaries.

Trade and the market

The other area where social class conflict is most visible is trade. In Rojava, this sector is currently delimited by the conditions of capitalist war.

What first caught my attention when I arrived in Qamishlo, Rojava's de facto capital, from the Derik province, where the border crossing of Semalka is located, was a long line of cargo lorries. In fact, it was the first observation I jotted down in my notebook. The Qamishlo market, which I visited a few days later, seemed surprisingly lively. It offered anything one could need at affordable prices. Although the market functioned under capitalist logic, this surprised me, as it was functioning within the context of a fierce war and an ongoing embargo.

As previously mentioned, the Economic Coordination body is organized into sectors. One of them is the Trade Committee. Before my long meeting with Zafer, who in 2018 was responsible for the Trade Committee, I had heard concerns and criticism about the organization of this committee from the movement's political cadres. The most common criticism pertained to its independent organization; that, though considering itself part of the social economy, it conducted business exclusively with merchants instead of seeking to establish a broader popular base for the market. Zafer mentioned that this criticism was the result of idiosyncrasies relating to trade in the current context:

> For now, commerce in Rojava operates as a free market system. That is, it is unregulated and does not base itself on socialist and democratic ideals. There are several reasons for the current situation: first, the system of the Ba'ath regime. Here, the Ba'ath regime implemented an economy based on consumption instead of production, and thus made society entirely dependent on the state and on trade. This society is used to being offered manufactured goods, consuming them and living off of them. Therefore, it is neither correct nor possible to define the current system of trade as a system of democratic or socialist values.
>
> So, then what is the current trading system based on? The classes are not yet fully developed and their reality in Rojava does not fit modern class analysis. For example, the terms "bourgeois," "proletarian," "worker" or "peasant." Here, a bourgeoisie has not yet developed, neither has there been a process of proletarianization, while most peasants are landless and poor. We cannot speak of landowners as such (axa, possessing both land and an armed force), but we can say that there are people who own large swaths of land. However, these lands are clustered in only a few villages. In Rojava, there is close to no private property. This is the current situation. Using these classifications, the state developed a trade system that would connect people here. That is, it linked society with itself by creating a trade system through the rich sectors, which are not bourgeois, but have capital. (Interview with Zafer, responsible for the Trade Committee, 2018)

Zafer further stated that this system was complicated by war and revolution. Before, the main players in trade were the regime and those with strong ties to the Ba'ath party. With self-governance, new traders from Iraqi Kurdistan were allowed take part. They acted as nodal points, attracting trade from Turkey and Iran, and directing it towards Rojava. Zafer (2018) makes clear that, as the Trade Committee, they have been trying to organize a different system for the past two years. In his words, they are trying to "strengthen the social-democratic aspects of business."

The Trade Committee is organized into four units or "commercial centers": the chambers of commerce, the trade directorate, the customs administration, and the trade cooperatives (interview with Zafer, 2018). The primary duty of the chambers of commerce is to draft trade-related transition documents, relying on the autonomous cantonal administration in order to gather traders together and facilitate their oversight. In Rojava, where there is no industrial production, one of the Trade Committee's two crucial functions is to manage customs on Rojava's borders. There are two main border gates that collect trade customs in northern Syria. One is Semalka, which bridges Iraqi Kurdistan (Başur-Pişxabur) and Syrian Kurdistan (Rojava-Kuzey Suriye-Derik). The other is Manbij, on Syria's northern border with Turkey. This border crossing was opened by U.S. forces, as Turkey has kept all customs gates in the north closed to all transit, including humanitarian aid, since 2013. The sole exception was in 2014, during the Kobane war.

Besides the Semelka and Manbij border crossings, there is also a lively domestic trade, from Syria's interior regions to its north. During regime rule, this trade involved the transfer of wheat and oil to the south and west of Syria, and the import of food products from the western regions. From the eruption of the civil war in 2011 until 2017, this trade was interrupted due to conflict and the presence of ISIS. Products made in Damascus gave way to those made in Turkey, Iran and China. When Raqqa and Deir ez-Zor were liberated from ISIS rule after 2017, trade with the southern and western regions revived. Due to a lack of internal border crossings, Asayish (NES's security forces) checkpoints were also tasked with monitoring commercial vehicles. The Administration of Border Crossing sets the customs duties together with the Pricing Committee and authorizes the flow of products in and out of the region. According to Zafer, in order to bring goods from abroad to Rojava, traders must meet two requirements: they must be from Rojava and they must have a permit from one of the trade directorates, which works in coordination with the Autonomous Administration. The communes confirm that the trader is from Rojava and the precise commune therein, while the authorization granted by the trade directorate confirms that the commercial activity is being carried out in order to meet the people's collective needs, and that the product traded is not already produced in Rojava or is not being produced in sufficient quantity (interview with Zafer, 2018). An issue frequently brought up in my interviews in Rojava was that the merchants authorized by the Trade Committee tended to be ENKS-PDK (Kurdistan Democratic Party) members. The adage repeated to me was that "those who died in the war were PKK and those who became rich [off of it] are PDK"[10];

---

10 These words were spoken at one of the commune meetings I attended. The Autonomous Administration has been criticized on this issue.

there seemed to be a sound basis for this claim. Zafer attempted to explain it away, saying "this is the war economy."

Rojava traders who import goods to Rojava thus support a national project, rather than the local autonomous project. They advocate for the independentization of western Kurdistan—that is, Rojava—from the rest of Syria. While this idea is championed by the PDK in Iraqi Kurdistan, in Rojava it is promoted by the ENKS. The logic behind this approach is that commercial capital can be transformed into production capital. The borders between state and nation, a dominant idea in Kurdistan, are the preconditions for the development of capital. According to Zafer, wartime conditions forced them to rely on ENKS-PDK traders. It was not possible to establish direct trade with Iraqi Kurdistan, since the Bashur government applied embargoes at will, though never completely sealed its border with Rojava.

> As our organization [the Kurdish Movement], we attempted opening trade companies through our associates in Bashur on several occasions. But when the Barzani government discovered this relationship, when they realized that the products were meant to reach us, they immediately shut them down. No company linked to us has ever been able to carry on working. (Interview with Zafer, 2018)

According to Zafer, this is the most visible face of the war economy, and the Trade Committee's task is to walk this tightrope, effecting balanced policies and trade that can avoid the closure of border crossings and benefit the people (interview with Zafer, 2018).

Rojava is in a process of intense contradictions. Furthermore, efforts to resolve one contradiction sometimes leads to the emergence of another. Chicken farming is one example. The chicken-feeding cooperatives, which were founded in 2018, successfully prevented the importation of Turkish chickens to Rojava, although they fall short of the region's ecological standards. In 2018, Serxwebun, Co-Spokesman of Rojava Cooperatives, told me that this move had been essential because they were unwilling to give money to Turkish companies and, furthermore, the Turkish chickens were often rotten, making people ill. Despite their utter disregard for the principles of the communal and ecological economy, they wanted to carry out their own chicken production (Interview with Serxwebun, 2018). I was also surprised when I realized that the chicken that was being sent as part of food rations to our commune by the TEV-DEM was a brand I knew from my time in Turkey. A comrade, who saw the shock on my face, grinningly explained "The Turks don't just send us bombs, but chickens, too. They are able to make all kinds of profit from this war." I did not know whether to laugh or cry. How utterly surreal!

It was thus gratifying to see that the chicken farming cooperatives I came back to in 2019 were now producing enough chickens to feed Rojava. Although the production was not organic, it is a noteworthy achievement, as it demonstrated people's ability produce their own food cooperatively. Even though the Economic Coordination body of Northern Syria and Rojava temporarily allowed chicken production under non-ecological conditions, it also encouraged communes to organize cooperatives raising "free-range" chickens in order to overcome this contradiction. This unique situation exemplifies the continuity of the anti-capitalist struggle within Rojava's present economic situation.

In 2018, I met with the political cadre who at that time oversaw the Semalka border crossing. He told me that the customs administration was unable to certify the quality of products passing through customs, and that they had received damaged and low-quality products on purpose. Proper inspections were impossible as there was no specialized laboratory in Rojava. He also said that that the customs administration was only able to check expiration dates, and lived in constant fear of the possibility of mass poisoning in Rojava.

> If a product is damaged or is of poor quality, we do not allow it to pass the border, but our knowledge is fairly limited, and we cannot check all products one by one! We are sending back mostly products from Turkey, which have the potential to turn into poison, we are not accepting them. (Interview with Ercan, responsible for Semelka Customs, 2018)

With these words, Ercan highlighted the insecurities implicit in a war situation. Zafer emphasized that they do business with traders they know and avoid doing business with those they do not (interview with Zafer, 2018). The Chamber of Commerce was created with the following objectives:

> First, the main objective of this center is to prevent the emergence of a bourgeoisie. To avoid the creation of a new layer between classes or inequality between classes. In striving for this goal, we also work with traders. We work with them to set prices, control the market, address their problems, avoid injustices or, for example, improve their relationship with the cantonal administration. In other words, the main objective is to avoid a widening income gap and the deepening of existing income inequalities—that is the duty of the Chamber of Commerce. (Interview with Zafer, 2018)

Zafer added that, through cooperatives, they were trying to extend society's access to capital. He clarified that their economic policy was not against capital, money or the market, but against their monopolization. Zafer's statement was clear and the definition he provided had never been articulated to me in this way:

> We also conduct our own business, but the capital that is created from this business does not go to a managerial class or to anybody else—the money collected works like a public bank on behalf of the people and is redistributed from there. For example, we carry out commercial activities, we obtain income from trade, and we provide our income to the people through cooperatives. In other words, there is no money that directly finances the movement or the Autonomous Administration. So, we're trying to make the capital we obtain accessible to all, to expand access to it; we are trying to prevent capital from concentrating in the hands of a few. This is our basic approach to commerce. (Interview with Zafer, 2018)

While trying to tame the capitalist market (that is, to organize the market), it stands to reason that the same commercial approach will be employed to create an alternative form of trade and exchange between commercial cooperatives. Analyzing global experiences of anti-capitalist organization, however, it becomes apparent that alternative approaches to trade have become stuck and uninspired, failing to break the hegemony of the capitalist market. Oft-discussed in meetings on alternative economies, realistic solutions to rival the capitalist market are few and far between. These discussions—on how to establish ties between communal and solidarity economies that do not transform self-management into a process of remunerated self-exploitation—center around two main points of deliberation. Firstly, the strengthening of local ties, particularly in relation to geographical proximity (Hernández and Martí, 2019). This includes solidarity-based trade, linking small peasant production and urban consumers, such as the organization of responsible consumption. Numerous attempts at this type of arrangement have been made; most are oriented towards ensuring food security and satisfying other basic needs.

Secondly—and perhaps harder to tackle—is how to develop macro- or international networks that can transcend the capitalist system at the country, continental and global level. These discussions have not progressed beyond sharing experiences. All attempts at an alternative face a number of challenges related to the capitalist market, such as the laws surrounding logistics, pricing, distances, taxes and trade. Any industrial work—such as industrial cooperatives or collectives—have no other choice but to produce for the capitalist market, under the conditions thereof. "For self-managed organizations and cooperatives, participating in the capitalist market, with its push towards competitiveness and a work rhythm that is defined by that logic, is a major contradiction. In the face of this tension, the question arises: what values should we build on in practice in order to transform the market and the relations it imposes?" (Trasol, 2017, p. 49)

Today, as products are assembled across multiple countries if not continents, the market's influence in shaping the production process is more pronounced than at any time before. Cooperatives, even as they produce in a self-managed and collective manner, must bow to and compete within market dynamics the moment they present their products for sale. "The fact that cooperatives and self-managed companies do not constitute a universe apart from the capitalist economy can lead to the internalization of these principles of competition, to the exacerbation of work subjected to hierarchical and authoritarian rules—in short, to self-exploitation" (Cattani, 2004, p. 27).

An example of perseverance in the face of this global challenge of capitalism, which was able to integrate a collective production process within an alternative process of exchange, is the Zapatista's distribution system for coffee, their leading export. Almost all Zapatista coffee production is collective. Local coffee cooperatives collect and sell the coffee produced in each *caracol*. This coffee is sold with the help of solidarity centers/groups that support the Zapatista's autonomy project. These centers, constituted of political groups and collectives, exist all over the world. The Zapatista movement highly values these solidarity centers for various reasons. For example, when the Mexican state attempts to pressure the Zapatistas, these centers are able to organize protest actions. Moreover, these centers are the point of sale for Zapatista coffee. Coffee cooperatives provide these centers with coffee, which is sold through local solidarity networks, and receive money in exchange. This money strengthens family economies and provides the political project in each community with a small source of income. The secret ingredient, which allows for the ubiquitous presence of Zapatista coffee from America to Europe and Asia, are these solidarity networks created in defiance of the trade monopoly of capitalism. The coffee is traded on a global scale; money, too, is used during this trade. However, the money is managed by political collectives with solidarity as its main objective.

An attempt at alternative trade in Rojava is embodied by the Hevgirtin cooperative. *Hevgirtin* means "common purchase" in Kurdish and refers to the common provision of needs. Founded in 2016, the Hevgirtin cooperative was established as an association of 12,000 families. The Trade Committee was tasked with conducting trade on behalf of the cooperative with some 380 million Syrian pounds raised from more than 25,000 contributors. Resat, my interview partner from the Hevgirtin administration for the Cezîre canton, said that in order to break the negative influence of the capitalist market and monopolistic-minded businessmen on the people and the revolution, they had to lower the prices for products that were now available on the black market because of the war (interview with the Hevgirtin Cooperative, 2018). Zafer added that the main objective of the Hevgirtin cooperative was to avoid price fluctuations in the market (interview with Zafer, 2018).

Product shortages and the flourishing of black markets are common wartime conditions. According to Zafer, the main reason there was no acute starvation, poverty and homelessness in Rojava, even as the war raged, was the continued existence of a working economy. This is also tied to "the Economic Committee's focus on social economy and democratic practices, such as the Hevgirtin cooperative" (interview with Zafer, 2018). At a monthly assembly meeting of the Hevgirtin cooperative, held in March 2018, which I attended, its members mentioned Hevgirtin's aim to corner the market, but failed to discuss its relationships with other cooperatives (Hevgirtin Cooperative Assembly, 2018).

An additional purpose of Hevgirtin is to sell products made in Rojavan cooperatives, with the intention of creating a market space for cooperatives. However, Hevgirtin, which is organized at the provincial level and has a sales shop in each provincial center, does not seem to have achieved this goal. In meetings I had with women's cooperatives, the women often complained that Hevgirtin refused to sell their products. When I asked Reşat about this contradiction, he told me that Hevgirtin did want to sell them, but that these cooperatives' products did not reach certain quality standards, that it was difficult to sell them because they were often rough-hewn. He added that women's cooperatives demand money even if the product is not sold or it spoils (interview with Hevgirtin cooperative, 2018).

A similar conflict arose around the Medya consumer cooperative, one of the first to open in Wan, the region that, after the Democratic Economy Conference in Bakur (Kurdistan-Turkey), functioned as a pilot for the democratic-communal economy. Founded under the principles of a communal market, similar to Hevgirtin, the Medya cooperative, which set out to ensure that small-scale producers and cooperative products can reach the market and consumers, was ultimately unable to perform that role, relying instead on selling the products of capitalism and distributing their profits among its associates. In fact, in Rojava, the general perception of Hevgirtin was that it had failed to act as a cooperative and instead became a bank that distributed its profits in accordance with the size of each family's capital contributions. According to people's perception, it had become an institution that reproduced capitalism and capitalist logic.

The Kurdish struggle's experience with an alternative economy is far from unique. No organization whose structure to sell and act as an intermediary that is cooperative-based has the capacity to be an alternative to the logic of the capitalist market. Exceptions to this rule are limited to political collectives that function on the basis of volunteerism. Essentially, they are solidarity cooperatives whose members often make a living doing other jobs—mostly of the capitalist kind. The day-to-day business and responsibilities of these cooperatives are managed as political activities in their own right and their members do not expect to benefit; the political end is to support alternative economic experiences. The hope of those involved is that they will move alternative economies into the mainstream—it is a long-term process towards joint liberation.

When I conducted my field research in 2019, the Trade Committee had been abolished and all trade-related activities had been transferred to the Trade Council of the AANES. The Hevgirtin cooperative had closed. Although an alternative trade model had not been built in the years prior to 2019, the Trade Committee's intention of establishing an alternative market were undeniable. With the abolition of the committee and the transfer of control to the Autonomous Administration, the Trade Council became the market's shepherd and overseer; it became the controlling force behind the liberal market economy. In other words, the local market became much more sensitive to financial fluctuations. The most important indicator of this change was the growing inflation recorded during the past year (2021).

Even though Hevgirtin closed, it represents a crucial experience of the Rojava Revolution's early years, marked by both positive and negative aspects. Thanks to the capital raised through the cooperatives, the Trade Committee was able to curb the development of a black market in basic products, such as sugar, cement, oil, boulghour (savar), rice, and tea. Moreover, in concert with the Pricing Committee of the Autonomous Administration, it was able to control market prices for these goods. Reşat considers this the social benefit of Hevgirtin:

> Perhaps Hevgirtin did not accept all products for sale, but it prevented merchants from price gouging. When we kept the price low, the traders had to keep it low. Therefore, society benefited. Although Hevgirtin's associates did not benefit, society benefited. This was Hevgirtin's main role. (Interview with the Hevgirtin cooperative, 2018)

Additionally, in the early years of cooperative formation, Hevgirtin provided crucial resources for the establishment of other cooperatives. The Lorin Cooperative, one of the women's cooperatives I visited in 2018, was assisted by Hevgirtin, which provided the means of production and the production site at the Hevgirtin cooperative building (interview with the Lorin cooperative, 2018).

Among the non-intermediate alternatives created in the field of commerce, the women's markets or communal markets established by the Women's Economy Committee (*aboriya jin*) in Dirbesiye, Derik and other provinces are well worth mentioning. Patriarchy's hold over commerce is strong; although women produce, they are made invisible in the sales process. The goods they produce become commodities and the target of competition through trade, which is in the hands of men. In other words, in markets under patriarchal control, women's labor is enslaved. Additionally, it is much more difficult for women to enter this sector, as in most Islamic societies in the Middle East female traders are generally frowned upon. For this reason, the Women's Economy Committee established women's markets and other spaces where women are able to bring their products directly to the consumer, which gives credence to the fact that women can offer an alternative approach to change. In women's alternative markets, sales or exchanges are carried out directly between producer and consumer, without any middlemen. The Spokeswoman of the Women's Economy pointed out that products are often exchanged, especially among women. Although this relationship in many instances takes place through the medium of money, this most powerful element of capitalism can also aid in the development of autonomy and establish alternative commercial and market relationships (interview with Delal, Spokeswoman of the Women's Economy Committee , 2018).

Cooperatives — The social economy's organizational foundation

A crucial element in the construction of autonomy is the creation of new forms of social relations. Cooperatives, especially, are fundamental to the organization of an alternative economy. If we understand autonomy to mean the struggle towards a way of life that is defined by self-determination, in order for the struggle to achieve actual social liberation, it is imperative to develop an alternative way of working that rivals capitalist labor, which "reduces the enormous wealth and the multicolor of useful work to abstract and unique work that generates value" (Holloway, Matamoros and Tischler, 2013, p. 15). Thus, the core transformations that alternative economies should bring about are tied to work. The first challenge of *la otra economía* (the other economy or the alternative economy) is to reaffirm the fundamental importance of work for individuals and society (Cattani, 2004, p. 27). A transformation of the way we work, based on concrete work that generates use value, can be the catalyst for the development of alternative social relationships. In other words, the will of every individual and, naturally, of the community as a whole, to decide how and to what end they will work lies at the heart of self-determination. In the capitalist system, this will is under the monopoly of capital, as individuals are made to sell their labor power. Robbed of the power over their own labor, they lose the ability to make decisions in all other spheres of life. Moreover, anyone who does not use their labor to satisfy their own needs, and in this sense lacks self-determination, cannot be part of revolutionary politics—no matter their inclination. Throughout history, labor regimes have provided the conditions for the enslavement or for the liberation of society. Therefore, in the present and future, as in the past, labor regimes will continue to be defined by how and to whose benefit the labor force is used.

The struggle for autonomy, thus, is not one fought against right-wing governments, centralist government systems, electoral politics, or differing conceptions of democracy; it is the fight of society against the monopoly/power of capital over the commodification of labor. In essence, autonomy is society's struggle to recover the ability to rule itself. As previously mentioned, such a struggle cannot be carried out by accumulating power, since power only begets more power. On the contrary, social liberation entails breaking the domination of capital over daily life. Thus, the structures that are to break this dominance and effect society's transition from slavery towards the condition for freedom cannot be centralist, statist, capitalist or patriarchal; they have to be structures in opposition to power.

In Rojava, the cooperatives represent a concrete, communal and anti-power way of working that is essential for the organization of the social economy. Cooperatives are the subject of discussion and experimentation not only in Rojava, but all over the world "since cooperatives are an unavoidable point of reference for any alternative economic proposal to capitalism" (Garcia Jané, 2012, p. 13). Cooperativism is a common topic of theoretical discussion among alternative economies. Its definition, as well as its practice, is heterogenous across these different fields. However, both cooperatives and cooperativism are not new concepts or structures. Since the first cooperative—Rochdale, founded in England in 1844 by 28 weavers—cooperatives have been discussed and experienced not only as economic organizations, but also as political and social structures.

A reflection on cooperatives: cooperatives against capitalism

Previously, I discussed the depth, breadth and variety of non-capitalist economies in the struggle against capitalism. Cooperatives offer a similar level of complexity. For instance, most cooperatives are capitalist, rather than anti-capitalist. Cooperatives that create capital through the union of their associates in order to jump start their economic production are generally favored by the public and encouraged by capitalist states. In Germany, where capitalism is highly developed, the state considers cooperatives part of its "intangible cultural heritage" (UNESCO, 2016). Reportedly, more than 7,500 cooperative institutions count a total of 20 million members (Deutschland.de, 2018). For this reason, cooperatives should not be analyzed as a unitary structure, but rather according to their content, how they work and what kind of political project they pursue. It would be naive to consider cooperatives anti-capitalist by their mere nature, without taking into account their limitations and contradictions.

Cooperatives can become an anti-capitalist force only when they form part of the politics of construction of a communal economy. As Katherine Gibson and Julie Graham write, "the communal economy is not a geographic or social cooperation, but a space for ethical and political decision-making; the community is not its basis but rather its result" (J. K. Gibson-Graham, 2010, pp. 18-19). Cooperatives are a part of this space for ethical and political decision-making and can be organized to aid in community construction, as they offer a new basis on which non-capitalist social relations can be organized.

Collective work is the essence of a cooperative. The reason work is carried out collectively is cooperatives' perpetual aspiration to achieve total equality among its workers. Not a liberal equality, which entails symmetrical rights for all, but equality in how work processes are constructed, where no one exploits or imposes themselves over anybody else. Workers come together to establish democratic relations in opposition to the dominant relations of exploitation and create cooperatives. Ranya, a young girl working at the Lorin Cooperative, one of the women's cooperatives I visited in Rojava in 2018, said: "We are equal here, we work together in solidarity. There is no one to give us orders. We decide everything by ourselves. When somebody needs something, we all help out" (interview with the Lorin Cooperative, 2018). She highlighted the equality between workers she felt and the role of solidarity in the culture of cooperatives. Since cooperatives are formed based on local solidarity and communal economies instead of competition and individuality, each cooperative is shaped by the unique existing cultural life of the communities in which it is developed (Özgen, 2014).

To achieve true equality, it is necessary to problematize and break the hierarchical and exploitative forms of production that were established to enable capitalist accumulation. In cooperatives that continue to use wage labor and are overseen by a dominant managerial class, exploitation and surplus are still practiced in the name of profit. Contracting salaried workers is fairly common in cooperatives. In these cases, a distinction between the cooperative's associates and hired workers is made. More often than not, workers do not have the right to participate in the cooperative's assembly nor to have a say in its decision-making. In contrast, when workers organize themselves into cooperatives, their objective is to eliminate distinctions in class (employer-employee) and profession (manager-managed) through collective work and role-rotation.

Theoretically, cooperatives have neither bosses nor profits; all associates have the same rights and the same stakes. A truly transformative practices in this regard is the implementation of a role-rotation system. This system, which entails alternating who performs the tasks necessary for a harmonious coexistence, is one of the democratic mechanisms in the arsenal of communal economies, especially in that of Latin America's Indigenous communities. Cooperative members eliminate the supposed professionalization that is inherent in the managerial role by carrying out all the management and coordination tasks on a rotating basis. Task rotation is applied to all spheres of work to ensure that everyone has the ability to carry out all tasks. In cooperatives without managers or bosses, the establishment of a permanent managerial class is prevented by a rotation system (Zibechi, 2014, p. 103), while the cooperative process and cooperativism become spaces for self-education.

Another core characteristic of cooperatives is the common ownership and joint control of the means of production. However, collective ownership alone is not enough; collective decision-making mechanisms are needed as well. Even if an agreement on collective decision-making exists, if the cooperative assembly does not actively push for its democratization and for wider participation, if all members of the assembly do not speak, express themselves and discuss differing opinions, if the fair participation of all members is not facilitated, decision-making will be concentrated among a few, and decisions and opinions that are considered to be collective will in truth only be made by a limited number of dominant members. Thus, cooperatives must actively work towards the democratization of its structures. The democratization of relations within cooperatives is to be addressed once the cooperatives have been established, thus bringing about a real collectivization process.

An important part of this process is the democratization of gender relations. In the usual mixed-gender collective structures, a common observation is that decisions-making is dominated by men. The percentage of women who express opinions and participate in discussions tends to be lower than that of men, even if the overall number of participants is equal. Under the hegemony of patriarchal relations, women find it difficult to express their opinions to the wider community. The powerful (not to say booming) way men express themselves, their positioning at the center of every discussion, and the lack of care given to the equal participation of fellow comrades only heighten women's reservations and anxiety. In order for women to be able to express their opinions and thoughts, cooperatives must make a particular effort to work towards the democratization of gender relations without simply basing themselves on the axiom that women have the right to participate freely. In other words, cooperatives must ensure that everyone has the same influence on decision-making. Understanding themselves as decision-makers, rather than simply being subject to decisions, is important not only for women, but for all members of cooperatives. This establishes cooperatives as a structure in which both relations of production and social relations are remodeled. As in all of the Kurdish Movement's spaces, women's participation in cooperatives is set at 50%. This does not mean that women represent exactly half of its members everywhere, but it does mean that their influence on decision-making is equal to half. Furthermore, all cooperatives are headed by a male and a female co-spokesperson.

In addition to equal representation and the co-spokespersons system, two other practices that were implemented in the Bakur cooperatives significantly advanced gender-egalitarian self-management. One of them, which was applied in the cooperative's assemblies as well as in all mixed spaces of the Kurdish Movement, was not to accept men's contributions before a woman had spoken first. Once the co-moderator opened the assembly, a woman was expected to take the floor and speak in order to start the meeting. At times, this entailed long interludes before someone decided to speak; other times women spoke without hesitation. This practice had two consequences. Firstly, after the first (female) speaker, other women felt more empowered to speak, paving the way for them to participate in the discussion. Secondly, there was a noticeable difference in the topics discussed in the assemblies when women were first to speak. Men prefer to talk about their earnings, while most women raise issues related to common life and the relationship between members. Thus, in cooperative assemblies, when women speak first and begin the discussion, the topics addressed tend to focus on reproductive instead of productive labor.

Another practice implemented in Bakur is that when the cooperative had too few female members, the men attended the assemblies with one of their female relatives. Relatives could remain as passive observers or participate actively in the discussion if they wished. Although this practice was rarely implemented, it is noteworthy. The women who accompanied the men to the assembly could be their mothers, wives, sisters or daughters. However, it was crucial that they be a female relative with whom the man lived. Through this practice, it was hoped that female relatives would become better acquainted with the cooperative, and begin to socialize domestic relations. One of the main arguments the women in Bakur made for the need to implement this practice was related to the care work that women carry out, which enables men to participate in the cooperatives. Making this care work visible within the cooperative should be considered a political achievement for the emancipation of women.

Another argument presented was the fact that men could hide the full extent of their income, while the presence of one of their female relatives in the cooperative assembly would prevent this. Furthermore, even if the men behaved democratically in the cooperative, they often continued to interact with women in an undemocratic and violent manner at home. Therefore, for the cooperative to effect social transformation, it had to achieve a dynamic that would extend into family life and weaken patriarchal relationships within the home.

With the disappearance of the Bakur cooperatives, the basis on which to continue these practices also vanished, however, it is worth making note of them and considering how these experiences of problematizing gender relations created a concrete practice to achieve their democratization—a topic only seldom discussed in the field of cooperatives.

Cooperatives are spaces of self-management. In such spaces, people can make free decisions about their work and their production process. Self-management is implemented when these aspects are jointly discussed in the cooperative assembly. In the context of Rojava, if a cooperative wants to be part of a community and of community relations, it is essential that its assembly be open to community participation, or that community self-management be carried out through other mechanisms. Cooperatives that work in conjunction with the community produce use value—that is, use value is the aim of production. This allows them to adjust their production process to the needs of the community. For example, in joint assemblies, the community can express which products are needed, how many and when, and the cooperative's production can be planned collaboratively. Thus, the cooperative, acting in accordance with the decisions of society within the framework of community needs, becomes a mechanism for the production of social equality. In contrast, the cooperatives that are disconnected from the needs of the community set their purpose as, first, to guide their production by exchange value rather than use value and, later, to find markets for their products. These cooperatives are thus condemned to the market, where relationships are established on the basis of value. Just as use value is the prevalent force shaping a cooperative's community solidarity, in the market, the predominance of competitivity ties a cooperative to exchange value. Contrary to popular belief, cooperatives are not static organizations, but rather social spaces that are shaped by fluid relationships.

To be clear, though they may become a part of the self-sufficient economy by producing based on use value, such cooperatives are not by necessity bound to systems of barter. Cooperatives that generate use value can make exchanges through "sales," that is, through the mediation of money, but this does not constitute a classical market, defined as an area dominated by exchange value, but rather a bazaar (marketplace), a phenomenon predating capitalism. When speaking of self-sufficient economies or communal economies, one should not assume that the community's production is intended only for internal consumption; historically, next to no community has had a closed economy that operated without any exchange with the outside. The exchanges between families, clans and communities were in fact the first forms of trade. In the process that followed, markets, caravans and trade routes were established. Trade was part of the communal economy and was understood as an activity that supplied raw goods in exchange for processed goods. This activity was carried out either through the direct exchange of products or by using a material that facilitated this exchange (money as a medium of exchange, C-M-C). Commodification entered the picture when brokers began to dominate trade routes and accumulate materials for exchange.

In capitalism, the medium of exchange is money, which dominates all relationships. The major difference between the market and the bazaar (in the classical sense) is that, in the former, exchange value became a mechanism for accumulating wealth in the form of money (money as a store of value, M-C-M then M-C-M'). The main elements that constitute the economy, such as needs, use value, work, communality, forms of production, profit, creativity and the marketplace were placed under the dominion of money. Today, these elements, which make the reproduction of life possible, are expressed in monetary terms; that is, they have been commodified. The economy was divorced from its original meaning to society. Therefore, the search for an alternative economy implies rediscovering the original, communal meaning of these concepts.

In summary, cooperatives have an anti-capitalist character only when they form part of the communal economy, where production satisfies collective needs and is defined by use value, and money is not the dominant regulator of relationships. Only in this way can cooperatives be emancipatory in the struggle against capitalism. Today, so-called producer cooperatives are fairly common, especially in the field of agriculture. In such cooperatives, farmers partner in order to sell their products. Their objective, generally speaking, is to protect their members against monopolistic traders during sales of a particular product, in a particular region. Sometimes, even the monopolistic traders themselves encourage farmers to organize under a cooperative in order to facilitate purchases. The main purpose of this type of cooperatives is to aid in price negotiations, that is, to obtain a fairer price for each sale, with no consideration for the conditions of production. In fact, landed farmers who participate in cooperatives may produce on the basis of exploitation, for example by employing wage laborers. The farmers' objective is not to generate use value in order to satisfy community needs, but rather to obtain the greatest possible benefit from the exchange value that they will sell to merchants. Thus, even if the purpose of such cooperatives is antagonistic to that of merchants', it does not contradict the logic of capitalism.

Another common example of trade or sales cooperatives are consumer cooperatives, especially those established in large cities. As their name indicates, they are cooperatives in which consumers jointly organize their consumption; they are usually composed of urbanites who are not themselves food producers and work in other economic sectors. Their members tend to consider themselves "conscious" citizens, although they rarely possess an anti-capitalist conscience and rather seek ethical, considered and organic consumption. Consumer cooperatives in large cities usually prefer to establish ties with small-scale producers or agricultural cooperatives that produce naturally, organically, ecologically, etc. In recent years, the ecological destruction and negative effects of industrial agriculture have prompted more and more consumers to establish these types of cooperative. That is, the conditions of production are increasingly being considered.

In addition to having to be environmentally-friendly, an emphasis is also put on exploitation-free production. Fair and natural production is encouraged and many consumer cooperative have been highly successful in this regard. Nevertheless, even in these cooperatives, the consumer's character is not properly analyzed. Their members perform capitalist jobs in capitalist metropolises and their consumption is guided by the income generated through these jobs. Consumer cooperatives do not provide products that are affordable to poor people; their products are generally aimed at high- and middle-income consumers. Consumer cooperatives—whose constituents intend to change their way of life only through consumption and not through work—may foster continuous small-scale production through the purchase/exchange of their product at a fair price, but fall short of creating a truly anti-capitalist dynamic that can effect social transformation. For a truly anti-capitalist exchange to take place, it needs to occur on the basis of use value produced for collective needs. Other forms of trade are inexorably capitalist and though they may be mediated by a cooperative, they dominated by capitalist market relations and value.

Cooperatives or cooperativism are not defined by any legal organizational structure or specific legal framework that regulates their inception. Nor can they be considered an institution. Instead, the essential element is the practice of societal cooperation, which is why the concept of cooperativism is preferred over that of cooperative, as it implies a collective mobilization rather than simply a structure. A cooperative's practice can be considered anti-capitalist cooperativism only when it is organized around the reconstruction of the commons and solidarity, community self-management, use value and its exchange, mechanisms (such as role-rotation) that democratize internal social relations or practices to guarantee gender equality and social emancipation, as well as non-capitalist forms of work. More than its legal structure, I consider it crucial that it exist in antagonism to capitalism. Furthermore, its importance lies not in how it was established, but rather the political process by which it arose. In other words, I want to analyze cooperativism as a movement arising as part of a political project, with the objectives of true emancipation and social liberation, going beyond merely establishing alternative economic forms. The experience of the cooperative movement and the organization of cooperatives in Rojava has laid bare a discussion on cooperativism in deep need of new concepts and perspectives.

The organization of the cooperativist movement in Rojava

Cooperatives were introduced as the third basic structure of democratic autonomy—after the assemblies and communes—as an organizational unit. The political training and education units of this tripartite organizational structure are called academies (*Bilim Aydınlanma Komitesi*, 2009). As I highlighted in the previous chapter's discussion on communes and assemblies, although Kurdish political actors consider these strictly organizational structures, during my field research I observed that, for society, the organization within communes and assemblies had a significance beyond that of a static structure. As it penetrated all imaginable spheres of daily life, such organization was able to spontaneously create dynamic movements, ushering in a self-determined social transformation from below. Communes and assemblies create permanent processes; what remains is not the structure itself, but the process, which is imbued with its own momentum. The Autonomous Administration of Northern Syria aims to extend cooperatives into the social base—into the communes and assemblies—and create a people's autonomous economy by establishing cooperatives throughout all sectors of the economy.

Rojava's first cooperativism initiatives were taken in 2016. However, the first public debate with the express goal of establishing such autonomous organizations took place at the First Conference on Cooperatives in Northern Syria, held on October 20 and 21, 2017.

The conference discussed the draft for a Contract on Cooperatives, "the preparation for training sessions on cooperatives by the economy academy" and "the cooperativization of previously-established cooperatives that failed to function in accordance with the aims of the social economy." In addition, other decisions made at the conference included "organizing the 'cooperative for each commune' movement"; "focusing on the organization of agricultural and livestock cooperatives," and "granting villages right-of-use over communal lands through cooperatives" (interview with Yekîtî, 2018). The draft "Contract on Cooperatives of the North Syrian Federation," prepared at the conference, stresses that not a single person in Rojava should remain without a cooperative, just as no one should be without a commune (Cooperatives Committee of North Syria – *Komîteya Kooparatîfên Bakûrê Sûrî*, 2017). Moreover, according to this document, "cooperatives must internalize the mentality and the paradigm of the democratic-communal economy, as well as its basic principles and approach towards economic problems." This means that "cooperatives cannot be limited only to economic production, since they are one of the basic pillars of any democratic society—both for their economic activities as well as for their support to other social areas." Consequently, "the cooperative does not cover only economic interests; it is a social organization whose objective is to satisfy the basic needs of society, which is achieved on the basis of collaboration, exchange, solidarity and self-management" (Cooperatives Committee of Northern Syria – *Komîteya Kooparatîfên Bakûrê Sûrî*, 2017).

In Rojava, cooperativism is organized as a movement (the cooperativism movement) so as to build the community economy of democratic autonomy. In other words, cooperatives are not expected to develop on their own, as in other parts of the world; the will and willingness of the people to establish them is not a determining factor. In short, cooperatives are not expected to form on the basis of class-based needs. Instead, they are understood as a project for political organization involving all sectors of society. Cooperatives are deemed the "dimension under construction" of democratic autonomy. This is attested to by the fact that the two political cadres who head the TEV-DEM are in charge of this work, acting as a Cooperatives Committee within the Economic Coordination body.[11] The cadres' task is to direct the organization of cooperatives, extending their influence by establishing cooperatives in all sectors of the economy. Additionally, Kongra Star has its own women's cooperatives committee.

11 The Cooperatives Committee is co-chaired by spokespersons, one of whom is a woman, who are swapped out every few years. The Kurdish Movement periodically rotates its political cadres; thus, the people I interviewed at the time have been replaced. However, since the Committee's work is the construction of autonomy, it is never dissolved. Its purpose and tasks were defined by the movement.

Although the Kurdish Movement had previous experiences with cooperatives in Bakur, cooperatives began to be organized in Rojava in 2016, the first of which was Hevgirtin, mentioned above. However, it was only in 2017 that the Cooperatives Committee began operating and started the cooperativism movement in Rojava. The cooperatives I visited in early 2018 were generally not more than two years old. During this period, the Cooperatives Committee centered their attention on building an underlying institutional structure rather than on establishing new cooperatives.

The House of Cooperatives (*Mala Kooperatîfa*) and the Union of Cooperatives (*Yekîtîya Kooperatîfa*)

Cooperatives began to organize much more widely in 2017. According to the Co-Spokesman of the Cooperatives Committee, coupled with the decisions made at the cooperatives conference in October 2017, this created the need to formally organize cooperativism in Rojava. In other words, the institutionalization of cooperatives was the fruit of necessity (interview with Serxwebun, Co-Spokesman of the Cooperatives Committee, 2018). One of the conference's lasting decisions was to establish a *Mala Kooperatîfa* (House of Cooperatives) in all provinces and a *Yekîtîya Kooperatîfa* (Union of Cooperatives) in all cantons of northern Syria. Once these organizations were inaugurated, the Federation of Cooperatives was brought into being in order to cover all types of cooperative units.[12] Its purpose is to popularize cooperatives, as well as act as a coordinator between them in order to create a network of cooperatives (interview with Serxwebun, Co-Spokesman of Rojava Cooperatives, 2018). Yet again, the creation of these institutions was a response to the needs of the movement for social transformation; it was not institutionalization from above.

Melsa, Co-Spokeswoman of the Cooperatives Committee, explains how the structures that emerged as a result of this process are related:

> The work of the cooperatives is new in Rojava; the comrades started working in this field a year ago. Frankly, we don't have many cooperatives. After the conference, several new cooperatives were established. As I said, since the peoples of Rojava are not familiar with cooperativism, our task is to go from one province to the next, meeting with people and discussing cooperatives. In the aftermath of the conference, we organized a *Mala Kooperatîfa* (House of Cooperatives) in each province. All the Houses of Cooperatives convene at the *Yekîtîya Kooperatîfa* (Union of

---

12 I am not always going to make reference to the organization of the women's economy (*Aboriya Jin*), but it should be noted that women's cooperatives have an identical organizational structure. It is called the *Mala Kooperatîfa* of *Aboriya Jin* and the *Yekîtîya Kooperatîfa* of *Aboriya Jin*.

Cooperatives) assembly. *Yekîtî*[13] is responsible at a cantonal level; they are responsible for all the Houses of Cooperatives. All problems and all projects arrive here; *Yekîtî* is where all decisions are made. In other words, *Yekîtîya Kooperatîfa* is an assembly of Houses of Cooperatives where all decisions about cooperative projects are made. We, as co-spokespersons, work mainly with *Yekîtî*. Our planning is arranged together with the colleagues from *Yekîtî*. They are our local partners, we train and appoint them for the organization of the social economy. They hold daily meetings. When needed, they let us know and we accompany them and attend their meetings. Sometimes we give seminars on cooperativism or other political issues. Or, if a cooperative is preparing to be opened, we go with them, see it for ourselves, and talk to the people. (Interview with Melsa, Co-Spokeswoman of the Rojava Cooperatives Committee, 2018)

Yekîtî's Co-Spokeswoman, Leyla, refers to the process of forming the House of Cooperatives as follows:

Now we have *Mala Kooperatîfa* in all provinces. While they were being established, we met with the people who had administrative positions in the different cooperatives and we introduced them to a number of confidence-building assurances to encourage them to participate in the House of Cooperatives process.[14] Our goal was to ensure that those who had established cooperatives before would guide the newly-established cooperatives and inspire people to participate in them. We wanted them to share their experiences with the people. However, when we decided to organize a House of Cooperatives in each province, we found that there were not enough cooperatives or members in each province to form them. Therefore, we organized a training program for cooperatives at the Economy Academy (*Akademiya Aborî*), bringing together people who had studied economics or done political work in the social field, that is, those who had had previous experience in self-organization. These comrades established the *Mala Kooperatîfa* in the provinces they lived in. The *Yekîtîya Kooperatîfa* was formed out of the unity of the Houses of Cooperatives. *Yekîtî* controls and supervises the Houses of Cooperatives. (Interview with *Yekîtî*, 2018)

The Union of Cooperatives (*Yekîtîya Kooperatîfa*) is a social and autonomous institution in terms of its institutional relations—it is not formally related to any

13 When talking about the *Yekîtîya Kooperatîfa*, their members refer to their institution as *Yekîtî* for short.
14 The assurances that Leyla mentions is the implementation of the *fon* system.

institution of the Autonomous Administration. Its theoretical and political relationship with autonomy is mediated by the Cooperatives Committee, as Melsa explains. This committee then reports back about *Yekîtî*'s concrete projects to the Economic Coordination assembly, convened monthly at the Economic Council (*Destaye Aborî*) of the Autonomous Administration. Therefore, although the latter does not intervene directly in the organization of the cooperatives, it is aware of the advances in the organization of cooperatives and considers the cooperativism movement's needs when taking general decisions about the economy.

The "Contract on Cooperatives" defines the duties of the House of Cooperatives as follows:

> The Houses of Cooperatives are tasked with supervising the cooperatives' operations, ensuring that they comply with the principles of democratic cooperatives in their rules and programs, establishing a relationship with the Cooperative Unit (*Yekîtî*), and collecting the monthly contributions for Yekîtî. (Cooperatives Committee of Northern Syria – *Komîteya Kooparatîfên Bakûrê Sûrî*, 2017)

Leyla affirms that this is the technical work of the Houses of Cooperatives, as their main objective is to organize society into cooperatives:

> The Houses of Cooperatives hold extensive open meetings with the people. They explain the objectives of cooperativism. What does the project mean, how do you start a project, how can you work collectively, how do you collaborate and share, how their cooperatives will grow and develop, etc. These are the main topics of the meetings. In fact, we are the Union of Houses of Cooperatives. People can also contact us directly to open a cooperative, but the relationship between cooperatives and the people is mediated directly by the Houses of Cooperatives. The *Mala Kooperatîfa* participates in the economic assemblies of its provinces and develops cooperatives according to the ensuing debates and decisions taken at its assemblies. It organizes commune meetings, working together with each commune's economy committee. In these meetings, the social economy's objectives are explained, how cooperatives fit into it, the vision of democratic autonomy, and, to this end, the communes' own needs are discussed. All community members attend the meetings and can make suggestions freely. These are discussed with consideration to the needs of the region and, if a consensus is reached on an economic proposal, the House of Cooperatives launches a cooperative project.

For example, yesterday, at a commune meeting, a decision was made to establish a cooperative bakery in the province of Girke Lege. Subsequently, we had a meeting with the Girke Lege House of Cooperatives and they informed us that they did not have the fund, so we discussed it. (Interview with *Yekîtî*, 2018)

The Houses of Cooperatives are organized in all the provinces as public spaces. People can enter at any time to chat, ask and consult. In other words, it is not an institution separate from or above the people, but instead works according to the wishes and decisions of the people. *Mala Kooperatîfa,* which, like any autonomous institution, always has tea boiling on the stove, is not only a point of contact for communication with the administration; it is also a place where horizontal, face-to-face relationships are built. Zibechi reminds us that one of the ways to dissolve the state is by creating spaces where relationships can develop through face-to-face encounters (Zibechi, 2014, p. 115). In the Houses of Cooperatives, as in Community Houses (Mala Gel), people gather to drink tea and talk about the economy. These conversations provide a window into how people perceive and feel about the current economy. In these discussions, one can hear references to the knowledge and vibrancy of the old forms of collective work, mutual support and solidarity, when people speak of the way "we used to do it."

Beyond that, they are spaces where criticisms of the organization and construction of the social economy can be expressed directly to those in charge of it. Often, people enter saying *"ez hatim we rexne bikim!"* ("I came to criticize you!"). One day, as I was drinking tea at the House of Cooperatives in Serêkanîyê province, a farmer came in saying exactly that. As the House's Co-Spokesman invited him in, saying *"kerem ke!"* ("go ahead!"), he turned to me laughing: "No one ever comes to congratulate, only ever to criticize." Perhaps one of the most remarkably creative practices of the Kurdish Movement in their organization across Kurdistan is the availability of spaces in which people can make criticisms to the movement as part of their everyday lives. To be part of the autonomous struggle means criticizing the struggle as well as constantly practicing self-criticism. This is the most revolutionary practice of the autonomist movement in Kurdistan: it is the criticism and self-criticism of an armed organization against its very existence.

The Houses of Cooperatives, which are usually deeply intertwined with local economy committees, are an original and unique experience, and it is indisputable that they play a vital role in assuring people's participation in the discussion and organization of the economy. Put otherwise, they make possible the socialization of the economy, as it is lived in Rojava.

Another responsibility of the House of Cooperatives is the collection of 5% of the income from all cooperatives, which is distributed as follows: 2% of the contributions goes to cooperative fund, another 2% is set aside for *Mala Kooperatîfa* and 1% goes to *Yekîtî*. With these contributions, *Mala Kooperatîfa* and *Yekîtî* support the creation of new cooperatives (Cooperatives Committees of Northern Syria – *Komîteya Kooparatîfên Bakûrê Sûrî*, 2017). However, since there are not enough cooperatives and the ones that do exist are not yet competitive enough, Melsa points out that this mechanism is not working well and that they have obtained the necessary financing for the creation of new cooperatives from Economic Coordination-affiliated companies—that is, from the companies that I call "factories without bosses." This "borrowed money" is transferred from these companies to the cooperatives. Thus, the construction of cooperatives is supported by the Economic Coordination body's other economic activities.

> For instance, a bakery or tailoring project was presented to a House of Cooperatives. Public meetings were held, prospects, expenses and potential income were calculated; capital contributions (sehm) were collected. But some people did not have money, so they could not participate. We may decide that some of them can participate without paying any sehm, but for others we can decide that they will participate with one or two sehm. In their stead, we pay the capital contribution. We are simply providing credit. But we, as a committee, can't decide to make this loan immediately. We make the decision after discussing it at *Yekîtî*'s monthly assembly. If the assembly decides in favor, the House of Cooperatives can give the loan; if their budget does not allow it, the request will reach *Yekîtî*. If *Yekîtî*'s budget cannot cover it, we can obtain it from the companies that are part of the Cooperatives Committee. In general, our contribution to cooperatives' starting capital is between 10 and 20%. The cooperative then pays back the money it borrowed when it starts turning a profit. That money is then re-circulated in order to help other cooperatives. (Interview with Melsa, Co-Spokeswoman of the Rojava Cooperatives Committee, 2018)

Melsa's account shows that, although institutions exist to organize cooperatives, it is not the kind of capitalist state-institutionalization that we are familiar with. It is not an institutionalization that creates a society/institution division and eliminates face-to-face or community relationships. Institutions like *Mala Kooperatîfa* or *Yekîtîya Kooperatîfa* have been organized to promote, facilitate and coordinate society's autonomous anti-capitalist organization. They were built to meet the needs of the struggle for autonomy and operate by popular decision-making.

They are not hierarchical in structure, but work as an assembly of cooperatives. Relations are democratic, horizontal and centered on the community. The ethical and moral principles of their struggle shape their relationships with other institutions. However, all institutional actions are based on belief in the Kurdish Movement. The political cadres of the Cooperatives Committee occupy their posts as a sign of people's confidence in the movement; people perceive their words and decisions as the decisions of the movement. The cadres themselves carry out their work according to the Kurdish Movement's directives. An aspect that illustrates the importance of the relationship of trust that has emerged out of the unity of this struggle is the fact that, in the meetings on cooperatives held in the NES's Arab regions, there have not been any immediate successes.

When I conducted my field research in the early months of 2018, the Houses of Cooperatives were in the process of organizing public meetings in each commune under the slogan "a cooperative for each commune." Each *Mala Kooperatîfa* held commune meetings all over their provinces and encouraged the communities to establish cooperatives to meet their collective needs and aspirations. In these meetings, which I attended together with the Houses of Cooperatives in various communes, the discussion was centered around how to establish cooperatives. Before economic discussions began, the martyrs (*şehîd*) were remembered with a minute of silence, after which the House of Cooperatives co-spokespersons gave a report on the general political situation. The Afrîn War, which was being waged as I conducted my first field work, and the Serê Kanîyê resistance, which coincided with my second research trip, informed the atmosphere and dominated the discussions at all meetings. Plans in solidarity with the wars' displaced were one of the main outcomes of these assemblies.

What I remember most from these meetings is that the communes' participants thought, and often demanded, that the House of Cooperatives should establish new cooperatives. When the Houses explained that they would only support the process and help them establish it themselves, the discussions became more realistic, as the fact that the communes had to be the ones to form their own cooperative raised the issue of collective contributions. As mentioned previously, in Kurdish communities, which have more trust in the movement, it was not difficult to obtain collective contributions; generally, Kurds, even as they pay their contribution, always try to negotiate with the movement.

In Arab communities, however, the co-spokespersons usually have a harder time making the people understand that the contributions they pay are going to be used directly to create cooperatives. I saw more of these doubts expressed during my first visit in 2018 than in 2019. Arabs tended to hesitate more before cooperating with each other as well as with Kurds. During a "a cooperative for each commune" meeting I attended in the Arab-majority Shaddadi region, a man stood up and asked: "What happens if the money we put up disappears?"—an expression of the general distrust of the Autonomous Administration and its political project in this region. For this reason, the development of cooperativism in Arab regions and communities is sluggish compared with Kurdish regions. My goal here is not to conduct an analysis based on ethnic dichotomies, but rather to emphasize that the development of cooperativism will continue to be slow as long as sufficient collective and political trust has not been built.

When Melsa pointed out that Kurds consider cooperatives to be the core of the economy, she clarified that this is also true of all peoples living in northern Syria. Nevertheless, as the Cooperatives Committee, they are fully aware that it will take time to explain cooperativism and cultivate people's trust and willingness to collectivize. It should be noted that throughout the Syrian War, control over many Arab regions of the NES changed hands frequently between armed groups. Their economies failed to stabilize as political stability, too, crumbled. None of these regions had a working agricultural sector. As their subsistence was threatened, many men became involved with groups such as al-Nusra Front and ISIS—even when they did not share their ideologies—simply for the economic incentive they offered. Families in these regions could not meet their basic needs. Melsa highlighted that the Cooperatives Committee was one of the first institutions to arrive in these regions after their liberation by Kurdish forces:

> Our objective is to bring a concrete project to the villages that will allow them to rebuild their lives. Cooperatives are the foundation of the social economy. It is the way in which they can organize their own economy. Our objective is that they organize their own economy through popular and democratic cooperatives. Through them, they can work for themselves, trade in their own markets and earn their own money. In this way, people can obtain the fruits of their labor. But we need time to achieve this; it can't happen overnight. First, the social ground must be readied. Other things take priority for a people recently liberated from war. They expect their daily bread as much as they expect us to assure their security. We tell them: "Build your own bakeries, we will help you; you will no longer need anyone to give you bread. Do not allow anyone to enslave you for food. Don't allow us to do that either. You are the masters of your own economy." We achieved results in some regions, but we need more time to reach the level we are striving for. (Interview with Melsa, 2018)

Melsa's remarks demonstrate that the Kurdish Movement considers the economy the basis for the self-determination of society. Its full expression is, essentially, the definition of autonomy.

One last aspect I would like to highlight in talking about the organizational structure of the cooperativism movement in Rojava is that the *Yekîtîya Kooperatîfa*, the *Mala Kooperatîfa* and all the cooperatives have two co-spokespersons—a woman and a man. In Rojava cooperatives, there is no cooperative presidency as exists in other types of cooperatives. This practice is crucial in establishing democratic gender relations. All cooperatives have rotating leadership positions as well. The cooperative assembly takes the decision of when leadership positions change, as it does for all other decisions related to the cooperative. The cooperative administration's main task is to report the results of the assembly, as well as the decisions and the plans of the cooperative to the House of Cooperatives. Each cooperative's co-spokespersons attends their province's monthly assembly of cooperatives—which is called and organized by the House of Cooperatives—where they present their cooperative's report. Once this assembly is concluded, the House of Cooperatives drafts a report on cooperative development in its province, which it submits to *Yekîtîya Kooperatîfa*'s monthly assembly. In addition to an evaluation of existing cooperatives, the *Mala Kooperatîfa* report also includes plans for establishing new cooperatives. Considering all opinions, suggestions and reports filed by the different Houses of Cooperatives, *Yekîtî*, the coordinating body between all of them, organizes the plans for cooperatives at a cantonal level and presents them as a report to the monthly meeting of the Economic Coordination body of the Federation of Northern Syria.

As I previously mentioned, the system of reports is vital for the Kurdish Movement, as it allows for the flow of information into all areas of the organization, while at the same time showcasing how all political decisions are harmonized with the political outlook of democratic autonomy. These reports are not sent to the relevant institutions; the institutions' co-spokespersons instead attend the assemblies with their reports. This practice guarantees that all autonomous processes occur face-to-face and in a democratic manner, transforming each meeting into an assembly and encompassing all of the movement's areas of organization—not just popular assemblies, but also economic, educational, self-defense and other assemblies. As each autonomous dimension is socially organized, they generate new spaces for assembly. Thus, each Rojavan becomes a participant and assembly member in the debates of several different assemblies, each in a sphere of life they form a part of and are directly affected by. In this way, decisions become increasingly social in nature and people turn towards communal assemblies in order to make decisions. The cooperatives, where communal assemblies are also commonplace, thus become a dynamic and popular movement.

As already indicated, cooperative assemblies are open to popular participation. Any person belonging to the local commune can take part, while the participation of the commune's economy committee in these assemblies is considered all but mandatory, if not an ethical-moral obligation in the context of the struggle for autonomy. This exemplifies the fact that autonomy is organized on the basis of an alternative ethic—a communitarian ethic that is neither capitalist nor hierarchical.

Several cooperatives have been organized under Rojava's cooperativism movement. Although agricultural cooperatives have had the biggest impact, thousands of others have collectivized their means of production or their labor force into diverse cooperatives, including sales, services and production cooperatives. In order to organize this economic sphere, which encompasses hundreds of thousands of people, hundreds of political cadres affiliated with the Cooperatives Committee, the House of Cooperatives and the Union of Cooperatives are dispatched each day.

Before I move on to an analysis of the problems, limitations and contradictions of Rojavan cooperatives, I would like to stress that, thanks to the mobilization of these cadres, cooperatives are becoming an autonomous movement. The fact that this mobilization is organized and has become a dynamic movement is a concrete indicator of anti-capitalist revolutionary practice in Rojava.

The dynamics and limitations of Rojava cooperatives

Make-destroy-remake: experiments in cooperativism

Cooperatives presuppose the reorganization of social relations on the basis of production as a form of emancipatory economic activity. Generally, the reorganization of economic relations gives rise to a novel structure/institution in the form of the "cooperative." However, I must emphasize that cooperatives are only one of the possible forms of economic union and organization. The objective of the cooperativism movement (*Mala Kooperatîfa, Yekîtîya Kooperatîfa* and the Cooperatives Committee) in Rojava is to build cooperatives as organizations of economic production. However, the vision that lies behind the struggle for autonomy in Rojava and the concrete on-the-ground reality, marked by ongoing war, are not the same thing.

Although there has been a continuing effort to organize cooperatives in Rojava since 2016, and new cooperatives have sprouted up continuously, cooperatives have also shown a lack of continuity as a single structure. Often, they dissolve after only a short existence or are abrogated by decision of the Economic Coordination body. This gives the impression that the organization of cooperatives has failed:

> The fact is that, from the very beginning, cooperativism, which took the path treaded by Israeli, German and French capitalist cooperatives, was enough to destroy the basis of Rojava's revolutionary resistance. We had very tough discussions, conflicts and confrontations around the topic of cooperatives. With the attempt by the liberal wing, which at the time dominated all levels of Rojava's administration, to introduce cooperatives into social life in the form of anonymous companies, cooperativism collapsed before it had had a chance to begin and the revolution lost its most important opportunity to spread into the social life (Acun, 2020).

Unlike Hikmet Acun, father of the Turkish socialist revolutionary Paramaz Kızılbaş (Suphi Nejat Ağırnaslı) who died in the Kobane resistance in 2014, who has lived in Rojava since 2015, I believe that Rojava is undergoing a process of making-destroying-remaking—that is, of experimentation. On this issue, one of the co-spokespersons of the KCK's Communal Economy Committee (Koma Ciwakên Kurdistan – Kurdistan Society Unit) states:

> Those who have carried out cooperative activities under the ruling regimes of the four parts of Kurdistan have no experience in organizing cooperatives according to the ideals of our system, neither our political cadres nor society. So, we don't know what would be the right way. We make it and then we destroy it; we make it again, we destroy it again. Our general organizational history is like this, too: it developed out of a practice of making and destroying. This is also the case in the field of cooperatives. But, to be honest, this practice is taking place more than is necessary. Many cooperatives have developed. At one point, the cooperatives counted approximately 50,000 members. But how did it happen? For example, when electricity was lacking, people were buying generators in each neighborhood and street commune and, since they produced their electricity communally, we were counting them as if they were cooperatives. In fact, in a way, they were, it was collective work carried out due to a collective need. On the other hand, we have quite a lot of land in our possession. We have developed cooperatives on these lands. People pool their contributions (sehm) and we give them the land so that they can produce communally. But these are not permanent coop-

eratives, since they used to change their members on a yearly basis; now they are changed every two years. The goal is that all people benefit. Well, we also consider them cooperatives, but, essentially, they lack an institutional structure. (Interview with the Co-Spokesman of the Communal Economy Committee, 2019)

This dynamic of making and destroying is one of the most important indicators that Rojava's Autonomy is undergoing a process of attempting to overcome its internal and external contradictions. For this reason, I believe that, in order to truly understand the contradictions of this revolution, rather than focusing on issuing precise judgments, we must concentrate on the changes, transformations and tendencies of this ongoing process. In this sense, I want to underline that the organization of the cooperative or alternative economy is not a process that has concluded, has been abandoned or whose goals have changed. The movement for democratic autonomy continues to build cooperatives, testing and searching for new models. Cooperatives continue to be organized as a movement aimed at creating an anti-capitalist social economy. In fact, although cooperatives have not (yet) become permanent operational units, cooperativism entails a practice that politicizes the quotidian activities of people in Rojava. Put differently, there has emerged a process of cooperativization without cooperatives.

In the following section I argue that the alternative economy and the organization of cooperativism must be understood within a comprehensive view of the politics of autonomy and be considered a fruit of autonomous organization, rather than discussing whether they exist or not. In this sense, I think it is important to focus on the actual internal and external difficulties and contradictions in this process, which limit the development of cooperatives, in order to uncover the potential and direction of the Rojava Revolution.

The search for a unique model of cooperativism

In Rojava, the first step towards the formation of a cooperative involves holding public meetings organized by the communes. The House of Cooperatives convenes the commune assembly in order to gather and discuss cooperativism. These meetings, which take place under the banner of "a cooperative for each commune," have two main objectives: to present to the people the idea of cooperativism as a political project and to discuss their collective needs and wants in order to direct the organization of cooperatives (interview with the Co-Spokesperson of the House of Cooperatives, 2018).

In order to organize an anti-capitalist economy, one must be able to answer three questions: What do we produce? How do we produce? For whom do we produce? (Trasol, 2017, p. 23). The answers to these questions determine the political project's transformative and emancipatory potential.

In Rojava, the questions of "What do we produce?" and "For whom do we produce?" are discussed within common spaces. Through community relations, people are able to carve out an autonomous space in which they can debate and discuss collective needs. For example, during meetings with community members held by the Economic Committee and the House of Cooperatives, attempts are made to define the collective needs of the community. However, the conversation is not reduced merely to hearing their needs. Discussions are also held to determine which of the commune's own/autonomous resources could be used to satisfy these needs, since cooperatives are based on commonizing the collective wealth. In many of the commune meetings I participated in, it was highlighted that common resources are not only material; the communal relations that bind the communities of Rojava are also sources of social wealth that can be tapped in order to organize cooperatives. Thus, the topics of discussion included communal forms of social life and what these forms of community life should look like concretely. Once a commune assembly decides to satisfy/produce their collective needs through self-organization, the House of Cooperatives proposes cooperativism as a political and economic project. The expectation is that cooperatives will be established, not as a model imposed from above, but as the product of discussions from below.

It should be noted that cooperatives are not a well-known phenomenon in the region, be it in Rojava or in other parts of Kurdistan. It is not a local or authentic concept, but rather a form of organization imported by the Kurdish Movement as part of its political project. Despite this, many other non-capitalist, collective and solidarity forms of economic organization exist in Kurdistan, in the shadow of capitalism, as Gibson-Graham describes it, including: the paletî (wheat harvest), the berî (communal milking), the bêş kirin (collective fundraising) and the hevra (collective). If we do not embark on a discursive and political effort to shine a light on such practices, to restore their dignity, vitality and potential, they will remain in the shadows (J. K. Gibson-Graham, 2010, p. 27).

It quickly became apparent that, in Rojava, cooperatives are often presented as the only form of alternative economic organization and that the Economic Committee does not make any effort to revive regional manifestations of communal organization or to use them as a basis for the organization of cooperatives. Cooperatives have thus not been readily accepted by the people, and even when they are, this does not necessarily mean that they are internalized. That is why, as Delal points out, more often than not, the decision to establish a cooperative is not taken after a single meeting. At times, dozens of discussions are held with the same commune, until the decision is eventually made (interview with Delal, Spokeswoman of the Women's Economic Committee, 2018).

> Our first objective is to generate a change of mentality, as this is a fundamental prerequisite for the formation of cooperatives. However, this should be a step-by-step process. We are, then, trying to effect a dual transformation. We can consider this a transitional process, in which capitalist modernity and democratic modernity exist simultaneously— that is how we can see the current situation. There may have been a revolution, but mentalities are still dominated by capitalist modernity, and that is very evident in everyday life. [...] We held dozens of meetings in order to introduce the concept of cooperatives into community discussions and we tried to generate practices on this basis. In other words, we put cooperatives on the people's agenda, but we cannot say that they are completely convinced. For example, when we propose cooperatives, we tell them to get together and start producing on their own and that they can also earn on their own; by taking out the mercantile middlemen they can even create their own markets. However, the first thing they ask us is how much they will earn. They ask us for guarantees of future earnings. When we tell them that this will be determined by their work in the cooperatives, they say no. They ask us to build it for them and to give them wages (fon) and that they will then work, because they see wages as a guarantee. We need to break with the "I stand to lose in cooperatives, but a salary serves as my guarantee" approach. Otherwise, even if a cooperative is established, as long as this mentality remains dominant, nothing will be achieved, because it will be reflected in their practice. (Interview with Delal, Spokeswoman of the Women's Economy Committee, 2018)

In fact, none of the community meetings I attended in 2018 resulted in the decision to immediately establish a cooperative. As Delal pointed out, a stable income was preferred over cooperation. Deeming safe and salaried work a privilege is far from exclusive to Rojava. In the context of global insecurity, hunger and destruction created by capitalism, many people all over the world share this opinion. In fact, most of the time, people stay away from political struggle lest they lose a paying job. Thus, one of the most important challenges that must be overcome in the fight against capitalism is the mentality that—under the weight of capitalism—wage relations are a guarantee.

That should be understood as the foremost objective of the meetings that are arranged with the communes, as well as Rojava's entire social organization—to produce a mental and emotional rupture with this system. Autonomous organizing is the continuity of that rupture. This entails not only an intellectual rupture or a critical position, but the creation of a collective practice of rupture too. In this sense, when, after long discussions, the commune is ready to establish a cooperative, the House of Cooperatives will take the position of coordinator of this process. Its main task is to ensure that the cooperative is established in accordance with the commune's decisions. At times, this practice is carried out in reverse, and the Cooperatives Committee assigns communes to cooperatives it has established in order to satisfy general needs.

> For example, we have a cooperative project that we have identified as a social need. But we, as the House of Cooperatives, cannot establish the cooperative. That is why we go and hold meetings on our projects with the communes. For example, we hold meetings with the communes of the city and tell them about the organization of cooperativism. Then we go to the village communes and explain the same thing to them. When they decide to pool their contributions (sehm), we then can coordinate the creation of a cooperative. It used to be different, but now we no longer accept contributors who will not work in the cooperative themselves. We often put up a 20% incentive, or lend money to those who want to work but are unable to gather the necessary fund in order to contribute. (Interview with the Co-Spokesperson of the House of Cooperatives, 2018)

Decisions regarding membership of the cooperative are made collectively in the commune. Since agricultural cooperatives are renewed every two years, the communes play an important role in this process:

> The planting season is approaching; we need to accept new members for the agricultural cooperatives. We call on the communes, we send letters, the communes meet at their communal houses. All those who want to participate put in a request with their communes. First, the communes themselves carry out an internal evaluation, then they send in their comments to the economic assembly or their province's economic committee. In this way, the number of applicants is ascertained, which is often well above the number needed. We pick them in accordance with the comments we received from the communes. (Interview with Delal, Spokeswoman of the Women's Economy Committee, 2018).

The first problem that arose at this stage is that the Economic Coordination body was unable to accept all of the petitions. That is why the membership of the cooperative is renewed every two years. The other problem—which inevitably arose with the formation of institutions and authority—is that members of the House of Cooperatives began enrolling themselves or their family members to participate in cooperatives whose construction they themselves were coordinating. When I asked about this situation, Delal explained that this was caused by two factors:

> Early on, in some places, the Houses of Cooperatives were established by comrades who were already members of a previously-existing cooperative. Therefore, there are comrades who, although they work in the House of Cooperatives, continue to be members in a cooperative. Previously, there was no system of salaries (*fon*), so these people were in charge of organizing cooperatives in the *Mala Kooperatîfa*, but received no salary for working in this position. When the autonomous organization began supporting the comrades who held social and political positions financially, the comrades from the Houses of Cooperatives were granted these benefits automatically. However, in some places, certain people from the Houses of Cooperatives engaged in fraudulent activity, becoming members of established cooperatives themselves or through their families. They didn't ask us. We began to notice it once we looked at the lists. I remember looking at a cooperative's membership list in which the names of two members were left blank. We convened a meeting and I asked the comrade from the House of Cooperatives: "Who are they, what commune do they come from?" She didn't say anything and started to cry. In short, we learned that her two sisters were members of one of our cooperatives. She argued that she did it because they were very poor. We have now prohibited this kind of situation. No one working with fund from our autonomous institutions can be a member of the cooperatives we have established. But they ask, they say, "Why can't my family participate in a cooperative?" They are right; they themselves cannot be a member, but one of their relatives could. We decided then that they were allowed to become members, but only if their communes make that decision.

> Now, we often face similar problems, but we don't want to prohibit from above; it's not right. But when we don't, we know that we are going to find ourselves in situations like this. Our concern is that the towns may think that the cooperatives are corrupt. That is to say, although our comrades may act with good intentions, it is nevertheless corrupt. [...] In other words, a revolution has taken place in Rojava, but the real

revolution will occur when these mentalities are changed. (Interview with Delal, Spokeswoman of the Women's Economy Committee, 2018)

As the previous testimony shows, the commune assembly is the arbiter of any given cooperative's membership. The commune can establish its own cooperatives or decide to have commune members participate in a cooperative organized by the Cooperatives Committee. It can do so by sending the references of their members to the *Mala Kooperatîfa*. Likewise, in some special cases, the Cooperatives Committee can make suggestions regarding membership in the cooperative.

Once the commune or the Economic Coordination body makes the decision to establish a cooperative and its members are chosen, the process of creating the means of production and their collectivization begins, which can be defined as the construction stage.

Generally, when looking at radical cooperative experiences throughout the world, "occupying" (or rather recovering) appears to be the most common route towards obtaining the means of production. In Argentina, cooperatives were created as a result of the recovery of factories by the workers, while many cooperatives of Indigenous peoples, such as the Zapatistas in Chiapas or those of the *Movimiento Sin Tierra* in Brazil, arose as a result of land occupation. In Rojava, the occupy/recover methods are not involved in the organization of cooperatives. The resources or means of production are created through "contributions," which, symbolically, entails the establishment of the cooperative as such. According to Zafer, of the Trade Committee, this constitutes a policy aimed at the "diffusion of capital across society":

> The living standards of society in this sense are not very bad, but our core policy is to communalize and collectivize them even more, to build a society that controls its own resources. People have very limited capital, and we are focused on avoiding the monopolization of capital and the formation of a bourgeoisie by diffusing this productive capital across the entirety of society, both in our commercial activities and in the cooperatives we organized jointly with the people. In other words, our policy is to guide society towards production through the dissemination of that capital. (Interview with Zafer, Responsible for the Trade Committee, 2018)

Zafer's use of the term "capital" is undoubtedly provocative. Yet what is really meant is the creation of a common capital through the pooling of fund, so that people who do not own the means of production can participate. Here, capital refers to a common production force/resource. However, it is an idea that can easily lead to precisely the inverse of what is intended if one does not clearly stipulate how the "diffusion of capital across society" should take place. Concretely, in Rojava, it has led to the practice of paying contributions (*sehm*) directly to the cooperatives. This creates a common capital that allows for the establishment of cooperatives. According to Melsa, these contributions are symbolic and were established for two reasons:

> We want people to see that they can create productive power when they cooperate with very small fund. The other [reason] is that they feel like part of the cooperative because they have put in their own money. Therefore, a hierarchical relationship between "us" and "them" cannot develop. If we were to put up the capital or all the means of production, they will see us as the state. (Interview with Melsa, Co-Spokeswoman of the Rojava Cooperatives Committee, 2018)

However, Hevrîn pointed to the example of her mother, who is a member of the Hevgirtin cooperative, and mentioned that, although many people contributed their small fund to the cooperative, they are not interested in its administration or production process (interview with Khalaf, 2018).

For Rojava's first cooperative, Hevgirtin, the buy-in was set at 30 dollars (1 *sehm* = 30 USD), while in Qesrik it was 100 dollars (interview with Zafer, 2018). Hevgirtin was formed by collecting sehm from 12,000 participants, establishing a common capital out of 25,000 single contributions. As there were no restrictions on how many single contributions a person could make, those with deep enough pockets bought up and became owners of several sehm (interview with Hevgirtin Cooperative, 2018).

At this point, members of Rojava cooperatives began to notice a problem—a problem which led the Economic Coordination body to take concrete action: the unevenly collected *sehm* generated unequal profits, as the cooperatives' membership rights were tied to the size of their contribution, rather than the principle of equitable distribution. The cooperatives' use of a profit-sharing model derived from capitalist companies, that is, of handing out a percentage of the profits equivalent to the percentage of contributions to the capital, caused Rojava's so-called cooperatives to be born with the defect of preserving, if not reproducing, existing economic inequalities. Hevgirtin was able to do a lot with the common capital it had been provided: it reduced market prices, avoided product shortages and financially supported the formation of other cooperatives, but it was unable to become a mechanism for the elimination of inequalities in profit distribution. On the contrary, it spearheaded the creation of cooperatives that lacked the understanding of what a Rojava cooperative was supposed to be, making the rich even richer (interview with Şerhat, Head of the Economic Coordination body in Derik, 2018).

When the Economy Committee supported agricultural cooperatives (by granting right-to-use over communal lands, diesel, water and energy support, seed support, support for tractors and other production equipment, as well as the purchase of the produce, etc.), their incomes increased, leading to the perception that they were an easy way to make money, and attracting opportunistic behavior:

> This is our main challenge in the Qasrik cooperative.[15] Four people, five people, 10 people from a single family were joining in. One family contributed 20 sehm. But poor families could only contribute one. So, there are serious imbalances in Qasrik. Those who have the money have obtained a lot of shares and earn a lot of money. We have intervened, we try to reduce it, but it continues to be a problem. (Interview with Delal, Spokeswoman of the Women's Economy Committee, 2018)

Melsa mentioned that this situation had been discussed by the Economic Coordination body and one of the decisions taken at the conference on cooperatives was that each family could own a maximum of three sehm. Even when two people from the same family join the cooperative, the contribution they can make cannot exceed three sehm. After this conference, at the end of 2017, in order to avoid greater inequalities, the Economic Coordination body made a special decision targeting cooperatives with a very high number of members, such as Hevgirtin and Qasrik, and returned the contributions of members who had bought in with more than three *sehm* at the time of the cooperative's foundation (interview with Melsa, 2018). At the time of my visit, at the beginning of 2018, the co-spokesperson of the Hevgirtin cooperative confirmed to me that they had reduced all contributions to three sehm (interview with Hevgirtin Cooperative, 2018).

Even so, in this ongoing process, the fact that all cooperatives continue to determine profit distribution by the percentage of contribution to the capital is indicative that, in the cooperatives, the logic of capital and the mentality of individual profit have remained intact. Nevertheless, the logic of cooperatives is not based on capital, but rather on common wealth: when all resources (money,

---

15 Qasrik is an agricultural cooperative, 120 kilometers west of Qamishlo, towards Aleppo. It was established in mid-2016, and by December had 5,000 members living in the cities of Tel Tamir and Dirbêsîyê. The largest cooperative in Cezîre in terms of size, diversity of departments, employees and participants, Qasrik covers an area of around 32,000 acres of rainfed and irrigated land in the area around Dirbêsîyê, where they grow cumin, maize, barley and wheat, and use greenhouses to grow vegetables such as tomatoes and zucchini. It has 4,624 members. Each share costs 50,000 SYP. Eighty people work in this cooperative, spread over five departments: livestock, rainfed agriculture, agricultural machinery and means of production, irrigated agriculture and livestock. One *sehm* = 100 dollars.

raw materials, machinery and labor power) are assigned to collective production, they become the communal foundation of a cooperative. The most common practice that ensures that the resource/production power that is created belongs to everyone, or to no one at all, is to repay members' contributions as the cooperative generates income.

The fact that the means of collective production of Rojava cooperatives are not communalized is problematic. Although the Cooperatives Committee is aware of it, they have yet to find a concrete solution (interview with Serxwebun, Co-Spokesman of the Rojava Cooperatives Committee, 2018). The formation of cooperatives through social contributions has been important in demonstrating to society that they can create a popular production power when they cooperate with their own resources, and that communal production can be organized based on cooperatives without it leading to the creation of a local or national capitalist class. Moreover, the commerce generated by Hevgirtin contributed to curbing the detrimental effects of the embargo and the black market, since it was able to supply basic necessities, and reduce prices in local markets, and led to the creation of a variety of food products. Qasrik, for its part, diminished the impacts of war by producing many of the basic necessities in its region. However, the main challenge remains that the means of production—essential to any real cooperative—are not communalized. Additionally, the fact that this discussion is not on the agenda of Rojava's cooperativism movement constitutes one of the main contradictions of this organization, in the context of the social economy.

Collective work-against-work

The aforementioned contradiction is also reflected in the collectivization of the labor force (or lack thereof), which is another problem plaguing Rojava's cooperatives. Regardless of how a cooperative's means of production and capital are obtained, people who unite and cooperate on the basis of their labor power are referred to as "worker cooperatives" in academia (ACI, 2020). In an alternative, non-capitalist economy, workers within collective work cooperatives—now masters over their own labor—are able to reconsider and define the nature of work. As mentioned before, for an economy to be considered non-capitalist, a non-capitalist form of labor is necessary. In order to rethink the nature of work, we must question what we will produce and under what material, emotional and ecological conditions (Uharte, 2019, pp. 33-34). In other words, what form of work is able to produce for the sake of society rather than capitalism. To answer these questions, we must put "the self-determination of the activities of our own productive force" at the center of the struggle for autonomy (Holloway and Hardt, 2012, p. 48).

Democratic-communal economies, then, entail a non-capitalist view of work. However, in Rojava, cooperatives are far from becoming a significant source of work or any other activity for their members. The price of contributions (*sehm*), which were kept artificially low in order for cooperatives to find a footing in society, led to people joining them in their thousands in order to come up with the initial common capital.

> The number of members of our cooperatives is very high. At first, the comrades, without a second thought, had not set an upper limit on the number of members, allowing everyone to join a cooperative. Yes, we want everyone to be part of a cooperative, but when the number of members is this high, families cannot gain an income high enough to allow them to survive on a subsistence level. Naturally, this situation generates mistrust towards cooperatives. In other words, we propose that they join the cooperatives, that they work collectively, but we cannot guarantee their livelihoods. That is why they have to engage in other capitalist jobs. (Interview with Melsa, Co-Spokeswoman of the Rojava Cooperatives Committee 2018)

The cooperatives that have been established up to this point are unable to generate jobs for thousands of people, which is why, most of the time, only a very small fraction of their membership can be employed by them. Cooperatives have been unable to establish a rotation system, whereby each member can work a number of shifts at the cooperative. Those members who work at the cooperative became salaried employees, as collective production cannot involve all members. Nevertheless, even those members who have not worked at the cooperative during a given year will collect their allotted profits every six months to a year. This makes the conditions of alienation and exploitation—fostered by the payment of wages to those cooperative members whose labor is used for production—permanent. Or in other words: it defines labor through the mediation of money.

Leyla, the Co-Spokeswoman of Yekîtî, pointed out that in Rojava's first cooperative experiences, collective work was an afterthought, while those who had the means became members simply by paying the sehm. As a result of discussions held at the Conference on Cooperatives, the practice was later banned:

> Because our objective is that the cooperatives' members work at the cooperatives. When someone who works all day in the city doing something else and, with their earnings, joins a village cooperative, they are not going to work at the cooperative, because their intention is to turn a

profit. When we realized that we had made a mistake, we started asking ourselves why we're enriching those who already had enough money. At the Conference on Cooperatives, we took decisions on this issue in order for it not to happen again. (Interview with Yekîtî, 2018)

In fact, the Contract on Cooperatives clearly states that, in Rojava, cooperatives are based on labor participation, while capital-based participation can only be accepted in "particular" cases (*Komîteya Kooparatîfên Bakûrê Sûrî*, 2017). When I asked Leyla about this particular section, she said: "We allow the elderly or martyrs' parents who are unable to work, or an engineer or an independent veterinarian who is collaborating, to support the cooperative by participating only through contributions" (interview with Yekiti, 2018). However, when we look at cooperative experiences in Rojava, even today, we observe that the degree of capital-based participation far exceeds that of a few particular cases. There are a large number of members who only obtain income from the cooperatives but are otherwise uninterested in its production process or its work. So much so that, when in some cooperatives no members wanted to work, these cooperatives, whose objective is to dissolve salary-based relationships, had no choice but to hire salaried workers, thus propagating internal capitalist dynamics—a glaring contradiction.

At one of the Qasrik cooperative's meetings I attended, I learned that some of the communal land that the Agriculture Committee provided to the cooperative was rented out to a single man and that 200 wage laborers worked on another part of the land where the cooperative was growing vegetables. The Qasrik cooperative, which has 4,700 members across the canton, half of whom are women, hired wage labor to harvest its vegetables. The cooperative's Co-Spokesman, whom I questioned about this situation, which had been recounted in a monthly report, said that none of the cooperative members wanted to work in the fields, so the House of Cooperative was forced to hire workers so as not to lose that season's produce. Additionally, the entire harvest was sold directly to a single merchant instead of being used to meet the needs of cooperative members and local communes (Qasrik Cooperative Assembly, 2018). Thus, the Qasrik cooperative's members did not carry out any work in the cooperative nor were they interested in using the produce to satisfy their own consumption—an approach in complete contradiction to the Contract on Cooperatives' definition of work.[16] Melsa confirmed that this situation is not unique to Qasrik:

16 "Work will cease to be a chore and instead become a cult to life itself. The walls of alienation built between life and work will be demolished. Priority will be given to the economic system that is based on use and mandatory exchange values, rather than the system that commodifies everything in society and transforms it into simple commodities. [...] A moral understanding that considers work as freedom, as well as the elimination of widespread unemployment, will satisfy all the essential aspirations and needs of society." (*Komîteya Kooparatîfên Bakûrê Sûrî*, 2017)

In most of our cooperatives, participation is not based on work; they put up the money and don't get involved. Especially in agricultural cooperatives, the mentality of seeking profit without getting involved in the production process is very dominant. We encourage members to work; we attempt to build work cooperatives. For example, in a dairy cooperative, we demanded that the cowherd and the veterinarian must also be members, therefore, they should work without remuneration. In most places, the herders were accepted as cooperative members through our efforts. I mean, it's only been a year since cooperatives have sprouted in Rojava and already they are plagued by many problems. We try to right the mistakes where we see them. The cooperative is a space where people can work and earn on their own, but in many of our cooperatives, the members invested their money and were never seen again. Some do not even show up to the assembly in order to discuss and make communal decisions about the cooperative. These are the serious problems.[17] (Interview with Melsa)

The co-spokespersons of the Hesekê canton economic assembly also highlighted the fact that cooperatives are not yet seen as workplaces and that this is one of the most important challenges to their political organization:

In the cooperative model that we envision, the members of the cooperative must work in it. The Houses of Cooperatives get many requests; people bring their projects. However, their expectations are often purely utilitarian, so the mindset we want to encourage hasn't yet taken root. For example, they will say that they will help us establish a cooperative; they want to put up their contributions and establish a cooperative, but they do not want to work there. When we ask who is going to work, they say that they will bring others, that is, that they will hire workers. This issue is one of the most challenging. (Interview with Hesekê Canton Economic Committee, 2019)

These circumstances led to the Hesekê Economic Committee's decision to shut down a number of cooperatives. During my research in 2019, Qasrik, Hevgirtin and many similar cooperatives were closed by the Committee due to their failure to "turn them into simple worker cooperatives" and because "their members failed to take responsibility for managing them" (interview with Şiyar, Co-Spokesman of the Rojava Cooperatives Committee, 2019).

---

17 Leyla, the Co-Spokeswoman of *Yekîtîya Kooperatîfans*, mentioned that at the *Yekîtî* assembly they made the decision to return the contributions of members who fail to attend three meetings of their cooperative's assembly and to eject them from the cooperative (*Yekîtî*, 2018).

The women's cooperatives, which initially were plagued by similar problems, attempted to include all the members in their work by reducing the number of members and introducing rotating work groups, which was never implemented in the mixed-gender cooperatives. In the agricultural cooperatives of aborîya jin (the women's economy), instead of paying wages, a fine was introduced for all those who failed to take part in the cooperatives' tasks:

> Membership in our agricultural cooperatives generally numbers 50 women. We divide the land among many cooperatives, each with 50 members. But 50 women don't have to go to work in the fields all at the same time. Instead, the women divide themselves into groups and each time a different group goes to the fields to work. When a certain group has to work but one of their members fails to show up, the cooperative imposes a fine. We do not consider this an appropriate decision, but our cooperatives discussed and decided for themselves. In other words, they say that it is necessary to be fair to those who work and those who do not. [...] For example, today we are going to clear the land. There are a lot of mice in the fields this season. We go and put poison in the mouse dens and fertilize the soil. This is a full day job, so all of the women go to the fields. Some did not show up; there are lists of members and those who do not come are marked, and the cooperative imposes a fine on them. They agree what the penalty will be together at the annual meeting. For example, this year, the penalty will be 2,000 pounds. Let's say, if 10 people don't show up, that comes to 20,000 pounds. This money is then distributed among those who worked. For now, this is the system we have; it has helped us solve some problems. (Interview with Delal, 2018)

The non-agricultural cooperatives established in recent years, especially women's cooperatives, have begun to overcome abstract labor with practices such as work rotation, penalties, reductions in the number of members, and more. In this sense, cooperatives have increasingly become spaces for collective work and have begun to move away from capitalist labor. This is not true across the board, as such developments were not present at the same time and at the same level in all of the cooperatives. Nonetheless, a new awareness of salary-free relationships has begun to take hold both in the Cooperatives Committee and the institutions linked to the cooperatives, as well as among the people. What is important to emphasize is that this happened as a result of the experience that was gained trying to organize Rojava cooperatives. In fact, the problematization of the material and emotional conditions of work, which determines the working conditions, as well as the conception and the logic of production, appears to be the natural next step for those cooperatives that have begun to experiment with collective work.

Many of the cooperatives that I visited in Rojava in 2018 had not experienced any kind of intervention in the production—or the logic and conception—of their labor. Textile cooperatives (generally employing only women) worked much like any capitalist textile mill. A work logic developed in which everyone had their backs turned to one another, no one looked at each other, and work was focused entirely on the product, not on any kind of collectivization.

I was able to experience first-hand how vital the transformation of the space and the flow-logic of work is when the members at one women's cooperative in Bakur (Kurdistan-Turkey), Eko-jin, rid themselves of the production line at a textile mill. The destruction of the production line, with its design based on Fordist logic and the exploitation of women's labor, and the reconstruction of the work process in accordance with the women's vision, allowed for the creation of a new and collective work process, face-to-face, punctuated by conversation and laughter. On rotation, women took on kitchen duties at the cooperative, preparing food they could all take home, and thus solving the issue of having to cook dinner for their families upon their return from work in the evenings.

For the women, the workshop ceased to be simply a space for production, becoming a space where they could interact with one another beyond work (Aslan, 2016). The fact that the production process became collective and enjoyable also meant that the workers were able to self-manage the production process; that is, self-management became part of the women's subjectification (*subjetivación*) on the basis of their own activity. When I asked members of Rojava's women's cooperatives about their experiences, two common aspects kept cropping up: no one bossed them around and their decisions were all made collectively. A woman from the Çarçela Restaurant, one of the first projects of the women's economy, who had worked in Derik since 2016, stated that, for her, working meant not only producing, but also organizing and being able to decide how to work:

> Here we work, it is true that we also receive money in exchange, but working at Çarçela is not the same as working in any other restaurant, because, first, there is no manager or boss here. Nobody can give us orders. None of us order the others. Sometimes we stay here at night to make *kutilk*.[18] We laugh, we joke, we sing. It is true that we are making money, but our goal is not just to make money—our main goal here is to organize ourselves. (Interview with Çarçela Restaurant, 2018)

18 Traditional Kurdish food that involves a long preparation process.

This demonstrates that, in Rojava, cooperatives are starting to overcome (managerial) power and hierarchies in the spaces of production. Despite its many contradictions, cooperatives are practicing direct and communal self-management, in which the entire economic process is decided on jointly by its members. The main reason for this rapid development is that, generally, in Rojava, assemblies have become a dynamic of everyday life. Joint decision-making free of state/managerial power plays a fundamental role in daily social emancipation and will surely be crucial for cooperatives' transformation and the resolution of their contradictions.

Each cooperative's assembly, the joint assembly of cooperatives in a particular region, held at the House of Cooperatives, and the *Yekîtî* cantonal assembly, are the spaces in which the problems of the cooperatives are being discussed and possible solutions are being proposed. Melsa mentioned that the cooperatives that meet in these spaces tend to visit and observe each other, while exchanging lessons learned:

> For example, a new farming cooperative (*sewaldarî*) will be established. In Derik, in one of the communes, we already have a farming cooperative. All the community members are members of the cooperative, they all take care of the animals and produce milk, yogurt, cheese, etc., and deliver it to the market themselves. For example, we say to those who want to establish a new farming cooperative that they should go there first, talk, discuss, observe, and then come and organize their own cooperative. In other words, an experience has been made already, a good example has been set. Take advantage of their experience so you don't start from scratch. (Interview with Melsa, 2018)

Cooperativism without cooperatives

The Kurdish struggle considers only cooperatives, and not institutions, to have the capacity to transform social relations:

> We are talking about a way of relating to one another, this is how we understand cooperatives, that is, as a space for collective work based on collective production and creating a collective life. That is the role of a cooperative within a socialist economy, a communal economy that serves us. It is the collectivization of work, the collectivization of society's potential, the collectivization of products and, through it, the collectivization of social life. (Interview with Şiyar, Co-spokesman of the Rojava Cooperatives Committee, 2019)

Agricultural cooperatives, which represent a majority of cooperatives in Rojava, are established on communal land for a period of two years. These lands are handed over to these cooperatives to serve the general economy and the women's economy. In addition, the Agriculture Committee grants the right-to-use of a fraction of the land to engineers (pispor), the seed center (bûhuz) and the seed company that reproduces seeds developed by the seed center (interview with the Co-Spokeswoman of the Communal Economy Committee, 2018).

> The distribution of the land in the past year [2017] was as follows: we held a meeting for six days and these decisions were the result. 100,000 hectares of land were given to the seed cultivation institution. During the war, we could not find seeds in Rojava. Some of the seeds we did find have increased in number; now they are working on reproducing good and authentically indigenous seeds. Our goal is to use these seeds both in cooperatives and to distribute them to farmers. *Aborîya jin* received 31,000 hectares of land. Only women can use these lands. 181,000 hectares are cultivated by the general economy cooperatives; 3,500 hectares were given to engineers in order to carry out projects that allow for the diversification of the produce. At the same time, we can say that they make a living from these lands, since they are organized as a cooperative. Apart from these, there are lands that are used by our various agricultural institutions. For example, the comrades who work in the Directorate of Agriculture in Dirbesiye requested 400 hectares of land and we gave it to them. Thus, while they farm different products, they also form a relationship with the land and go beyond being simple office workers. [...] Everyone who makes use of these communal lands is landless. This is our distribution of communal lands in the Cezîre canton for this year. Every year we re-evaluate this distribution. There are 500,000 hectares of land here. As I said, we give most of it to cooperatives. But, as you know, people here don't work in the fields throughout the 12 months; they only work during the productive season. (Interview with the Co-Spokeswoman of the Communal Economy Committee, 2018)

Wheat and barley, the most common agricultural products in Rojava, do not require much manual labor, as their cultivation is mechanized. Farmers simply wait for the winter and spring rains after sowing in autumn. In the region of Mesopotamia, which includes Rojava, wheat has been watered by natural rainfall for thousands of years. Regular irrigation is almost exclusively used in more arid areas, such as Raqqa and Deir ez-Zor, located in the south of northern Syria.

After the construction of irrigation canals in these regions (in 1960), agricultural production was centered on cotton. Although climate and rainfall in the region have seen drastic changes in recent years, traditional farming is still mostly carried out without additional watering. In Cezîre, harvest season begins in early May. This is when agricultural cooperatives are most active and most work is carried out, even partially. In the years before the revolution, the harvested wheat would then quickly be sold to the state. Now, it is sold to the agricultural directorates of the Autonomous Administration.[19]

When agricultural work is seasonal, so too are the cooperatives that carry it out. After long discussions, the Cooperatives Committee decided to re-build agricultural cooperatives every two years—that is, to collectivize two years' worth of agricultural production, allowing everyone to benefit from the communal land. The cooperatives, whose members are renewed every two years, are not permanent structures. They are not established as a cooperative institution. Rather, the commune members cooperate to carry out the two-year production process together. Every two years, the Agriculture Committee convenes a number of communes and announces that it will grant use rights over some of its lands to individuals in order to form a cooperative. The communes are asked to recommend potential members to the Cooperatives Committee. The selected individuals then collectively purchase seeds, pesticides and other agricultural inputs with their contributions and work the land that the Agriculture Committee has assigned to them for the next two years.

After these two years, the land is again available for collective use by a new cooperative. This practice has two consequences: since cooperatives are not established as institutions and the land is not given in perpetuity, cooperative work does not develop into a continuous and quotidian economic activity for their members. Thus, members of agricultural cooperatives often engage in other economic activities in order to assure a regular income that can sustain them through the entire year. This is true even if they are able to secure a livelihood for half of the year with the income obtained from agricultural cooperatives alone. Şiyar, the new co-spokesman of the Cooperatives Committee, whom I met in 2019, stated that these types of cooperatives can be a temporary solution:

> This practice emerged as a temporary solution to the immediate problems of people who suffer from poverty—unable to earn a living

19 As I mentioned before, the Autonomous Administration and the Economic Coordination body have yet to intervene forcefully in the functioning of the agriculture system, since the old system still remains in place. The AANES today makes purchases of wheat and barley before the harvest season, just like the Syrian state used to. In addition, each year, the Syrian state still determines its own purchase price of wheat and barley for all of Syria, although the vast majority of farmers prefer to sell their produce to the Autonomous Administration's agricultural directorates.

or feed themselves—as a result of the war. Today, communalization has been achieved through the cooperativization of production, granting right-to-use over lands that were previously in the hands of the state, but without turning them into property. Traditional farming in these places focuses exclusively on the production of different types of grain, given that there is no infrastructure or water resources that would allow irrigation-based agriculture to be carried out in this region. This is why cooperatives have not always been able to create work-based collectivization: rainfed farming has no minimum requirement for work. We don't consider the cooperatives that we have now to be real cooperatives. Rather, they are just temporary workarounds; in other words, they are a remedy for people's poverty, but in their current condition, they do not play the role in the collectivization of work that we strive for.

Now, when we approach this issue ideologically, we cannot say that they are cooperatives, but considering the conditions of war and geography, we see that they are nonetheless beneficial to the people. Though far from ideal, we have to find a way to adapt the current organization to the communal economy even as we face the pressures of war, without losing ourselves in judgement of this or that flaw, and, even though it has worked as a solution so far, we have not yet been able to create a vision for the future. Apparently, our political training has not been enough. We have been able to achieve some level of development through experiences and mistakes alone, but, from now on, we need to be in an organization that will make it possible to achieve a real communal economy. (Interview with Şiyar, 2019)

Many members of the Economic Coordination body, like Şiyar of the Cooperatives Committee, expressed similar self-critiques about their inability to develop cooperatives:

On the subject of building cooperatives and the economy, I must say that we were not able to, or that we simply have not done it. We cannot do long-term and stable planning, there are several reasons for that; but we can do the following: we can organize society based on leadership, self-management, and the search for political solutions; we can even carry out some of its practical activities in the beginning, and we can extend them credit and financial independence and support as much as possible, so we can achieve an economic or cooperative organization, organized according to its unique dynamics.

Serok (Abdullah Öcalan) says that society is already producing and living communally and collectively. What remains to be done is to apply it to the moral and political society, that is, to organize society. What is not organized? Does society not produce? Yes, it does. Does society not transport? Yes, it transports. Does society not sell? Of course, it sells. Are people not a part of the social market? Yes, they are a part of it. In short, they sell and buy every day, but society has a fragmented and scattered the economy, based solely on the capitalist experience, and it lacks a science-based production process.

So, what we have to do is to organize this fragmented and scattered economy. We can organize it whichever way: in the form of a units, cooperatives or chambers. When everything from production to reproduction is organized, no one will be able to destroy it. If the government or the system changes, these organizations will be the defensive shield of society, because people who know that they own their economy will defend themselves. That's what we haven't been able to do so far. As I mentioned, there are many reasons for this. However, some of our comrades don't believe in democratic socialism and do not believe that a democratic communal economy can be built. Honestly, a segment of our movement's comrades believes only in state-based commercial activity. (Interview with the Co-Spokesman of the Communal Economy Committee, 2019)

The fact that political cadres are able and willing to issue such self-criticisms is in itself liberating. Nonetheless, in my opinion, it leads to two contradictory conclusions: on the one hand, it creates a dynamic base for new revolutionary practices by ensuring that the organizational work is constantly being evaluated and does not become a fixed model; on the other hand, it reveals the cadres' own recognition of their incapacity to do what they should have been able to do as a movement—a mindset that often prevents them from recognizing and valuing practices that do not fall within their political perspective. People's spontaneous practices resulting from amassed real experiences are thus sacrificed in favor of party orthodoxy.

As I emphasized earlier, the experiences of the "factories without bosses" were criticized for not being true cooperatives and, eventually, these factories were transformed into the Autonomous Administration's own financial resources. Cooperatives are expected to shape their identity along the lines of the communal and democratic cooperative model espoused by Öcalan. According to my own observations, this two-year experience with cooperatives has had a positive impact on the people's and the movement's appreciation of cooperativism.

Those who have experienced and internalized cooperatives as political process and as a practice for two years are in the best position to open new cooperatives in other economic sectors after the end of their term. Serê Kaniyê province's bakery cooperative, *Kooperatîfa Mezopotamya ye Nanpêjîyê*, was established from the pooled incomes of former members of an agriculture cooperative. In Derik, a group of women established a new tractor service cooperative, which bought its vehicles from the profits its members made in an agricultural cooperative (interview with Delal, 2018). The Co-Spokesman for the Communal Economy Committee emphasized that, based on the experiences gained in agricultural cooperatives, society was coming to realize that they could "go at it together" (*bi hevre karkirin*):

> [...] our agricultural cooperatives have serious problems; the Agriculture Committee supports them by providing seeds, fertilizers and diesel. The cooperatives' members only have to work and organize their administration and assembly, but they find it difficult [...] However, despite all the problems they face, they are very useful in disseminating the idea of cooperatives within society. The people who plant, care, harvest and sell collectively throughout two years come to understand that it is possible to go at it together, and that it is done better together. (Interview with the Co-Spokesman of the Communal Economy Committee, 2019)

In other words, although former members cannot continue working together as an agricultural cooperative once they lose access to the land, they establish cooperatives in other sectors. In fact, many smaller cooperatives are established outside of the agriculture sector, such as bakeries, canneries, bottling plants, lentil processing plants, textile mills, canteens, communal markets, greenhouses, natural poultry farms, and so on. Such cooperatives have become permanent and ensure the livelihoods of many of its members. In summary, the cooperativism that is generally presented as democratic autonomy's fourth organizational base has found a space on the people's agenda thanks to these experiences.

Communes have developed and been witness to endless collective experiences, even if they do not establish themselves as cooperatives. Hevre, working in the village of Cerûdîye, recounted the experience of his village commune, where cooperativism is not necessarily understood as a communal project that is created by collecting fund, but rather as the purest form of the organization of communal life.

Serok tells his comrades, "You may not believe it, but if I were to leave Imrali,[20] I would go live in a village and start organizing society from

---

20 Imrali is an island in the Sea of Marmara, in Turkey. Since 1999, Abdullah Öcalan has been imprisoned in total isolation on this island.

there." This idea of his changed my vision of the struggle. I was insistent to the movement that I wanted to go to a village. That's how I got here. When I arrived, this town was surrounded by garbage. Not because the farmer lacks love for his land, but because garbage is something that belongs to capitalism. Before, it did not exist in their lives because, normally, anything that was thrown out would dissolve into the soil, but plastic is not like that. That's why they don't know what to do with all the garbage, they start throwing it out on the outskirts of town.

Now, when you arrived, did you see a single piece of garbage on the road? I remember my first visit to this village; before I even got to it, I saw mountains of garbage. As soon as I arrived, the first thing I thought was: we have to clean up that garbage. So, one day, when I grabbed a bag and started collecting garbage, at first, only the children came to help, but then, one by one, the villagers came as well. For a week, we cleaned the outskirts of the village with the participation of a majority of the people. This made a noticeable difference; we found that we could deal with the rubbish together. Ten days after my arrival, the town was now very clean and people trusted me. After all, I'm not from the village, I don't own a house or lands there, they only knew that I had come to organize their commune. They didn't necessarily have to trust me, but through clearing the garbage we have established a foundation of trust, which I have tried to explain.

The village also had a stony field, where the animals grazed. But it was difficult for the sheep. I said, "Let's clear the field." Now my colleagues would say, "Let's establish a cooperative, let's organize so that people become cooperative members." But the villages have their own subsistence economies, even in this exaggerated situation. Therefore, if I now told them to form a cooperative, they would say that they do not need to. Why am I saying that? Because I think it's necessary to create a unit, but if we tell them in a language they don't understand, they're going to reject it. We must build a unity of hearts, a unity of enjoyment. For example, as Marx says, "work is like love"; the point is to make them see collective work as love. When they say work, they mean something they constantly repeat and get tired of. So, it must be something that they like the work done.

For example, when we went to clear the stony field, people gathered stones while drinking tea, laughing and dancing. At that time, they did not know if the work they were doing was useful, but being together was joyful for them. It was the end of winter when we cleared the field. When spring came, the grass sprouted in that field and the farmers joked that our animals were going to die from a full stomach. Beautiful grass and lots of it also meant lots of milk. With a lot of milk, a lot of cheese, yogurt and butter were also produced. They produced much more than they needed.

In the past, most of them did not speak to each other, they had conflicts of identity and faith. But now solidarity and unity have developed between them. So, they started proposing to do things together. They told me that they had a small common field; they wanted to plant sesame there but didn't have the seeds. The comrades from agriculture helped out; we found the seeds and planted sesame all together. Now, we are building a kona jiyan (house of life) with the collective profit from the sesame. In fact, we gave some sesame to a women's cooperative to make tahini. The comrades also supported us during this process.

Curiously, there is an *axa* (landowner) in this town; if someone did have a problem, they would go to his house, discuss it there, but, instead, the commune is building its own communal house. The *axa* afforded us no help. He lost all of his power in the eyes of the people. So why am I telling you this now? Because Economic Coordination is sometimes too narrow-minded. *Serok* does not speak of a communal, social and democratic economy, just for the sake of saying something. Many of our comrades understand the economic part, but do not take into account the social part. They say "commune," "cooperative," but they approach it as if they were only institutions. Now, without establishing a cooperative, we did a lot of collective work, we produced, we created *kefxweşî* (joy) and their self-sufficient economies became stronger. You can see that this town is on the border with Turkey, they asked for the formation of self-defense groups and now we are preparing to form them. (Interview with Hevre, Cerûdiye Commune, 2019)

Once I had finished my conversation with Hevre, we ate with the villagers; later on, we visited the school and the orchard that they planted for the town's martyrs. A tree had been planted for each person who had fallen in the war. Although the trees were still young, the cucumbers they planted at the base of the trees were already beginning to bloom.

While, in Rojava, we cannot yet speak of a communal economy organized by cooperatives, collectivization and "going at it together" as forms of communization are central aspect of village life. Cooperativism is central to people's day-to-day discussions as well as to the adoption of new practices. Therefore, I must re-emphasize that cooperatives as standalone structures or production-only spaces are difficult if not impossible to find. However, if we look for cooperativism in the new relationships revealed to us by democratic autonomy it appears almost everywhere. Therefore, it is difficult to write about Rojava without fully grasping the extent of the organization of cooperatives and the contradictions that arise from the organization of the social economy, but we must also change our expectations and approach. This is equally imperative for all those who observe Rojava's autonomy from the sidelines as well as for those who seek to organize it from the inside.

The Lessons of the
Rojava Revolution

An anti-capitalist autonomy

Those who discussed, supported and shared their ideas and struggles with me, and those who read this work, have a problem with the capitalist system. The Kurdish struggle and the peoples of Rojava, who are the subjects of the Rojava Revolution, also have a problem with capitalism. This problem is the defense of life against capitalism, that is, building an anti-capitalist life in order to live with dignity.

Throughout this book, I have talked about the Kurdish struggle and how it developed under the leadership of the PKK since 1978, becoming a popular movement (Kurdish Movement). Rojava, the region where the reflexive and organizational transformations of this struggle became revolutionary practices, shows that the project of autonomy built from below constitutes anti-capitalist politics. Following the Syrian civil war that began in 2011, the Kurds first declared autonomy in 2012 in large Kurdish cities, such as Kobane, Afrîn and Qamishlo. In 2014, they created a system of cantons and autonomous governments in these cities and throughout Rojava (western Kurdistan, along the northern border of Syria). In 2017, autonomy took on the form of autonomous regions, like the Democratic Federation of Northern Syria, which encompasses the entire region of northern Syria and east of the Euphrates River. It is a process of territorial organization that transcends the territorial and shows that autonomy is moving towards a more diverse popular base and, therefore, towards the formation of a confederal democratic autonomy of the peoples—instead of a single and identical autonomy only for the Kurds—thus diversifying their social, religious and ethnic base.

This research looked at the changes, transformations, contradictions, conflicts and tendencies that were evident during this seven-year period (2012–2019). The analysis of this period reveals that the Rojava Revolution and its autonomy has entailed a series of contradictions and conflicts, and the tendencies that it followed were determined by the practices proposed to overcome them. Since 2003, with the contributions of Abdullah Öcalan and the anti-state and anti-power debates of the movement that began at the beginning of the 1990s, the Kurdish Movement has made democratic autonomy and democratic confederalism a new horizon of struggle. However, the way in which autonomy was built in practice was simply a definition of common ethical principles of struggle. Thus, although the autonomy of Rojava was built within the framework of democratic confederalism in the form of principles—democratic, ecological, women's liberation—and forms of organization—communes, assembly, cooperative, academy—it has been lived in the context of various subjectivities.

My research has shown that some of these subjectivities are related to the organizational structure of the Kurdish Movement, while others are anchored in past and present geographical, social, political and historical aspects of Rojava.

The subjectivities that guide the organizational transformation of the PKK in the Kurdish Movement are:

- The origins of the Kurdish Movement in the traditional Left playing an important role in the formation of the Kurdish Left, which, despite separation, defined its goal of struggle as the search for a Kurdish socialist state.
- Questioning the nation-state on the basis of a critique of the experience of real socialism, which only produced state capitalism.
- Gender relations caused conflicts between women and men within the organization, leading to a questioning of patriarchy and power relations, and defining them as the main social problem.
- Women organize on the basis of anti-patriarchal struggle.
- The organization transforms methods, such as critique-self-criticism-platform-report, into methodologies of political formation, analyzing power and capitalist modernity as reproduced by individuals.
- These methods strengthen horizontal relationships with the people, since they question hierarchical relationships, giving rise to a process in which the people matter to the organization and the organization matters to the people, which eliminates the classic separation between organization and society.
- Finally, and at the end of this whole process, the revolution becomes a popular revolution, based on the self-determination of the people, with the aim of building autonomy against the state, patriarchy and capitalism. In this process, the PKK went through ruptures and continuities, including the transformation of the Leninist and vanguard party into a popular movement that made possible the creation of a popular revolution.

Therefore, I talk about the Kurdish Movement, and I refer to the subjectivity of this historical background. One of the things that this research affirms is that the Kurdish Movement, as a revolutionary organization, has the ability to adapt to the needs of the struggle and this translates into practical politics. In fact, inasmuch as the transformations that take place in the organizational structure and in the horizon of struggle respond to the needs demanded by the process of struggle, they determine the present of Rojava, just as they determined its past and, without a doubt, will determine its future.

We have seen that, although Rojava is part of "Greater Kurdistan," different geographical, social, political, historical and temporal subjectivities coexist within it, which are decisive for the revolutionary process and the construction of autonomy, and for this reason they cannot be thought of only in the context of the struggle of the Kurdish people.

Rojava has always been politically related to Bakur. Those who participated in the 1925 Seij Said rebellion established the Xoybûn organization in 1927 in Syria (present-day Lebanon) and led the Mount Ararat Rebellion (1929–1930) in Bakur. The presence of the PDD, founded in Bakur, in the Bekaa Valley (Syria) in the 1980s and the enormous work it carried out in those years in the Kurdish community of Rojava is also important to understanding how the Kurdish Movement was organized in this region. Many young Kurdish men from Rojava became PDD guerrillas and fought in different parts of Kurdistan. When the civil war in Syria began, they returned to Rojava to defend their land and their families, and formed the YPG and YPJ, declaring democratic autonomy. The PYD, which is the most important political party in Rojava, has been organized in the KCK system since 2003. This shows a constant connection between the political terrain of Bakur and that of Rojava. Although there is no organic relationship between the organizations of Rojava and Bakur, there is indeed a political and intellectual relationship that explains why, when the war in Syria began, the Kurds distinguished themselves from other opposition groups—whose objective was to seize state power—by proposing democratic autonomy as the third way (*xeta seyemin*), and why that vision was easily accepted by society.

The autonomy movement in Rojava has been socially accepted, not only by the Kurds, but also by other ethnic and religious groups. However, it would be incorrect to claim that everyone in Rojava has welcomed it. Although the majority of Kurds have rallied around the TEV-DEM and adopted the policy of democratic autonomy, the ENKS, linked to the PDK in Bashur, promotes the idea of a Kurdish state with nationalist approaches, and continues to constitute an emotional contradiction for the Kurds of Rojava.

In addition, Arabs and Assyrians, other important components of autonomy, are not fully involved in this project for fear or expectation that the Syrian state still exists in Rojava and northern Syria. While it still exists in practical terms and coexists with the autonomy of Rojava, it is not correct to say that there is a "dual power," as is often claimed, because the Syrian regime has lost its power and the autonomous government is not looking to build a new power; on the contrary, it rejects power. The current situation is one of powerlessness and there is always the risk that democratic autonomy could collapse and the Syrian state could re-consolidate its power.

Moreover, although autonomy has created policies that allow everyone to participate, the hostility between Arabs and Kurds that dates back to the colonial period affects their full acceptance in non-Kurdish societies. The fact that democratic autonomy has not yet been fully accepted at the social level, prevents the Kurdish Movement and the autonomous government from taking radical decisions to deepen it, such as land reform or the elimination of the presence of the army and the Syrian regime police in the region.

The deprivation of citizenship of the Kurds with the 1962 census, and the subsequent expropriation that prohibited them from owning property; their conversion into slave laborers on state lands; and the policies of cultural assimilation, colonization and oppression, greatly subdued and depressed society. This situation has meant a very slow participation in the process of autonomy, decision-making, and the development of practices and, therefore, a social transformation that is not taking place at the pace expected by the Kurdish Movement. Likewise, the Kurdish Movement—that is, the Kurdish people, who are already politically accustomed and very active in Bakur—has been forced to mobilize the peoples of Rojava, a difficulty that perpetuates the contradiction in which some cadres of the movement who had renounced their vanguard role have had to return to it.

The Turkish state often attacks civilians in the cities and cantons of Rojava located on the border with Turkey, which is facilitated by the fact that the Euphrates River, which crosses this region, is controlled by Turkish dams. This allows the Turkish state to use water as a strategic weapon throughout Rojava, especially in the Cezîre region, whose fertile lands in Mesopotamia made it the breadbasket of the Syrian state. It is the richest region in the Middle East after Kirkuk and Mosul in Iraq, with its oil reserves (which led to an international imperialist dispute). This has exposed Rojava and northern Syria, where they are trying to build anti-capitalist autonomy, to constant attacks and possible conflicts between regional and international powers.

These conflicts and the oppressive war apparatus, coupled with practices such as direct invasion, depopulation and destruction, have given rise to an oppressive and compressive process that is expected to lead to institutionalization (nationalization) and capitalization. As the co-spokesperson for the communal economy said, "The current situation in Rojava is a conflict between democracy and centralization" (2019). We can read this situation as a conflict between autonomy and the state, between the anti-capitalist being and capitalism.

In Rojava, international powers are exercising a conscious policy of supporting the line of the PDK-Barzani against the line of the PKK-Öcalan, that is, of supporting the statist struggle against the anti-state struggle. And since the Kurds have more spaces liberated from the state and capital, international powers are encouraging the idea and the possibility of creating a Kurdish state. Meanwhile, as local communities try to build a democratic nation in Rojava, international and regional powers are forcing the Kurds into a dialogue about "national unity" under the threat of war. These repressive apparatuses are trying to erode and break the anti-capitalist and anti-patriarchal elements of autonomy, utilizing the policy of subsuming this struggle into a weapon of capitalism, to destroy what is against it. Ultimately, when it cannot block the flow of social transformation (revolution) or articulate it within capitalism, that is, make it part of capitalist relations and mentality, it not only carries out an annihilating attack against Rojava, but also against all territories of anti-capitalist struggle.

That is why this research did not treat the Rojava Revolution as an experience or place free from capitalism. Even as the revolution takes place, capitalism as a phenomenon and concrete understanding is striving to exist and dominate in Rojava to counter the revolutionary process (counterrevolution), as are the state and power, or patriarchy, visible in the form of ISIS.

Most importantly, this research shows that as the practice of autonomy grows and people become subjects that strengthen and deepen its process, the material conditions of the struggle against capitalism—in the words of the Kurdish Movement, the self-defense of autonomy—will also be strengthened. Today, the autonomy of Rojava has promoted a radical social transformation, by achieving the coexistence of different ethnic and religious identities in conditions of peace and equal participation in Autonomy, through the policy of a democratic nation coupled with the participation and organization of women transforming gender relations in society. Both practices, the democratic nation and the self-organization of women, have guaranteed that the revolution and autonomy do not create privileges for any group, class or identity, thereby fostering an experience that can build true social emancipation.

In my research on the autonomy of Rojava, looking at the experiences of communes and popular assemblies, I noticed that autonomy has been built as a relationship and not as an administrative structure. Despite this, until now, the perspective of the autonomy of the Kurdish struggle, as well as the readings on the autonomy of Rojava and the original accounts of the Kurdish Movement, describe the communes, assemblies, cooperatives and academies as four structures of the administration of Autonomy and define them as static structures. However, my research in Rojava shows that as Autonomy is the reorganization of social relations, communes and assemblies are (non-physical) spaces in which social relations and certain (non-static) ways of relating to each other are reproduced. The most important evidence of this is the reestablishment of relations within the communes where daily life is configured from the perspective of democratic autonomy. The communes are organizing themselves in various areas—education, health, self-defense, justice, economy—and as a community, they are producing the tools and policies to cover their own collective needs and practicing democratic autonomy in everyday life. The coexistence of different political positions, religious and ethnic differences, which in the past meant daily conflicts between peoples, have ceased to generate hostilities, because people recognize that their differences can coexist within a commune, which is based on the reorganization of community life for autonomy. I am not suggesting that these conflicts have disappeared, but I have found that the practice of autonomy, as a principle of identity between the struggle and life, is increasingly eliminating the basis of conflict in society.

The assemblies, established from the perspective of a democratic nation, are the most important practice in making the aforementioned possible. The field research carried out in Rojava shows that all the decision-making processes have been carried out in the form of assemblies, as well as in the assemblies called for elections, and in the systems of delegation and representation of the Autonomous Administration. The widespread organization of democratic autonomy according to the dimensions of democratic confederalism, the establishment of their own assemblies, the mobilization of the people through assemblies to make common decisions in all spheres, from communes to cooperatives, from associations to the countryside, ensure that the way in which assemblies are practiced generates an organizational experience that is itself mobilizing.

After 5 p.m., there is an assembly meeting for almost everyone; the reciprocal reporting system between the lower and higher assemblies, the participation of the people, and the fact that the assemblies are not only spaces for decision-making, but also where skills are developed in order to make common decisions, and they are controlled directly by tekmil (presentation of reports that include criticism and self-criticism about the performance of the tasks), shows that all the people of Rojava participate directly—through their voices, their decision and their actions—in the process of building autonomy through one or more assemblies.

Rojava constitutes a historical experience in the sense that it demonstrates that democracy/direct participation can actually be practiced and implemented through the assembly as a movement. Likewise, it recreates the meaning of revolution and transcends the limits of autonomy, which are often based on territory and identity. In this sense, communes and assemblies are important revolutionary practices that generate social transformation and emancipation without creating a state or taking power. Society can govern itself, determine its own destiny despite all the contradictions, proving to the people of Rojava and the whole world that this can be achieved in a democratic way.

For this reason, democracy autonomy is increasingly accepted and constitutes a social system that is integrating more and more people. It is true that institutionalization, the mediation of money through the fund system, and the creation of a class of officials represent a constant risk to this process. However, the communes and institutions created from below, based on common decisions in assemblies, and those who are paid to provide social services in these institutions while being under the control of the assemblies and congresses of the towns, are capable of overcoming the risk of establishing hierarchies or placing themselves above society.

The practice of communes and assemblies based on the idea of the democratic nation, the self-organization of women, and the level attained by the revolution today have generated a significant social transformation in the face of the destruction of the war, but the revolution's ability to continue to achieve social emancipation depends to a large extent on limiting and eliminating capitalism in Rojava. As my research reveals, carrying out the decisions made in the communes and assemblies requires the creation of more non-capitalist spaces and relationships. Although concrete daily life and the process of autonomy confirm it once again, the Kurdish Movement has always been aware that non-capitalist economic relations are necessary to create a social revolution, which is why it has implemented a policy in this sense, and has defined it as the organization of a communal democratic social economy in the context of democratic autonomy.

The Kurdish Movement, whose goal is to collectivize cooperative-based production, has been striving to organize the social economy since the beginning of autonomy. In the early years of the revolution, it focused on meeting the collective needs of society under conditions of war through neighborhood assemblies and, since 2014, it has tried to develop a sustainable and self-sufficient social economy by communalizing land through cooperatives.

A social economy that faces conditions of total economic and political embargo lays bare the contradictions of the revolutionary process, the construction of democratic autonomy. While capitalism tries to integrate Rojava into institutionalization with its weapons of war, nationalization, embargo, famine, and so on, and sometimes with the idea of peace, and to force the people to assume capitalist relations, the Kurdish Movement tries to restrict capitalism (resist capitalism) and strengthen the economic self-management (economic self-defense) of the people against capitalism, by creating new spaces and non-capitalist communal relations. This process is, in itself, a process of struggle and resistance, and it has very different edges. Thus, while the Kurdish Movement strives to empower people through a social economy based on self-sufficiency and self-management, so that they become decision-makers in the economy, NGOs, whose intervention is spreading through the international coalition against ISIS, try to frustrate the politics of autonomy by implanting monetary relations mediated by financial aid or micro-financing projects, and treating people as victims. In this way, they are contributing to the creation of a dependent and obedient society, as in other parts of the world, and generating a psychology of despair.

Moreover, since 2018, Rojava has been gradually occupied by the Turkish state through the Turkish-backed jihadist forces under the name of the Syrian National Army (*Suriye Milli Ordusu*, 2017), depriving and destroying the subsistence economy of the people and displacing them to refugee camps that are also part of these policies. According to the December 2019 report of the Rojava Information Center (RIC), when Serîkanîyê was occupied in October 2019, some 800 tons of wheat and 1,500 tons of fertilizer from the collective production of six cooperatives were transferred to Turkey, and the Mesopotamia bakery cooperative was confiscated by the jihadists (Rojava Information Center, 2019, p. 29). In January 2018, when cooperatives started producing olive oil, Afrîn was occupied by the "Olive Branch Operation" (*Zeytin Dalı Operasyonu*) of the Turkish state; the Kurds were displaced and their orchards and olive oil cooperatives were taken over. Presumably through Turkey, olive oil from Afrîn was sold to European countries, such as Spain and Switzerland (BBC News, 2020).

These events show that the economy in Rojava is being seriously attacked, which makes it difficult for people to get involved in the organization of the social economy, because, as the Co-Spokesperson of the Serîkanîyê House of Cooperatives said, "What is the use of working the land if the enemy will come and take everything? And with the war, everything was looted and destroyed" (Ashref, 2020). Despite this, the creation of spaces where people can meet, places of collective training and dignity, where the people of Rojava say "Here nobody governs us, we decide everything ourselves," revalue the meaning of autonomy in the face of the policies of capitalism and the war of dishonor, obligation and impoverishment.

When I analyzed the social economy and the economy of women (*aboriyajin*) organized within the framework of this process, I saw that it is still not possible to speak of a permanent and continuous situation. However, Rojava is learning from its own experience in the midst of certain conditions and contradictions that are being identified and limited. As we know, there is no recipe for how to organize an anti-capitalist communal economy; it is about learning through experimentation and investigating other anti-capitalist experiences, for example, that of the Zapatistas. In all sectors of the organization, the social economy—agriculture, industry, commerce, cooperatives and the women's economy—are directed by the Economic Coordination body. The TEV-DEM (general economy committee), Kongra Star (women's economic committee), the economic council of the autonomous government (*destaye abori*) and the co-spokespersons of the economy of the cantonal assemblies all participate.

As we have seen, a committee is formed for each economic sector within the framework of this coordination and, although it acts to develop and expand its sectoral organization and to communalize the production of its sector, the most evident policy in all sectors is to create cooperatives. However, despite the fact that the discussion about cooperativism has been carried out for a long time in the Kurdish struggle, one of the aspects that most hinders the establishment and management of cooperatives is their lack of permanency. Most of the cooperatives in Rojava, to varying degrees, have collapsed or moved away from a social economy perspective. The cooperative committee stated that it was constantly researching other world experiences and that it wanted to create its own cooperative models, but has not done so yet (interview with Serxwebun, Co-Spokesman of the Rojava cooperatives, 2018). Despite this, and even though there is no model with a clear structure, my research shows that cooperatives in Rojava create original methods and experiences.

Within the framework of the cooperative movement organized by the Committee of Cooperatives, Houses of Cooperatives (*Mala Kooperatîfa*) have been created in each province and, at the cantonal and regional level, the Union of Cooperatives (*Yekîtîya Kooperatîfa*), with the aim of organizing cooperatives and solving their problems and needs collectively. The Union of Cooperatives, known by the name of *Yekîtî*, essentially functions as the union of the cooperative houses and fulfills an important function, providing financing during the establishment phase of the cooperatives, while the Houses of Cooperatives carry out the processes of implementation.

The sectoral planning and the line of work of the cooperatives, widely organized at the provincial, cantonal and regional level, are carried out jointly in the

Houses of Cooperatives and *Yekîtî*, acting in a complementary fashion. The assemblies of the Houses of Cooperatives, which are attended by the co-spokespersons of the cooperatives, and the *Yekîtî* assembly, which is held after these assemblies with the participation of all the co-spokespersons of the Houses of Cooperatives, are spaces for mutual learning, in which collective solutions are proposed for the cooperatives. The mutual reports presented during these assemblies constitute a kind of collective training method for the cooperative process and prevent hierarchical divisions and subordination between institutions. This ensures that social relations within the economy are established on a democratic basis. For example, this prevents the Houses of Cooperatives, which only have the obligation to coordinate and establish the cooperatives and support the production processes, from trying to put themselves above the cooperatives and make decisions in their place; or, if communication is not transparent, one can easily express this in the criticism section of the reports presented by the cooperatives.

Another original aspect of the Rojava cooperatives is that self-management transcends their workers and includes the communes themselves. The cooperatives, built according to the decisions and needs of the communes, are also self-managed by the communes themselves. This is an example of the Kurdish Movement's commitment to self-management belonging not only to class but to society, which ensures that the relationship between the economy and needs will not be broken. The Committee of Cooperatives or the Houses of Cooperatives meet with the communes, discuss their collective needs, the economic opportunities, and what they want to produce and how. If a commune decides to organize itself as a cooperative, they provide it with the necessary support. This support may be required for production, including the allocation of communal land, the provision of means of production and inputs such as seeds, fertilizers or gasoline, and for sociopolitical training, ranging from the establishment of cooperative relations, to democratization, the promotion of self-management capacity and gender equality.

Every two years, the Houses of Cooperatives ask the communes to nominate people for the cooperatives they are going to organize on communal lands. Under this two-year rotation system, the communes appoint different communizers for the agricultural cooperatives. When I looked at the process of cooperatives on communal lands, I saw that while they are not permanent institutions, they nevertheless follow a set of agreements and relationships typical of cooperatives. That is why I refer to this practice of cooperatives in Rojava as "cooperativism without cooperatives." By changing the members of agricultural cooperatives every two years, a system implemented four years prior, the movement has tried to ensure that everyone experiences cooperativism through collective work, and benefits from the communal land. Those who have experienced cooperativism in this manner have established cooperatives in other sectors, since the income obtained in their first cooperative experience has provided them with the necessary resources to create new cooperatives, without the need for *Yekîtî* financing.

The development and continuity of cooperatives has revealed a series of critical problems for the future of autonomy. The Kurdish Movement's build-destroy-rebuild approach leaves no time for cooperatives to mature. The cooperatives have not been able to become a work area for their members because they are temporary and the type of production carried out, such as growing wheat, does not require much work. As a result, cooperatives are treated as companies that provide temporary and collateral income. The fact that people continue to prefer regular salaried jobs over the insecurity of cooperativism is an obstacle in Rojava and must be overcome in order to achieve the creation of a social economy. If these obstacles are overcome, cooperatives can develop in Rojava with the desired speed and intensity; the social economy can reach a stronger and deeper level. During my research in Rojava, I saw how relations of community, collectivity and solidarity strongly determine everyday life there. Although cooperatives are not developed as a model, the communal social relations that develop around cooperatives are increasingly decisive, since the Kurdish Movement and the autonomous government, through the Economic Coordination body, offer overwhelming political, social and economic support in this field.

The experience of the Rojava cooperatives and other experiences that have been observed and investigated in different parts of the world for many years show that the transformation of cooperatives into a true anti-capitalist force is possible only when they become part of a popular social movement. Cooperatives that do not have strong relationships with the community and do not produce to directly meet the needs of the community face the problem of "finding the market to sell." Seen in this way, community cooperatives have the opportunity to produce on the basis of use-value and can even sell their products to people in the community for money; in these cases, even if there is an exchange value, it does not reach a level that dominates the collective activities of the cooperative.

If a cooperative is not directly related to the community and does not produce for a defined need/use-value, even if it is based on collective work, it is dominated by exchange value from the moment it has to sell its product under capitalist market conditions. Therefore, the relationship that the Kurdish Movement established between the cooperative and the commune is vital to creating anti-capitalist power and an economy based on use-value. As seen in Rojava, this relationship can be translated into a cooperative that is organized based on the needs of the community and on its decisions; or a cooperative organized independently of the community, with the intention of getting rid of exchange value as part of the process of creating its community. This second approach can prevent the subsuming of cooperatives to capitalism and the market, especially in the case of anti-capitalist struggles and economies whose center is in the cities. The community relationship that is based on production for the collective needs of the community can transform cooperatives into a social relationship. Thus, cooperatives are not only a unit of collective production, but can become the fundamental bases of the anti-capitalist economy.

Antagonistic autonomy

Women and the women's movement have always had an antagonistic existence within the Kurdish Movement. A series of determinations and analyses, ranging from questioning gender relations, to questioning power, denying the state, defining patriarchy as the oldest system of domination and hierarchy, and affirming that society cannot be liberated if women are not truly emancipated in the fight for freedom, has had an important impact, both reflective and organizational, in the transformation of the PKK into a popular movement.

Since 1992, women, who have been producing anti-patriarchal practices since they created a self-organization (the original organization), have organized on the basis of women's autonomy, in accordance with the determination of democratic autonomy as the horizon of struggle in 2003. In fact, today the women of Rojava participate in co-representation, co-presidency, co-participation (50%), speaking as co-spokespersons and have an active veto in all areas of autonomy. Women's presence implies not only their physical participation, but also an active participation that ensures that all decision-making processes of autonomy must be, first, a decision made by women. Furthermore, for the first time in the world, the women in Rojava have organized their own autonomy under the Congress of Women (Kongra Star). Women's autonomy, organized in the form of their own communes, assemblies, cooperatives, academies, self-defense units (*YPJ-Asayişajin*), women's houses (*Malajin*), is not a parallel structure in any sense; rather, it operates as an antagonistic organization, as an antagonistic autonomy that constantly determines and recalls the principles of mixed autonomy.

The work of the Women's Economy Committee (*Aboriyajin*), affiliated with Kongra Star, has turned women into subjects of the economy. Into subjects of the creation of their own practices and economic areas, such as greenhouses, irrigated agricultural areas and orchards established to diversify products, cooperatives (bread cooperatives) and women's cooperative markets built in all the provinces, in which the free exchange of products operates, making the solidarity of women a practice that guarantees that daily life is organized on the basis of use-value and needs. Even if an industrial factory is established, the main questions facing the economy and women's cooperatives in Rojava are concentrated around how to create it as a cooperative; how to organize collective work; how to create the space and design of production in an anti-patriarchal way; how to meet the needs of the communes. The transformation of patriarchal relations and gender roles in the economy, and the presence of women to guide it towards sustaining life, are the fundamental pillars of the social transformation defined by the women's movement. This process requires a hard fight; as Kongra Star spokesperson Evin Swed says, the presence of women in the economy shows a dialectical link to their organizing in other areas:

> *Malajin* is where the women's justice commissions that deal with women's issues are located. Right now, from the problems that come from there, we see that women are being mistreated for not having economies; but we would be wrong if we said that if women worked everything would be fine; in a society where justice is in the hands of men, even if women had money, they would be oppressed; that is, everything must be rearranged together. That is why we organize ourselves in Kongra Star, not only in one area, but in all areas related to women's lives (Swed, 2019).

This means organizing the autonomy of women, an autonomy that will be antagonistic because it will exist in contradiction with mixed autonomy, that is, with democratic autonomy.

A self-critical revolution

> Some of our cadres do not believe in democratic autonomy; some of our cadres do not believe that a social and democratic economy can be built; some of our cadres only believe in state-based businesses or economic activity. They do not remember that the wealth, the land, the buildings, also the place where we are now, even the clothes we wear, belong to the people; they don't think about this, they don't have this outlook. That is why they come as director, manager, minister, president or worker of any institution anywhere. They think that when three or five coins enter the organization's box, when they enter the organization's box, not society's, they think that there is a profit, but this is a loss. The organization does

not tell us that we are going to organize their economy, none of their cadres has ever told anyone, neither Serok nor the movement give that perspective. But some cadres are looking at it like that. They try to be like a manager, like a worker, but not like a cadre of the organization. They don't wonder *ez kî me?* (who am I?), I also belong to the people, much less the clothes we wear; he belongs and owes himself to the people. Isn't that what they are fighting for? Didn't they participate because of it? But they can say this; they say that this property remains in our hands instead of going to the cooperative, to the assembly. Is that possible?

There may be a logic to this, up to a point. They may say that we cannot transfer all this wealth at once, that we must transfer it gradually, but in the end, our goal is to transfer it all; the oil wells, the biggest factories, the millions of hectares of land that we have and that belong to the people and that must be transferred. To whom will we deliver them? To popular organizations. What are popular organizations? Communes, assemblies, cooperatives, local governments, municipalities. So, we plan, we say that we will transmit the following this year, this and this, perhaps we will also transfer it wrong, we will transfer what must be transferred to the cooperative, to the municipality. But it is not a problem if we do it wrong, we can fix it. We can solve problems. These are details. Now, this is already another mind; this mind is in the organization, so we don't worry when we see contrary positions. I mean, this mind is in the organization and in the movement, but it's not in the picture. Of course, not all, but a part of our paintings do not have the same perspective that the movement has. [...]

These situations are sometimes invisible just because we are now at war, but we know that the problem with these cadres is their approach, it is their statist-possessive understanding, and this mentality is one of the ones that affects us the most. For example, as a cadre, I can't be the director of an institution, I don't want to be. And if they offer me to be the president of Rojava, I still don't want to, I have the responsibility to organize the economy, but I'm not an economist either and I don't need to be an economist. In other words, the economy is not my job, the economy is the work of the people. My task is to support society in this process; let society do every job for itself. What is my role in this process as a leader? To promote democratic processes. For example, the people still think about the logic of the state; they say that all local economic activities should be linked to the economic council of the autonomous

government (*destaye aborî*). Now the peoples are saying this, if everything depends on the aborî detachment, where will autonomy be? That
would mean centralizing the entire economy. Right at that moment,
the cadres must play their role if they see a possibility that autonomy is
moving away from democracy, they must rest on democratic ground.
This is the only task of the cadre. (Interview with the Co-Spokesperson
of the Communal Economy Committee, 2019)

This political cadre of the Kurdish Movement shares the criticism and self-criticism that the political cadres who work to organize the social economy made. In
Rojava, it is common for the movement's political cadres to express self-criticism
regarding a revolutionary position and practice, something that is not common
among traditional revolutionaries. The Kurdish Movement and the Rojava Revolution show that only revolutionary processes that integrate the people and accept
them as subjects of the revolutionary process can create true transformations and
social emancipation.

The experiences of Rojava and Chiapas tell us that organization and organizing are necessary for the anti-capitalist struggle to succeed. At the same time,
they teach us that this objective cannot be achieved through hierarchical organization and vanguard revolutionaries. This organization must have a constant
self-critical approach and not place itself above the people and the community.
Self-criticism eliminates fragmentation between the organization and society,
destroys the idea that the organization leads society towards the truth, listens to
the forms and methods of self-determination of the people, renews its structure
and mechanisms when conflicts and contradictions arise, after listening to the
people.

The Rojava Revolution has been possible because the Kurdish Movement
became a self-critical organization and learned from its experiences before the
revolution. However, for the Rojava Revolution to deepen and continue creating
social emancipation, both for the Kurds and for other peoples, the Kurdish
Movement must continue to build a self-critical revolution, overcoming the
contradictions and conflicts in Rojava through the same mechanism of self-criticism. This effort has been observed. Rojava is playing a historical role in the
continuity of the Kurdish struggle, as the place where the revolution takes place as
an experience that transforms the content of the revolution, in a process in which
both the society and the movement are being transformed.

Bibliography

Abdurrahim Özmen y Emir Ali Türkmen, E. D. (2014). *Kürdistan Sosyalist Solu Kitabı.* İstanbul: Dipnot.

Abdullah Öcalan Sosyal Bilimler Akademisi. (2012). *Demokratik-Komünal Ekonomi.* Qandil: Azadi Matbası.

ACI. *Alianza Cooperativa Internacional.* Obtenido de ¿Qué es una cooperativa de trabajo?: https://www.faecta.coop/index.php?id=que-es-cooperativa-de-trabajo (2 August 2020)

Acun, H. Rojava Devrimi ve Kürt Devrimci Hareketi nereye gidiyor? (K. Dergisi, Interview) Access: 19 June 2020. http://komundergi2.com/hikmet-acun-rojava-devrimi-ve-kurt-devrimci-hareketi-nereye-gidiyor-komun-roportaj/

Akkaya, A. H. (Director). (2005). *Ateşten Tarih* [Film].

Akkaya, A. H. (2013). Kürt Hareketi'nin Örgütlenme Süreci Olarak 1970'ler. *Toplum ve Bilim,* 88-121.

Akkaya, A. H. (2015). Kürt Hareketi'nin "Filistin Düşü". En J. Jongerden, A. H. Akkaya, & B. Şimşek, *İsyandan İnşaya Kürdistan Özgürlük Hareketi* (pp. 75-99). Ankara: Dipnot.

Altuğ, S. (2018). Suriye Arap Milliyetçiliğinde Vatan ve Suriyelilik (1919-1939). *İ.Ü. Siyasal Bilgiler Fakültesi Dergisi,* pp. 71-94.

Altuğ, S. Türkiye, Hafız Esad'ın Arap kemerini genişletiyor. (I. Aktan, Interview) (29 October 2019)

Amnesty International. *Turkey: Deaths in Custody.* Access: 16 November 2020, Amnesty International Newsletter: https://www.amnesty.org/download/Documents/200000/nws210011989en.pdf (1st January 1989).

ANF. *YPJ: Dedican la victoria de Raqqa a Öcalan y a todas las mujeres.* ANF Spanish :https://anfespanol.com/mujeres/ypj-dedican-la-victoria-de-raqqa-a-Oecalan-y-a-todas-las-mujeres-1513 (19 October 2017).

ANF. *Encamnameya Konferansa Aborî ya Rojava hat aşkerakirin.* ANF News: https://anfkurdi.com/kurdistan/encamnameya-konferansa-abori-ya-rojava-hat-askerakirin-49261 (18 October 2015)

Anweiler, O. (1975). *Los Soviets en Russia* (1905-1921). Madrid: Biblioteca Promoción del Pueblo.

Ashref. Ex member of the Economy Office of Serekaniye. (R. I. Center, Interview) https://rojavainformationcenter.com/2020/11/explainer-cooperatives-in-north-and-east-syria-developing-a-new-economy/ (8 November 2020).

Aslan, A. (2012). *Azgelişmişlik ve Kalkınma Sorunsalı Kıskacında: Sermayenin Mekansal Örgütlenişi ve Batman Örneği.* Istanbul, Bahçelievler, Turkey: University of Marmara, Institute of Social Sciences.

Aslan, A. (2014). *Demokratik Ekonomi Konferansı: Bireyci Kapitalist Bir Ekonomiden, Toplumsal Komünal Bir Ekonomiye.* Toplum ve Kuram/Zan Enstitüsü: http://zanenstitu.org/demokratik-ekonomi-konferansi-bireyci-kapitalist-bir-ekonomiden-toplumsal-komunal-bir-ekonomiye-azize-aslan/

Aslan, A. (2015). Construction of Democratic, Ecological and Gender Libertarian Communal Economy in Kurdistan. *Challenging Capitalist Modernity II: Dissecting Capitalist Modernity – Building Democratic Confederalism* (pp. 160-172). Köln: International Initiative Edition.

Aslan, A. (2016). Demokratik özerklikte ekonomik özyönetim: Bakur örneği. *Birikim*(325), pp. 93-98.

Ayboğa, E., Flach, A., & Knapp, M. (2017). *Revolucion en Rojava.* Madrid: Descontrol.

Ayboğa, E., Flach, A., & Knapp, M. (2018). *Rojava Devrimi: Komünalizm ve Kadının Özgürleşmesi Savaş ve Ambargo Kıskacında.*

Bárcenas, F. L. (2011). Las autonomías indígenas en América Latina. En *Pensar las autonomías: Alternativas de emancipación al capital y el Estado* (pp. 67-102). Mexico: Sísifo Ediciones, Bajo Tierra.

Badiou, A. (2010). İdeası Komünizm Olan Şeyin Gerçeği de Sosyalizm midir? In A. B. Zizek, *Metis Defterleri: Komünizm Fikri (Berlin Konferansı, 2010)* (pp. 11-22). İstanbul: Metis.

Balibar, E. (1978). Marx, Engels y el partido revolucionario. (Era, Ed.) *Cuadernos Políticos*(18), pp. 35-46.

Balibar, E. (2018). *The Idea of Revolution: Yesterday, Today and Tomorrow.* Columbia University: http://blogs.law.columbia.edu/uprising1313/etienne-balibar-the-idea-of-revolution-yesterday-today-and-tomorrow/

Batatu, H. (1999). *Syria's peasantry, the descendants of its lesser rural notables, and their politics.* Princeton: Princeton University Press.

Bayık, C. (2017). ¿Cómo puede Oriente Próximo liberarse a sí mismo del caos? En E. Ayboğa, A. Flach, & M. Knapp, *Revolución en Rojava* (pag. 15-27). Madrid: Descontrol.

Bayrak, M. (1994). *Kürdoloji Belgeleri.* Ankara: Özge Yayınları.

Bayrak, M. (2009). *Kürtlere Vurulan Kelepçe Şark Islahat Planı.* Ankara: Özge Yayınları.

Bayrak, M. (2013). *Kürtler ve Ulusal-Demokratik Mücadeleleri Gizli Belgeler-Araştırmalar-Notlar.* Ankara: Özge Yayınları.

Baysal, N. (2014). *O Gün.* Istanbul: İletişim.

BBC News. (31 January 2019). *Turkey in a pickle over Syrian olives.* Obtenido de BBC: https://www.bbc.com/news/blogs-news-from-elsewhere-47069403

Beşikçi, İ. (1990). *Devletlerarası Sömürge Kürdistan.* Paris: Insitut Kurde de Paris.

Bilgin, D. (2018). Bulut Yağmuru/Kobanê siperlerinde direniş hikayeleri. Istanbul: Mezopotamya Yayinevi.

Bilim Aydınlanma Komitesi. (2009). *Kürt Sorununda Çözüme Doğru: Demokratik Özerklik.* Qandil: Weşanên Serxwebûn: 146.

Bookchin, M. (2014). *Kentsiz Kentleşme: Yurttaşlığın Yükselişi ve Çöküşü.* Istanbul: Sümer Yayıncılık.

Bozarslan, H. (2008). Kürt Milliyetçiliği ve Kürt Hareketi (1898-2000). En *Modern Türkiye'de Siyasi Düşünce: Milliyetçilik* (Vol. 4, pag. 841-871). İstanbul: İletişim.

Bruinessen, M. v. (2012). *Kürdolojinin Bahçesinde (En el Jardín de la Kurdología).* İstanbul : İletişim Yayınları.

Caffentzis , G., & Federici, S. (January of 2014). Commons against and beyond capitalism. *Community Development Journal, 49*(S1), i92–i105.

Cattani, A. D. (2004). La Otra Economía: Los Conceptos Esenciales. En A. D. (Organizador), *La Otra Economía* (pp. 23-30). Argentina: Editorial Altamira.

CHP Merkez Yönetim Kurulu Somut Politikalar Çalışma Grubu. (1998). *Doğu ve Güneydoğu Bölgesi'den Göç.* Ankara: Cumhuriyet Halk Partisi.

Cliff, T. (1990). *Rusya'da Devlet Kapitalizmi (State Capitalism in Russia, Bookmarks, Londra,1988).* Istanbul: Metis.

Commission of the Preparation of the Democratic Economy Conference. (2014). Ekonomi Konferansı Bileşenlerine. *Demokratik Modernite,* pp. 71-78.

Committee of the Agriculture-Komîta Çandinî-Sewaldarî. (2017). Bangewazî Ji Bo Kooperatîfên Çandinî (The call for Agricultere Cooperatives). Cezire.

Conde, G. (2013). *Turquía, Siria e Iraq: Entre Amistad y Geopolítica.* México, D.F. : El Colegio de México.

Conde, G. (2017). Geopolíticas y Antigeopolíticas de La Cuestión Kurda en Perspectiva Histórica. *ISTOR*(70), pp. 51-72.

Coraggio, J. L. (2019). La economía social y solidaria como alternativa a la economía de mercado. En V. M. otros, *Cauca, café con raíces: caficulturas, agroecología y economía social y solidaria* (pp. 61-74). Cauca: Editorial Universidad del Cauca.

Çelik, A. (2020). *El genocidio armenio en la memoria colectiva kurd.* Middle East Research and Information Project (MERIP). Access: 25 September 2020. https://www.academia.edu/44117321/El_genocidio_armenio_en_la_memoria_colectiva_kurda_2020_

Cooperatives Committee of the Northern Siria-Komîteya Kooparatîfên Bakûrê Sûrî. (2017). Hevpeymana Kooperatîfana Federasyona Demokratîk a Bakûrê Sûrî (Contract on Cooperatives of the Democratic Federation of Northern Syria). Derîk.

Daly, G. (2010). Komünizmin Avatarları. En A. B. Zizek, *Metis Defterleri: Komünizm Fikri (Berlin Konferansı)* (pag. 22-47). İstanbul: Metis.

Dean, J. (2014). *Komünist Ufuk*. Istanbul: Yapı Kredi Yayınları.

Deutschland.de. *Creando valores en común*. Deutschland.de: https://www.deutschland.de/es/topic/economia/cooperativas-ejemplos-de-alemania-y-de-todo-el-mundo (5 July 2018)

Dinç, N. K. (2017). *Ezidilerin 73. Fermanı Şengal Soykırımı*. Istanbul: Zan.

DTK. (2011). Demokratik Özerklik İlan Belgesi. Diyarbakir. https://www.kcd-dtk.org/

DTK. (2014). 'Demokratik Ekonomi Konferansı' sonuç bildirgesi açıklandı. Access: IMC Tv: http://www.imctv.com.tr/2014/11/09/demokratik-ekonomi-konferansi-sonuc-bildirgesi-aciklandi/

Duman, Y. (2016). *Rojava: Bir Demokratik Özerklik Deneyimi*. İstanbul: İletişim.

Economy Assembly of the Democratic Federation of Northern Syria (2017). The Cooperatives Contract of Democratic Federation of the Northen Syria.

Engels, F. (1884). *The Origin of the Family, Private Property and the State*. Online Version: Marx/Engels Internet Archive (marxists.org).

Engels, F. (1978). *Ütopik Sosyalizm ve Bilimsel Sosyalizm*. Ankara: Sol Yayınları.

Erdal, M. (2018). Modernizmi Özsel Olumsuzlama Pratiği Olarak Devrim. *Demokratik Modernite*(24), 20-29.

EZLN. (1996). Discurso inaugural de la mayor Ana María. *Primer Encuentro Intercontinental por la Humanidad y contra el Neoliberalismo* (pp. 1-5). Chiapas: Revista Chiapas. https://chiapas.iiec.unam.mx/No3/ch3anamaria.html

Fırat, Ü. (2006). Ümit Fırat ile DDKO Söyleşisi. (L. R. BÎR, Interview)

Frye, M. (1983). *The Politics of Reality: Essays in Feminist Theory*. Trumansburg, NY: The Crossing Press.

Garcia Jané, J. (2012). Autogestión y Cooperativismo. *Papeles De Economía Solidaria*(3), pp.9-15.

GÖC-DER. (2013). *Türkiye'de Koruculuk Sistemi: Zorunlu Göç ve Geri Dönüşler*. Istanbul: Göç Edenler Sosyal Yardimlaşma ve Kültür Derneği.

Gökcan, Ö. (2018). Suriye'nin Kürt Meselesinin Tarihsel Seyri (1946-2011). *Türkiye Ortadoğu Çalışmaları Dergisi*, 5(2), pp. 159-189.

Göksel, O. (2017). Revolutionary And Libertarian Islam: A Divergent Islamic Perspective On Modernity. *The Journal of Academic Social Science*(48), pp. 144-162.

Graeber, D. (2002). "The New Anarchists". *New Left Review*(13), pp. 61-73.

Graeber, D. (2012). *Anarşist Bir Antropolojiden Parçalar*. İstanbul: Boğaziçi Üniversitesi Yayınları.

Gutiérrez Aguilar, R. (2014). *A Desordenar! Por una historia abierta de la lucha social*. México: Paz En El Árbol.

Hacettepe University Institute of Population Studies. (2004). *Migration and Internally Displaced Population Survey in Turkey*. Ankara : Hacettepe University Institute of Population Studies. Access: 28 September 2020 http://www.hips.hacettepe.edu.tr/tgyona/4maytgyona(eng).PDF

Hafıza Merkezi. (2020). *Türkiye'de Zorla Kaybetmeler Gerçeği*. Hakikat, Adalet, Hafıza Merkezi: https://hakikatadalethafiza.org/turkiyede-zorla-kaybetmeler/

Hernández, J., & Martí, J. (2019). CTO. Trabajo comunitario agrario en Traslasierra. En J. Martí Comas, & U. M. Luis, *Repensar La Economía desde lo Popular: Aprendizajes colectivos desde América Latina* (pp. 115-141). Barcelona: Icaria Editorial.

Holloway, J. (2010). *Kapitalizmde Çatlaklar Yaratmak*. İstanbul: Otonom.

Holloway, J. (2011). *İktidar Olmadan Dünyayı Değiştirmek*. İstanbul: İletişim.

Holloway, J. (2015). Presentación del Seminario realizada por John Holloway. En F. M. John Holloway, *Zapatismo: Reflexión Teórica y Subjetividades Emergentes* (pp. 21-35). Buenos Aires: Herramienta.

Holloway, J. (2017). *Öfke Günleri: Paranın Hükümranlığına Karşı Öfke*. İstanbul: iletişim.

Holloway, J., Matamoros, F., & Tischler, S. (2013). *Olumsuzluk ve Devrim: Adorno ve Politik Eylemcilik*. Istanbul: Otonom.

Horkheimer, T. W. (2013). *Teori ve Pratik Üzerine Bir Tartışma* (1956). İstanbul : Metis.

HRW. (2009). *Repression of Kurdish Political and Cultural Rights in Syria*. New York: Human Right Watch.

International Crisis Group. (2014). *Flight of Icarus? The PYD's Precarious Rise in Syria*. Brussels: International Crisis Group. https://www.justice.gov/sites/default/files/pages/attachments/2015/05/29/icg_050814.pdf

Internationalist Commune of Rojava. (2018). *Make Rojava Green Again*. London: Make Rojava Green Again.

Jineoloji Academy. (2016). *Jineolojiye Giriş*. Qandil: Jineoloji Akademisi Yayınları Azadi Maatbası.

J.K. Gibson-Graham. (2010). *(Bildiğimiz) Kapitalizmin Sonu: Siyasal İktisadın Feminist Eleştirisi [English Edition: The End of Capitalism (As We Knew It)]*. Istanbul: Metis.

Jongerden, J., Akkaya , A. H., & Şimşek, B. (2015). *İsyandan İnşaya Kürdistan Özgürlük Hareketi*. Ankara: Dipnot.

Karayılan, M. (2011). *Bir Savaşın Anatomisi: Kürdistan'da Askeri Çizgi*. Neuss, Alemania: Mezopotamya Yayınları.

KJA (Koma Jinen Azad). (2016). *The report of the "Kadın Emeği"*. Mardin: KJA.

Knapp, M. (2017). Historia de Rojava, Panaroma Histórico. En A. F. E- Ayboğa, *Revolución en Rojava* (pp. 55-80). Madrid: Descontrol.

Kongra-Star. (2016). *About the work and ideas of Kongra-Star, the Women's Movement in Rojava*. Qamishlo: The Committee of Diplomacy of Kongra-Star.

Mayer, M. (2013). *Squatting in Europe: Radical Spaces, Urban Struggles, Squatting Europe Kollektive*. New York: Automedia.

McDowall, D. (2004). *Modern Kürt Tarihi (The Modern History Of The Kurds*, I.B.Tauris, 2005, New York). Ankara: Doruk.

Moisés, Subcomandante. (2015). Resistencia y Rebeldía Zapatistas I. *El Pensamiento Crítico Frente a la Hidra Capitalista I* (pp. 137-150). Chiapas : Cideci-UniTierra.

Moisés, Subcomandante. (2015). Resistencia y Rebeldía Zapatistas III. *El Pensamiento Crítico Frente a la Hidra Capitalista I* (pp. 163-180). Chiaspas: Cideci-UniTierra.

Mohammadpour, A. and Soleimani, K. (2019). "Interrogating the tribal: the aporia of 'tribalism' in the sociological study of the Middle East," *The British Journal of Sociology*, 70 (5), pp. 1799-1824

Nail, T. (2014). Deleuze, Occupy ve Devrim Edimselliği. En S. Özer, *Gezi'nin Yeryüzü Kardeşleri: Direnişin Arzu Cografyaları* (pp. 257-295). İstanbul: Otonom.

Nail, T. (2018). Devrim. *Demokratik Modernite*(24), pp.11-16.

Negri, A. (2010). Ortak Olanın İnşası: Yeni Bir Komünizm. En A. B. Zizek, *Metis Defterleri: Komünizm Fikri (Berlin Konferansı)* (pp. 163-175). İstanbul : Metis.

Negri, A., & Hardt , M. (2004). *Çokluk: İmparatorluk Çağında Savaş ve Demokrasi*. İstanbul: Ayrıntı.

Öcalan, A. (1988). *İşte APO, işte PKK.* (M. A. Birand, Interview)

Öcalan, A. (1995). *PKK 5. Kongresine Sunulan Politik Rapor*. Köln: Serxwebun.

Öcalan, A. (2001). Sümer Rahip Devletinden Demokratik Uygarlığa *(From the Sumerian Priestly State to Democratic Civilization)*. (AIHM Savunmalar). Köln: Mezopotamya Yayınları.

Öcalan, A. (2004). *Bir Halkı Savunmak*. Weşanên Serxwebûn 135.

Öcalan, A. (2005). *Demokratik Konfederalizm*. Cologne: Weflanen Serxwebûn 142.

Öcalan, A. (2007). *Devlet*. Abdullah Öcalan Sosyal Bilimler Akademisi.

Öcalan, A. (2009). *Demokratik Toplum Manifestosu: Özgürlük Sosyolojisi* (Vol. III). Weşanên Serxwebûn 149.

Öcalan, A. (2011). *Ortadoğu'da Uygarlık Krizi ve Demokratik Uygarlık Çözümü, Hawar yayınları*. Hawar Yayınları.

Öcalan, A. (2012). *Kürdistan Devrim Manifestosu: Kürt Sorunu ve Demokratik Ulus Çözümü*. Diyarbakır: Ararat.

Öcalan, A. (2013). *Liberar La Vida: La Revolución de Las Mujeres Kurdas*. Colonia: International Initiative Editon.

Öcalan, A. (2014). Endüstriyalizm (Kapitalizm) ve Ekoloji. *Demokratik Modernite*(11), pp. 7-24.

Öcalan, A. (2016). *Demokratik Ulus (Democratic Nation)*. Colonia, Alemania: International Initiative Editiona & Mezopotamya, Neuss.

Özgen, N. (2014). Komünal Ekonominin İnşasında Yerel Bilgi: Dayanışma Ekonomisi. *Demokratik Modernite*(11), pp. 42-50.

Özkaya, A. N. (2007). Suriye Kürtleri: Siyasi Etkisizlik ve Suriye Devleti'nin Politikları. *Usak*, 2(8), pp.90-116.

PKK. (1978). PKK Kuruluş Bildirgesi. *Weşanen Serxwebûn* 25. Serxwebûn.

Provence, M. (2005). *The Great Syrian Revolt and the Rise of Arab Nationalism*. Austin, TX: University of Texas Press.

REAS. (2020). *Carta de Principios de la Economía Solidaria*. El Portal de La Economía Solidaria: https://www.economiasolidaria.org/carta-de-principios

Reuters. (2019). Russia Takes Part in Talks Between Syria and Kurdish-Led SDF. Reuters: https://www.reuters.com/article/us-syria-security-turkey-kurds-damascus-idUSKBN1WS0MY

Rojava Information Center. (2019). *Turkey's War Against Civilians*. Qamishlo: Rojava Information Center.

Ross, K. (2015). *Lugo Comunal El Imaginario politico de la Comuna de Paris*. Madrid: Ediciones Akal.

Rûdaw. (2016). *Esad'ın 42 yıl önce Kürtler'e yaptığı....* Rûdaw: https://www.rudaw.net/turkish/kurdistan/2406201614

Ruggeri, A. (2012). Un balance de las empresas recuperadas, una década después de la crisis de 2001. *Papeles de Economía Solidaria*(3), pp. 15-23.

Ruggeri, A. (2018). *Autogestión y Revolución de Las Primeras Cooperativas a Petrogrado y Barcelona*. Buenos Aires: Calloa Cooperativa Cultural.

Ruggeri, A., Wertheimer, M., Galeazzi, C., & García, F. (2012). Cuadernos Para La Autogestión #1. *Autogestión y Cooperativismo*. Buenos Aires: Centro de Documentación de Empresas Recuperadas.

Santiago, J. S. (2017). *Economía Política Solidaria*. Mexico City: EÓN.

Savran, S. (2011). Devlet mülkiyeti: Toplumsal mülkiyete giden yol. *PGBSosyalizm*(19). https://pgbsosyalizm.org/?p=152

Schmidinger, T. (2016). *Suriye Kürdistaninda Savaş ve Devrim (Krieg und Revolution in Syrisch-Kurdistan: Analysen und Stimmen aus Rojava)*. Istanbul: Yordam.

Schøtt, A. S. (2017). *From the Forgotten People to World-Stage Actors: The Kurds of Syria*. Copenhagen: Royal Danish Defence College.

Social Contract of Rojava (Rojava Toplumsal Sözleşmesi). (2014). Qamishlo, Siria.

Social Contract of the Democratic Federation of Northern Syria. (2016). Qamishlo, Siria.

Subcomandante Insurgente Marcos. (June 9, 1995). *La historia de los espejos*. Enlace Zapatista: https://enlacezapatista.ezln.org.mx/1995/06/09/la-historia-de-los-espejos-durito-iv-el-neoliberalismo-y-el-sistema-de-partido-de-estado-durito-v/

Subcomandante Insurgente Moisés. (2015). Ser Zapatista. En C. S. EZLN, *El Pensamiento Crítico Frente a la Hidra Capitalista I* (págs. 34-39). Chiapas: Enlace Zapatista.

Taştekin, F. (2015). *Suriye: Yıkıl Git, Diren Kal*. Istanbul: İletişim.

Tejel, J. (2015). *Suriye Kürtleri: Tarih, Siyaset ve Toplum (Syria's Kurds: History, politics and society)*. İstanbul: İntifada Yayınları.

The New York Times. (13 October 2019). *Trump Orders Withdrawal of U.S. Troops From Northern Syria. The New York Times:* https://www.nytimes.com/2019/10/13/us/politics/mark-esper-syria-kurds-turkey.html

Tischler, S. (2008). Prólogo. En F. M. John Holloway, *Zapatismo: Reflexión teórica y subjetividades emergentes* (pp. 13-21). Buenos Aires: Herramienta.

Tischler, S. (2011). Adorno: Öznenin Kavramsal Hapisanesi, Politik Fetişimzm ve Sınıf Mücadelesi. In S. Tischler, J. Holloway, & F. Matamoros, *Olumsuzluk ve Devrim: Adorno ve Politik Eylemcilik* (K. Tunca, Trans., pp. 117-137). İstanbul: Otonom.

TRASOL. (2017). *Levantando trabajo sin patrón: cooperativismo y autogestión.* Santiago: Quimantú.

TRASOL. (2017). *Trabajo Sin Patrón: Experiencias y Reflexiones de la Autogestión.* Santiago: Quimantú.

Türker, Y. (2011). Sunuş: Üvey Kardeş Dilinden. R. C. Danışman, in *Bildiğin Gibi Değil: 90'larda Güneydoğu'da Çocuk Olmak* (pag. 9-17). İstanbul : Metis.

Uharte, L. M. (2019). I. Macro Teórico: (Re)construyendo alternativas económicas emancipadoras de la base. Referentes teóricos y dimensiones de análisis. En L. M. Uharte, & J. Martí Comas, *Repensar la economía desde lo popular: Aprendizajes colectivos desde América Latina* (pag. 11-52). Barcelona: Icaria Antrazyt.

Ulugana, S. (2010). *Ağrı Kürt Direnişi ve Zilan Katliamı* (1926-1931). İstanbul: Peri Yayınları.

Ulugana, S. (2019). Zilan'da yapılan soykırımdır. (B. Balseçer, Interview) Access: 7 November 2019, de http://yeniozgurpolitika.net/sedat-ulugana-zilanda-yapilan-soykirimdir/

UNESCO. (2016). *La Lista Representativa de Oatrimonio Cultural Inmaterial de la Humanidad.* Berlin: UNESCO. Access: 10 October 2020, https://ich.unesco.org/es/RL/la-idea-y-la-practica-de-mancomunar-intereses-colectivos-en-cooperativas-01200

Vladimir I. Lenin, (2010). *Ne Yapmalı?* İstanbul: Agora Kitaplığı.

Yarkın, G. (2019). *İnkâr Edilen Hakikat: Sömürge Kuzey Kürdistan.* Kürd Araştırmaları: http://kurdarastirmalari.com/yazi-detay-nk-r-edilen-hakikat-s-m-rge-kuzey-k-rdistan-26

Yörük, E. (2012). *Zorunlu Göç Ve Türkiye'de Neo-Liberalizm.* Bianet: http://bianet.org/biamag/insan-haklari/118421-zorunlu-goc-ve-turkiye-de-neoliberalizm

Yusuf, A. (2015). Rojava Deneyimi Bağlamında Sosyal Ekonomiyi Düşünmek: Temeller ve İlkeler. En J. Jongerden, A. H. Akkaya, & B. Şimşek, *İsyandan İnşaya Kürdistan Özgürlük Hareketi* (pp. 261-290). Ankara: Dipnot.

Zibechi, R. (2006). *Dispersar el Poder: Los Movimientos Comp Poderes Antiestatales.* Buenos Aires: Tinta Limón.

List of interviews

All interviews by Azize Aslan

Ahmed (11 February 2018). The Co-spokesperson of the Directorate of Agriculture of the Autonomous Government.

Kawar Villager. (2014). Kawar.

Asmîn. (18 February 2018). The member of the industry committee.

Ciwan. (11 February 2018). Co-spokesman of Dirbesiye Agriculture Administration.

Axarî Committee (9 March 2018). Land Committee.

Agriculture Committee-Komîta Çandinî-Sewaldarî. (2017). Call for The Agricultural Cooperatives-Bangewazî Ji Bo Kooperatîfên Çandinî. Cezîre.

Heseke Canton Economy Committee. (15 December 2019).

Hevgirtin Cooperative (March 2018). The Member of Administration of Hevgirtin Cooperative

Lorin Cooperative (February 2018).

Co-spokesperson of the Cooperative House (March 2018). The meetings of "a cooperative for each commune".

Co-spokeswomen of the Committee of the Communal Economy. (2 February 2018). Management of Communal Lands

Co-spokesman of the Communal Economy Committee. (December 2019). General Evaluation.

Delal. (March 11, 2018). The spokeswoman of the women's economy committee (AborîyaJIN).

Ercan (April 2018). The responsible for Semelka Customs

Haydar. (28 January 2018). Co-spokesperson of the Economy Committee for TEV-DEM.

Hevre (24 December 2019). The Cerûdiye Commune (Gûndê Cerûdiye)

Jinda, & Mohammed. (14 December 2019). Co-spokespersons of the economic committee of Qamishlo Canton

Khalaf, H. (9 March 2018). The Co-president of the Economic Council

Kongra-star. (2018). The spokeswoman of the Women's Economy (AborîyaJIN)

The Assembly of Hevgirtin Cooperative (25 March 2018). Qamishlo, Rojava.

Melsa. (18 February 2018). The co-spokeswoman of Rojava cooperatives

Mizgin. (18 March 2018). The Axarî (Land) Committee

Çarçela Restaurant, (February 2018). Meeting with the women of the Çarçela Collective.

Şerhat. (March 13, 2018). The Member of the Economic Coordination body in Derik.

Serxwebûn. (February 2018). The co-spokesman of Rojava Cooperatives.

Şiyar. (December 2019). The co-spokesman of Rojava Cooperatives.

Swed, E. (25 December 2019). The spokesperson of Kongra-Star.

Yekîtî. (19 March 2018). The Co-spokeswoman of Cooperative Unit.

Yunis, T. (9 December 2019). Hevserokê Meclisa Rêveber a Rêveberiya Xweser a Herêma Cizîrê (The co-president of the Autonomous Government of Region Cezîre).

Yusif, P. (9 December 2019). The co-president of the Assembly of Qamishlo Cantonment.

Zafer (21 February 2018). The Responsible for the Trade Committee.

List of abbreviations

AANES or Autonomous Administration: The Autonomous Administration of North and East Syria (*Rêveberiya Xweseriya Demokratîk* in Kurdish)

SNC: Syrian National Council

DTK: Congress of the Democratic Society (*Demokratik Toplum Kongresi* in Turkish, *Koma Ciwaka Democratik* in Kurdish)

DTP: Democratic Society Party *(Demokratik Toplum Partisi)*

ENKS: Kurdish National Council *(Encümena Niştimani ya Kurdi li Suriye)*

FKDC: Democratic Front for the Liberation of Palestine *(Al-Jabha al-Dimuqratiya Li-Tahrir Filastin)*

GAP: Southeast Anatolian Development Project *(Güneydoğu Anadolu Projesi)*

HPC: People's Self Defense Forces *(Hêzên Parastina Ciwake)*

ISIS: Islamic State Iraq and Syria

Kongra-Star or Yekîtîya-Star: Northern Syrian Women's Congress

MGRK: Assembly of the Peoples of Kurdistan-Rojava *(Meclisa Gel a Rojavayê Kurdistánê)*

PÇDKS: Party of the Democratic Left of Syrian Kurdistan *(Partiya Çepa Demokrata Kurdi)*

PDK: Kurdistan Democratic Party of Iraq – *Partiya Demokrata Kurdistan a Irak*

PKK: Workers Party of Kurdistan

PYD: Democratic Union Party *(Partiya Yekîtîya Demokratik)*

QSD: Syrian Democratic Forces *(Hêzên Sûriya Demokratîk)*

NGARK or NAR: The Economic Development Center of Rojava *(Navenda Geşkirina Aborîya Rojavayê Kurdistanê)*

TEV-DEM: Democratic Society Movement

UAR: United Arab Republic

YPG: People's Defense Unit *(Yekîneyên Parastina Gel)*

YPJ: Women's Defense Unit *(Yekîneyên Parastina Jin)*

Some institution names

Aborîya jin: Women's Economy

Aborîya Ciwakî: Social Economy

Asayish: Society's Guard

Destaye Aborî: The Economic Council

Destaye Şaredarîyan û Ekolojî: The Municipalities and Ecology Council

Mala Kooperatîfan: Houses of Cooperatives

Mala Kooperatîfan Jinan: Houses of Women's Cooperatives

Yekîtî- Yekîtîya Kooperatîfan: Cooperatives Unit

Yekîtîya Kooperatîfan Jinan: Women's Cooperatives Unit

Cities and regions[1]

Kurdish Name	Official Name	Part of Kurdistan	Official (Colonial) Country
Afrîn	Afrin	Rojava	Syria
Aleppo	Alepo	North Syria	Syria
Amed	Diyarbakir	Bakur	Turkey
Amûde	Amuda	Rojava	Syria
Êlih	Batman	Bakur	Turkey
Cezîre	Al Jazeera	Rojava	Syria
Deir-Ezzor	Deir-Ezzor	North Syria	Syria
Dêrik	Al Malikiya	Rojava	Syria
Dersîm	Tunceli	Bakur	Turkey
Dirbêsiyê	Ad Darbasiyah	Rojava	Syria
Girêsipîyê	Tell Abyad	Rojava	Syria
Girkê Legê	Al-Muabbada	Rojava	Syria
Hesekê	Hasaka	North Syria	Syria
Hezzo	Kozluk	Bakur	Turkey
Hilvan (Curnê Reş)	Hilvan	Bakur	Turkey
Kawar	Düzcealan	Bakur	Turkey
Kobanê	Ayn al-Arab	Rojava	Syria
Mêrdîn	Mardin	Bakur	Turkey
Mosul	Musul	Bashur	Iraq
Qamişlo	Al-Qamishli	Rojava	Syria
Qoeser	Kızıltepe	Bakur	Turkey
Raqqa	Raqqa	North Syria	Syria
Roboskî	Uludere	Bakur	Turkey
Serîkanîye	Ras al-Ayn	Rojava	Syria
Sêwreg	Siverek	Bakur	Turkey
Şhingal	Sinjar	Bashur	Iraq
Şirnex	Şırnak	Bakur	Turkey
Tabqa	Al-Thawrah	North Syria	Syria

1 One of the policies of the colonization of Kurdistan has been the renaming of Kurdish settlements. Throughout the book, the names of villages, provinces, cities, and regions are used in their original Kurdish. The purpose of this table is to support the reader for geographical mapping.

Other books of interest

Slave King: Rebels Against Empire
Basem L. Ra'ad

Slave King recreates a slave revolt in Sicily led by a Syrian magus turned leader, circa 140-132 BCE, decades before Spartacus. He forges a coalition of slaves, farmers and herders to defeat Roman legions and establish an egalitarian polity. The novel challenges ancient sources to speak for the oppressed.

ISBN 9781990263521 • 216 pages • $25

Mental Health & Human Rights in Palestine
The life of Gaza's pioneering psychiatrist Dr Eyad Serraj
Waseem El Serraj

This is a biography of the life of Dr Eyad El Sarraj, Gaza's pioneering psychiatrist and founder of the Gaza Community Mental Healthcare Programme, written by his son, Wasseem El Sarraj. It is also a history of Palestine with a focus on Gaza.

ISBN 9781990263378 • 132 pages • $21

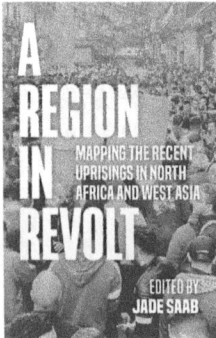

A Region in Revolt
Mapping the recent uprising in North Africa and West Asia
Jade Saab

A wave of mass protest movements spread across North Africa and West Asia, including Sudan, Algeria, Iraq, Lebanon and Iran. The mass protests have much in common, but each protest movement operates under different conditions that cannot be ignored. This book paints a clearer picture of these movements and draws out lessons to inform future struggles.

ISBN 9781988832616 • 178 pages • $20

Struggling to be seen
The travails of Palestinian cinema
Anandi Ramamurthy, Paul Kelemen

Palestinian filmmakers face challenges to give expression to the national narrative. This book explores the political, economic and cultural contexts that impact on Palestinian film production and some of the barriers encountered in profiling and screening Palestinian films.

ISBN 9781988832807 • 84 pages • $17.50

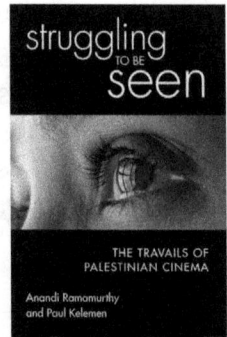

ALL PRICES IN U.S. DOLLARS

www.ingramcontent.com/pod-product-compliance
Lightning Source LLC
Chambersburg PA
CBHW071352280326
41927CB00041B/2904

9781990263712